Playing the REITs Game

Playing the REITs Game

John Wiley & Sons (Asia) Pte. Ltd.

Other Wiley Editorial Offices

John Wiley & Sons, Inc., 111 River Street, Hoboken, NJ 07030, USA
John Wiley & Sons Ltd., The Atrium, Southern Gate,
    Chichester PO19 BSQ, England
John Wiley & Sons (Canada) Ltd., 5353 Dundas Street West, Suite 400, Toronto, Ontario
    M9B 6H8, Canada
John Wiley & Sons Australia Ltd., 42 McDougall Street, Milton, Queensland 4064, Australia
Wiley-VCH, Boschstrasse 12, D-69469 Weinheim, Germany

Library of Congress Cataloging-in-Publication Data

ISBN-978-0-470-82204-3

Wiley Bicentennial Logo: Richard J. Pacifico
Typeset in 11-14 point, Bembo by Superskill Graphics Pte. Ltd.
Printed by Markono Print Media Pte. Ltd.
10 9 8 7 6 5 4 3 2 1

Contents

Foreword

T he market capitalization of Asia Pacific's listed real estate market is second only to the US.

The listed property trust market got under way in Australia in 1971, and the market capitalization is now worth over $80 billion. Thirty years later, the real estate investment trust (REIT) market emerged in Asia (with the launch of the first Japanese REIT in 2001). Since then the growth has been phenomenal, with Japan, Singapore and Hong Kong leading the way. In the space of five years, market capitalization grew to around $60 billion and it is estimated that this number will double by 2010. The growth has been exponential, with over half the REITs now listed having been launched in the last two years.

We have also seen the markets in Japan, Singapore and Hong Kong maturing and developing much more quickly than was the case in the US and Australia; innovations which took longer to appear—such as cross-border offerings and specialized trusts—have already been introduced in these markets.

However, we are just at the start of the journey. In Asia, the proportion of real estate in securitized vehicles such as REITs is very low. Asia has the most under-securitized real estate sector in the world, with only about 4% of real estate held in these structures. This includes Japan, which at the time of writing has 41 REITs and accounts for about 65% of Asian REIT market capitalization. There are numerous trends and drivers that virtually assure the continued rapid growth of this exciting sector.

One of the major reasons for the popularity of REITs is that they are a proxy for investment in direct real estate. With assets being predominantly real estate, high levels of distribution and no tax payable at the corporate level, an investment in a REIT is akin to a direct property investment but with one distinct advantage—liquidity. If an investor wants to dispose of his or her interest in the real estate he/she just needs to sell the shares on the exchange. It also enables investors to acquire interests in quality real estate that would otherwise not be possible.

In their "pure" form they are regarded by investors as "low beta" (low risk) securities and many studies have been undertaken globally which establish the risk/return benefits of an allocation to REITs in a balanced portfolio of investments.

With this extraordinary growth and interest in REITs, this book is very timely and extremely valuable. There is nothing currently available that is dedicated to this investment class and that covers such a broad range.

Dominic Whiting explains what a REIT is in simple, easy to read language. For all their popularity, as with any investment there are risks and the book very clearly analyzes why some REITs have performed well and why investors have not fully embraced others. It should be essential reading for any investor. Various approaches to regulation around the region are also examined. This is important as the markets that have tended to work best are those that have the most effective regulatory foundations.

I commend this book to all participants in the real estate investment trust sector.

Peter Mitchell
CEO

Peter Mitchell is the chief executive officer of the Asian Public Real Estate Association (www.aprea.biz). The Asian Public Real Estate Association is a non-profit industry association that represents the listed real estate sector in Asia Pacific. It works to encourage greater investment in the listed real estate sector in the region through the provision of better information to investors, improving the general operating environment, encouraging best practices and generally unifying and strengthening the industry.

Acknowledgments

I'd like to thank my employer, Reuters Co. Ltd., for giving me the opportunity to report on the burgeoning world of property investment in Asia and for giving me permission to write this book. In particular, Jack Reerink, Eric Hall and Tony Munroe have given me much encouragement, and I also appreciate being able to draw on the expertise of numerous other colleagues in bureaux across the continent.

A correspondent is nothing without sources, so I am grateful to everyone in the property industry who was generous enough to share their time and knowledge. Many are quoted at length in the book, but I would like to especially thank Matt Nacard at Macquarie Securities, Anthony Ryan at JPMorgan and Michael Smith at Goldman Sachs for taking my frequent phone calls. I have cited the positions of sources and their companies at the time they spoke to me, although I recognize that some of the people quoted in the book have since moved onwards (and upwards), and will continue to do so.

Thanks also to C.J. Hwu, who came up with the bright idea of a book on Asian REITs and who subsequently prodded me to get it done, and the rest of the team at John Wiley and Sons.

Last but not least, I'd like to thank my wife Atchara and my sons Kim and Ben for not appearing to miss me too much on Saturday mornings.

Playing the Asian REIT game

The board game Monopoly is popular around the world for its simple encapsulation of the ins and outs of property investment. Cash in hand, a player moves around the board, deciding what property to buy, assessing the market price and the potential for rental income, and hatching plans for growth through buying more land and building houses and hotels. Landing on "chance" exposes the player to risks, such as building repair costs.

Following the same basic themes, this book explores the very concrete world of real estate investment trusts (REITs), an investment option that is becoming more mainstream as new markets are established around the world.

It focuses on developments in the newest REIT markets in Asia, which are helping property investment go global, and outlines the experiences and views of the landlords, investment bankers, and trust managers who are pioneering new investment products in those markets. The book also examines the roles of the regulators and trustees who are seeking to ensure the new markets are healthy and investors are properly informed and protected if need be.

Key questions are answered, including: What are the regulatory and tax issues that can affect new REIT markets? Which types of property are offered in the various REIT markets? How do you value it? And how do you view and handle risks associated with inflation, higher interest rates and property cycle downturns? This book also gives a detailed history of the new markets and talks about how individual investors can learn from professional fund managers.

Rules of the game

How to go global?

Thanks to real estate investment trusts (REITs), an investor can now own a piece of property in New York, Paris, Tokyo, Sydney, or even Seoul or Kuala Lumpur—without being a multi-millionaire first.

If Singapore consumer confidence starts to stir, shop around for luxury malls. When Malaysia says it is on the brink of signing a free trade agreement with China, store the investment in some warehouses. But if yet another earthquake sends shivers through Japanese markets, it might be time to quickly ditch those 30-year-old office blocks.

Just as stock markets have given investors access to a myriad of companies, and bond markets let investors lend to governments and companies around the world, new and fast growing REIT markets allow property to be traded from minute to minute in the United States, Australia, and now several countries in Asia and Europe.

Asian governments in particular have been queuing up to draw up regulations to allow REITs to set up, giving tax breaks as encouragement, as they realize investors need a wider choice to better balance risk than the traditional offerings of stocks and bonds.

Authorities are aware that healthy REIT markets often invigorate property markets with a rash of new deals for buildings that might not have changed hands for years otherwise. Trusts also improve property market transparency. They increase information flows by setting a benchmark of how the capital markets value different types of buildings in different cities and countries. They are also obliged to communicate with their investors about the performance of their properties.

Property accounted for $830 billion of the world's stock market capitalization at the end of 2006, but some industry experts believed the emergence of new REIT markets would help the value of listed property grow to $1 trillion by 2010.[1] Asia's REIT market alone was tipped to treble to around $160 billion in four years from 2006.[2]

For the global investor, REITs will be difficult to ignore.

What is a REIT? (And how do you say it?)

REITs are so new to most of the world that many journalists reporting on them mispronounce the acronym, often to sneak a play on words into their headlines, such as "Making the REIT choice," or "Time to get it REIT."

So a very basic definition of a REIT might not go amiss.

In its simplest form, a REIT breaks down the ownership of a building, or more often a group of buildings, into units that are sold to investors and usually listed on the stock market—a way of "securitizing" property. Most of the income from the buildings, typically 90-95%, must be paid directly to investors as a dividend on a regular basis, for example twice a year.

Conditional on the high payout, most countries allow for "tax transparency"—taxation of income only at the investor level rather than at the company level—to ensure that REITs better mimic the concept of personal ownership of property.

This is a major advantage. Whereas investors in a normal property company stock would in effect pay tax twice—corporate tax and tax on dividends, REIT investors only pay a tax on dividends, at their personal tax rate. As a result, more of the revenue from the property assets flows through to investors than would be the case for traditional listed property companies.

REITs are generally regarded as a half-way house between stocks and bonds.

Like bonds, where the borrower makes a steady flow of interest payments to the investor, REITs offer a relatively secure and steady income from their dividends. This income is usually quoted as a yield—as a percentage of the market price of the trust's units. So if units are being traded at $100 and the trust announces an annual dividend of $6.50, the yield is 6.5%.

Just like bonds, if the unit price moves higher in market trade and the dividend holds steady, the yield falls. If investors are so keen on this hypothetical REIT that they push up the price of a unit to $105, the $6.50 dividend now yields 6.2% to a new buyer. The investor's return on the original $100 paid for each unit would combine the $5 capital gain (a 5% rise) with the $6.5 dividend payout (6.5%)—a total of 11.5%.

Generally bond prices rise, and their yields fall, if investors are worried about economic prospects and want to switch away from riskier investment in company shares and into something with a safe income stream.

But REITs tend to follow share prices rather than bond prices because trust investors react in similar ways as stock investors to twists and turns in the economy, which tend to dictate property business cycles.

Unlike bonds, the income from REITs is not fixed, and that is why trusts will often trade at least two percentage points above government bonds, to compensate for the extra risk.

Rents can rise, and they usually do if the economy is thriving, or if not enough new buildings are being built to satisfy demand. But rents can also fall if the property cycle turns downward and there is an oversupply of buildings. The value of a building will also rise and fall depending on the health of the property market.

And just as with rents, a property's worth can be held hostage to a host of other factors, from the construction of a new underground railway line nearby, to storm damage or the discovery of asbestos in the roof. A REIT investor should be on the look out for anything that might jolt the smooth running of the property, and keep an especially close watch on management.

It is up to trust managers, who receive fees for their work, to increase the dividend yield for investors. They could, for example, cut costs with more efficient power consumption, or renovate the buildings to attract tenants willing to pay more rent. Or they can borrow and ask investors for money, by selling more units in the trust, to buy buildings that are earning more rent than the current yield of the REIT—what is called a "yield-accretive" acquisition.

Put simply, a building on the market at $1 million, and annual rental income after expenses of $60,000 is giving a yield of 6% (this "net property yield is also often referred to as a building's "capitalization rate," or cap rate). The 6% would be attractive for a trust that is trading on the market at a 5% yield. But investors in a trust yielding 6.2% would raise their eyebrows if their trust manager opted for a deal of only 6% because it would reduce their dividend payouts—unless they were sure rents were about to rise steeply soon.

In some countries, REITs are also allowed to develop property—buy land and put up new buildings—which can bring in hefty returns. But often, REITs are not allowed by market regulators to build, and this lack of development risk, as well as the tax breaks, can be one of the factors differentiating investing in a trust from investing in shares in a listed property firm.

The *right* pronunciation of REIT in English rhymes with "sweet"—or at least that seems to be the consensus among the investment bankers who set up the trusts, and the managers who run them.

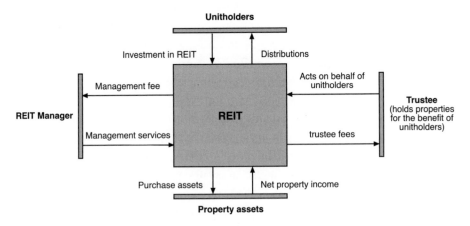

Why invest?

A glance at the price movement of REITs in some of the world's newest markets, Japan and Singapore, raises the question: why do the investment bankers and fund managers touting these securities insist on selling them as steady investments which give decent and fairly predictable returns?

After all, units in Singapore's CapitaMall Trust, a shopping mall REIT formed by developer CapitaLand Ltd., more than doubled in price in the first two years after the trust listed on the Southeast Asian island-state's stock exchange in mid-2002. Japan's biggest trust by 2005, Nippon Building Fund, also saw its price almost double in its first three years of life.

Hong Kong's Link REIT, formed with shopping malls and car park spaces sold by the city's housing authority in the world's biggest initial public offering by a REIT, saw its share price jump as much as 70% in its first month of trade in late 2005.

These kinds of steep capital gains are common, though largely unique, to nascent REIT markets, and that is why property investors should set their sights beyond the established markets of the United States and Australia. Experience has shown that the returns can amply reward the risks associated with untried markets.

A couple of explanations stand out.

Firstly, the price of some public share sales could be regarded in hindsight as generous to investors. The first trusts to list in a new market lack precise price benchmarks, and can only make a rough guess at how well they will be received by investors. But as investors became accustomed to the new securities and better understood their characteristics, REITs took off in Japan and Singapore, drawing growing volumes of firstly local, and later, foreign funds.

The spread between REITs and 10-year government bonds narrowed to about 2 percentage points from about 3 percentage points in the first couple of years in Japan and Singapore—reflecting a change in perceptions of relative risk in investing in REITs.

But there is also a concrete business spur for big capital gains in new REIT markets. Trusts in young markets can usually buy buildings, and therefore increase revenues, much more easily than their counterparts in the mature Australian and US markets.

For example, in Australia, about 70% of investment grade property is already in the hands of REITs—both unlisted and listed property trusts (LPTs), as they are called there. Prizing the remaining buildings away from landlords at the right price is likely to be difficult.

A healthy REIT market will typically push up prices for buildings on the open market. Whereas a landlord might have sold a building that gave its buyer a 9% yield in the past, he would know that a trust that yielded 7% would be more than happy to pay a higher price. The trust could pay a price that translated into an 8% yield and it would still be a good deal for its unit holders.

Singapore and Japan have both seen this yield compression, but as it is happening, REITs can still pick up bargains. And as more investors buy into REITs, they push down unit prices, meaning more expensive, lower-yielding buildings will also suddenly fit the bill as yield-accretive acquisitions.

In Japan, a country with $1.27 trillion of investment-grade property, the scope for acquisitions is huge for trusts that can trace their history back no farther than 2001.

However, for a more considered, longer-term view of REIT returns, it is best to look at the world's deepest and oldest market, that of the United States, which in 2006 had about 180 trusts with a combined worth of just over $300 billion.

Trusts were introduced in the early 1960s, and have been through various cycles, including a 1980s property market boom and a subsequent crash during the "savings and loans" crisis, which ultimately sparked a spurt of growth in the REIT industry.

After deregulation allowed them to compete with banks, savings and loan institutions took on risky ventures to give their customers higher deposit rates, but a mix of mismanagement, failed property speculation and in some cases fraud brought the industry crashing down. A US government body auctioned off buildings from failed investments, presenting the ideal opportunity for new REITs to pick up buildings cheaply. The REIT market mushroomed.

In fact, it was the US "savings and loans" example that spurred some Asian governments to establish REIT markets in the wake of the 1997–1998 Asian economic crisis to help the process of corporate restructuring.

REITs have performed well in the US partly because property values recovered in the 1990s from the savings and loan crisis but also because investors grew to accept the trusts as a serious asset class as property markets stabilized.

US equity REITS gave an average annual total return of 13.4% between December 1972 and December 2005, outpacing most other major US investment options.[3]

Over the same period, US large stocks gave an average 11.2% annual gain, and US bonds gave average yearly returns of 8.9%. Only US small stocks, with 14.9%, beat the REIT market's annual returns.

Diversification

Given the history of impressive long-term returns, it is hardly surprising that investment portfolios benefit if a sizeable chunk of capital is set aside for REITs. But the argument for REITs becomes even more compelling when the low correlation between REITs and stocks and bonds is taken into account. Because REITs will not necessarily move in tandem with other investments, investment managers can use them to reduce a portfolio's risk.

As investors better understood the characteristics of REITs in the US, the correlation between returns from US trusts and those from stocks measured by the S&P 500 index has actually fallen, to about 0.25 in the late 1990s from 0.64 in the 1970s. The correlation between REIT returns and 20-year bond returns fell to 0.16 from 0.27 over the same period.[4]

A portfolio containing a minority allocation to REITs would have seen higher returns and lower risks than a portfolio of only long-term bonds, stocks and treasury bills over much of the lifespan of the US REIT market, according to research by consultants Ibbotson and Associates.

The data showed that $10,000 invested in the non-REIT portfolio in 1972 with dividends reinvested would have grown to $219,049 by 2000. A second portfolio with a 10% REIT allocation would have reached $227,000, while a third that contained a 20% REIT allocation would be worth $238,349.

A bigger global market will now also allow much more diversification among REITs. Investors will have more choice within the staple asset classes of retail, office, residential and industrial property as well as more offbeat choices such as homes for the elderly and prisons. There are even suggestions of an igloo REIT.

But more importantly, investors can choose between countries at different points on the property business cycle. For example, if a dangerous property bubble has formed in the United States, maybe it is time to look at Japan, where land prices are just emerging from a slump lasting a decade and a half.

Research shows that securities investments in the same property type in different countries have a lower correlation than investments in different property types—for example, office, retail and industrial—within one country. To reduce risk, a property investor should diversify across national borders and preferably, across property types in different countries.

Liquidity

Because buildings are expensive, for most people, buying a home will be the biggest single investment decision of their life, and it will probably be their only type of property purchase. Small-scale property investors might buy a local house or apartment to rent out, and if that is successful, start to accumulate properties.

Few individuals, or even companies, can buy a whole office building or shopping center costing millions of dollars. Even those who can afford it will probably get a headache selling later, because it will not be easy to find a buyer for such a large asset who will pay the asking price. In cities where buildings seldom change hands, putting an exact value on a property is difficult.

REITs have essentially changed the nature of property investment, allowing investors to put as much or as little money as they want into a particular set of buildings. As REIT units are easily traded on the stock market, or "liquid," an investor does not have to worry about being unable to sell. And because the market price is always quoted, an investor will always know how much the property investment is worth. Trusts are also obliged to provide detailed reports on their operations, giving information about buildings and the general property market that otherwise would be difficult to find.

The bandwagon

About half a million people, or one in every 14 Hong Kong citizens, signed up for what would have been the territory's first REIT at the end of 2004, only to

US REIT Returns vs Stocks and Bonds

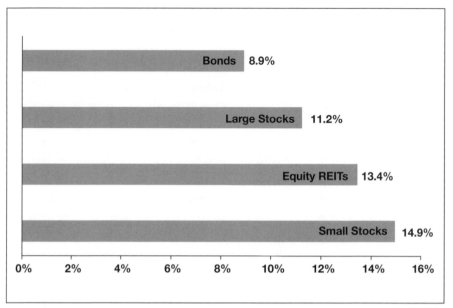

Source: Ibbotson and Associates/NAREIT (2006)

Return and Risk for Three US Investment Portfolios

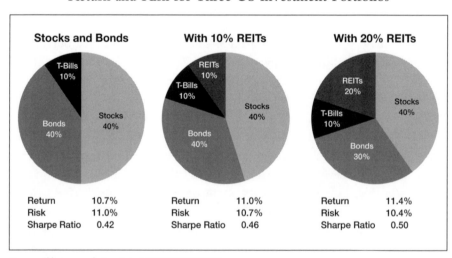

Source: Ibbotson and Associates/NAREIT (2006)

Correlations Among Various Asset Classes

		1	2	3	4	5	6	7	8	9
1	**Global REITs**	**1.00**								
2	Direct Real Estate - US only	**0.01**	1.00							
3	Equity - Developed countries	**0.30**	0.11	1.00						
4	Equity - Asia only	**0.20**	−0.07	0.74	0.75	1.00				
5	Equity - US only	**0.28**	0.11	0.94	0.94	0.58	1.00			
6	Fixed Income - Developed countries	**0.09**	0.01	−0.12	−0.13	−0.15	−0.06	1.00		
7	Fixed Income - US only	**0.08**	−0.03	−0.10	−0.10	−0.10	−0.03	0.88	0.19	1.00

The following indices were used as proxies for the respective asset classes:
Global REITs (GPR 250 REIT Index), Direct Real Estate - US only (NCREIT), Equity - Developed countries (MSCI World), Equity - Developed + emerging (MSCI ACWI), Equity - Asia only (MSCI AC Pacific), Equity - US only (S & P 500), Fixed Income - Developed countries Citibank (Citibank WGBI), Fixed Income - Emerging markets (EMBI Global), Fixed Income - US only (Lehman Aggregate).

Property Market Correlations Across Different Regions

Country	US	UK	Netherlands	France	Hong Kong	Australia	Japan
US	1.00						
UK	0.39	1.00					
Netherlands	0.31	0.44	1.00				
France	0.28	0.46	0.49	1.00			
Hong Kong	0.30	0.24	0.26	0.20	1.00		
Australia	0.29	0.22	0.21	0.20	0.24	1.00	
Japan	0.07	0.14	0.14	0.11	0.11	0.02	1.00

Source: S & P, Citigroup World Property Index, ING Clarion. Local Currencies.

have their hopes dashed when a 67-year-old public housing tenant mounted a legal case that postponed the initial public offering.

The $2.8 billion Link REIT, 130 times subscribed by retail investors, defied most expectations in Hong Kong, a property-mad city but a place where many analysts thought investors would be much more interested in the prospect of quick gains from traditional stocks rather than a yield product such as a REIT.

As it turned out, many investors were fed up with rock-bottom bank deposit rates, but were also wary of the volatility of traditional stocks—especially after the dot-com bubble popped and debunked all the investment hype surrounding technology firms in the late 1990s.

When the Link REIT overcame its legal hurdles and eventually listed on the Hong Kong stock exchange in November 2005, shares shot up 15% on the first day of trading thanks to strong buying from investors all around the world.

The Hong Kong market was to stutter later in 2006 for various reasons, but analysts predicted that REITs were here to stay.

With interest rates at almost zero in Japan under the government's "ultra-easing" monetary policy designed to flood the economy with cash to end more than a decade of stagnation, the Japanese REIT market has also experienced similar enthusiasm from individual investors. Individuals held about 20% of Japanese REIT units in late 2004, up from just 14% when the market started in 2001. Japanese financial institutions owned around 55% of REITs, with regional banks plowing a lot of their cash into the market because they were struggling to find reliable corporate borrowers. Foreign investors held about 10%.[5]

However, the main catalyst for growth in REIT markets across the world is coming from traditional large-scale property investors such as pension funds and insurance companies that need steady returns to cover long-term liabilities.

On the basis of a body of research into portfolio modeling, the general consensus among pension fund managers now appears to be that 10-20% of their investment should be devoted to property.

In most countries they are far behind that, partly because of the perceived high risk of putting millions of dollars into just a few "illiquid" assets—which is what buying big office blocks or shopping malls is like. In Japan, property accounted for less than 2% of pension fund investment in 2005. It was only 4% in France, nearly 5% in the U.K. and nearly 6% in the US. Pension funds in the Netherlands led the way with an average 10% allocation.[6]

Investing in "physical" property, in other words buying entire buildings, is attractive in terms of diversification because their returns have extremely low, and in some cases negative, correlation to those of stocks. But REITs, despite a higher correlation with stocks, are becoming more popular among pension funds and insurers because they give quick and easy global exposure and asset variety and, very importantly, are easy to offload if necessary.

With populations aging across the world, pension funds are desperate for REIT markets to grow and will probably be the main investors.

The proportion of the world's population in retirement was forecast to increase by more than a third to 21% over 15 years from 2006, with the post-World War II "baby boomer" generation putting an especially large strain on pensions in developed countries.[7]

In Asia, the United Nations estimates that the number of people over 65 will quadruple by 2050, when they will represent 18% of the total population, about three times the level in 2006.

Japan will have roughly one retired person to every two of working age by 2025, a higher ratio than any other major industrialized nation.

In China, the burden on the working population, and the need to find solid investments to fund pensions, will probably be even more acute. The population profile is aging because of a "one-child policy" designed to shrink a 1.3 billion population in a society that traditionally favors male babies.

"There'll be a big need for yield product," said Kurt Roeloffs, a managing director at RREEF, a unit of Deutsche Bank, of the prospects for a REIT market in the world's most populous country. "If China doesn't do it, we'll have a lot of grumpy old men."[8]

Tapping Asia's growth

Rapid economic growth and urbanization makes Asia probably the most exciting region for property investment in the world.

New buildings are crowding the continent's booming cities, providing a flow of new property investment opportunities but also lifting the price of increasingly scarce land and existing office blocks, shopping malls, factories, warehouses, apartments and houses.

In the decade to 2003, South Korea, for example, was among the fastest growing economies in the world, recording an average 5.4% climb in gross domestic product (GDP) each year. Malaysia and Singapore, with 5.3% growth, followed closely, and that was during a period marred by the 1997-98 Asian economic crisis, which sparked a short but sharp region-wide slump. In comparison, Germany and Italy managed just 1.4% and 1.7% average yearly growth respectively over those 10 years.

But China's dizzying economic ascent, driven by massive investment into manufacturing for export, is now fuelling demand and economic growth in the region. China, averaging 8.9% economic growth in the decade to 2003, was notching up growth of more than 9% in both 2004 and 2005, and 10% in 2006.

India, as it also opened up to foreign investment, saw its economy expand more than 7% in 2005 and 9% in 2006, as global companies outsourced back-office jobs and call centers to the country, sparking a construction boom.

As new manufacturing and service-sector jobs are created, millions of Asians are moving to cities every year, creating demand for all types of buildings.

The number of Asians living in urban areas grew to 1.22 billion from 540,000 between 1975 and 2000. With 40 million people moving to Asian cities every year to find better education and job opportunities, the U.N. estimates that by 2020 half of the continent's population will live in urban areas, compared with 35% in 2006.

By 2015, Asia will account for 12 of the world's 21 mega-cities. Four of them, Tokyo, Mumbai, Dhaka and Delhi, will have more than 20 million residents with Shanghai, Beijing, Jakarta, Kolkata, Osaka, Karachi and Manila each home to more than 10 million.[9]

But the rapid growth of cities presents its own difficulties for property investment. Once-fashionable areas can lose their glitter in just a couple of years, as new roads or a new airport direct business to an up-and-coming district. A bustling shopping center can empty almost overnight if a glitzier venue moves in down the road and pulls in brand-name retailers.

Following the Asian economic crisis, many global investors perceived the region's markets as relatively risky compared with other parts of the world. In many countries, property bubbles contributed to the economic crash. Too much building by overzealous developers with easy credit ended up flooding property markets in Bangkok, Singapore, Kuala Lumpur and Hong Kong with homes, offices and shops that no one wanted to buy, saddling banks with mountains of bad loans.

In hindsight, the experience was probably a good lesson for Asia's property industry. Across the region, banks became much more cautious in their lending for big property projects and developers started to attach more importance to market research, as well as good planning and design.

Investors are now learning that to generalize about a region that stretches from Tokyo to Phnom Penh to Mumbai in any way is unwise.

"A couple of years ago, Asia was seen as a high-risk region," said Robert Lie, the Asia head of the property arm of Dutch financial services group

A snapshot of Asia's REIT markets in 2006

Market	Number of listed REITs	REIT market capitalization	Average dividend yield	10-year bond yield
Japan	40	$39.18 billion	3.6 %	1.66 %
Singapore	13	$12.85 billion	4.9 %	3.01 %
Hong Kong	4	$6.46 billion	5.0 %	3.97 %
South Korea	8	$840 million	7.7 %	4.98 %
Taiwan	7	$1.76 billion	3.8 %	1.95 %
Thailand	9	$835 million	7.4 %	4.8 %
Malaysia	8	$657 million	6.9 %	3.8 %

(as of November 2006. Source: CBRE Research)

ING Groep NV.[10] "What I see now is people have much more knowledge and appreciation of the real risks. It's not just one high-risk region; there are different types of countries with different phases of maturity."

Lie said Dutch pension funds, for example, were keen to gradually increase the proportion of their property holdings allocated to Asia to about 20-25% from about 10% in 2005.

According to consultants Jones Lang LaSalle direct investment in Asia-Pacific property totaled $94 billion in 2006, up 43% from a year earlier, with cross-border flows accounting for about a third.

A survey in late 2005 of 180 banks and fund managers in Asia, Europe and North America by property consultants DTZ supported the idea that property investors were keen to move into Asia. The survey found that 40% intended to increase their cross-border property holdings in Asia within two years, with China, Australia, Hong Kong and Japan the most popular destinations.

The main sources for new investment would be Singapore, Hong Kong, Australia, the US and Germany, said the head of global research at DTZ, Joe Valente. "There's no shortage of capital," Valente said.[11] "What there is, is a shortage of investment-grade stock."

And that is where Asian REITs enter the scene.

REIT players—Fund managers

All sorts of people invest in REITs. You have individuals, who are often referred to as "retail investors." They will either buy REITS on their own through a stock broker or through online trading sites, which are often run by banks. They can also hold them through mutual funds, which may be general in nature, completely devoted to REITs or specialize in property securities, including REITs. Some retail investors will trade actively, even on a daily basis, while others might set up a portfolio for the long term—investing in REITs, with their steady income, over 15 or 20 years can be a perfect way to set up a personal pension.

On the other hand, there are "institutional investors," such as pension funds and insurance companies, which also like to invest in property because it gives the kind of steady income plus capital gain that meets the needs of their long-term liabilities. Although such investors have typically invested in direct property, in other words they have bought up entire buildings, they are starting to look at REITs.

A manager of funds for retail investors and a manager of a property fund for an institutional investor give their opinions here on Asia's new REIT markets.

"We know the story, and it's a good one"

Chris Reilly is in charge of investing in Asian property at Henderson Global Investors, an investment management firm with about $119 billion in assets under management globally.

Henderson offers funds that invest in REITs around the world to individual investors in Europe, Australia and Singapore, so it is hardly surprising that Reilly is enthusiastic about the securities. The Henderson funds typically invest about 75% of their capital in REITs, with the rest in shares in traditional property firms.

Reilly believes that the new REIT markets in Asia will mushroom because of both growing demand and a steady supply of buildings, as landlords increasingly see that selling to REITs can be highly profitable. But in 2005 and 2006, demand was outstripping supply, driving up the price of REIT units across Asia and therefore offering investors high capital gains.

"Demand has been broadening out," Reilly said. "There are global property securities funds interested, and there's a lot of capital flowing into those funds from retail investors. A lot of institutional investors are interested in getting into the space and are looking to buy that type of product. There are funds of funds, enhanced index funds, hedge fund investors."

"It's on a lot of people's radars now and the coverage of the sector is growing," he said. "There's no secret that risk-adjusted returns have been good, so the story spreads quite rapidly."

"So when IPOs (initial public offerings) are coming up, my impression is they are not restricted to specialist real estate investors like Henderson, but a whole band of people who say 'we'll have a piece of that please. We know the story, and it's a good one'."

Reilly said pension funds will be among the main institutional investors in REITs over the longer term.

"It's quite a simple set of metrics for them," he said. "Bond yields are very low so they're expensive to buy. So if you can find inflation-hedged assets that are delivering income and better yields, it's an attractive asset class."

"Pension fund allocation to real estate is increasing and the increase is not so much into the physical asset but into the securitized asset. Many institutional investors lack the skill sets needed to manage physical assets and so seek alternative exposure."

"The flow of property being packaged into REITs will continue as long as it is more profitable for landlords to sell the buildings into trusts than to other potential buyers," Reilly said.

Generally, investors will pay higher prices for REITs than the underlying buildings would fetch on the physical property market because the REIT units are "liquid" and better diversified, Reilly said.

"There's a kind of arbitrage going on, but it's a difficult arbitrage to originate because to actually go through the exercise requires a lot of capital," he said, offering an example of a company that wants to set up a REIT with Chinese buildings.

"Imagine you assemble, say, 10 offices in China, do all the IPO work which requires some capital and some risk. If you bought the asset for an 8% or 9% yield in China and you sell to the market at a 6% yield, you're certainly making money. You've just made 30-50% on your investment."

"The capital markets are prepared to buy this liquid real estate paper at a lower yield than the underlying real estate for a variety of reasons, such as liquidity, diversification, and expectations of future growth in value and rents," he explained. "And until expectations and yields move the other way, it will continue to happen. Of course the rationale becomes less compelling as yields move higher on the capital market."

Many of the buildings packaged into REITs will come from owner-occupier companies that want to free up capital for investing in their main businesses, according to Reilly.

"It's quite unhelpful to have large assets that are low-yielding on the balance sheet. They can sell it and take a leaseback on the asset, and let the REIT manager deal with the real estate side of it," Reilly said. "There's a recycling of capital option here. It wouldn't have been possible if there wasn't any buyer for the real estate. But what you've got now, the REIT is the end demand."

And which REIT markets in the Asia Pacific region will thrive?

Japan is "ahead of the game," Reilly said. "Singapore is rapidly developing. It's already old news in Australia."

Korea will probably develop a REIT market "if they free up the system and the regulatory issues," he said, adding that Taiwan's market will also grow. Thailand and Malaysia will develop slowly, according to Reilly.

Investors should expect Hong Kong to offer so-called "cross-border" REITS that include property in China because they offer more yield, he said.

Mostly "curious"

Although REITs are being marketed as the answer to all the investment problems of pension funds and insurance companies, many are not yet prepared to jump on the bandwagon.

Ben Sanderson, who makes property investments for British insurance firm Prudential Plc., said he is not likely to switch soon to REITs.

Correlations between US REITs and stocks have fallen over the years, but Prudential still regards the trusts as stocks and will probably only invest in REITs as part of its equity market allocation of around 40-45% of the billion pounds it has to invest. Prudential earmarks about 35% for bonds and 15-20% to property.

"REITs are not quite equities or direct property, they're something in between," Sanderson said. "We don't think they replicate physical property. The only people who say they do are the people who sell the REITs." But Sanderson leaves the door open for what he calls "tactical" investment in REITs—short-term investment, maybe to take advantage of cheap valuations in REIT markets.

Sanderson is a supporter of REITs, though, believing that they will have a positive knock on effect on property markets.

"I'm curious, interested and enthusiastic, in that order," he said. "I'm curious to see what the effect will be on other parts of the business. Whilst we're not interested in investing in any of the REITs in (Asia), we know that they are affecting the playground we're operating in and that might happen in the U.K. as well. Things like the way in which it increases transparency, the way in which it changes the risk premium being put on property. It gives you another exit route which reduces the liquidity risk of property."

Endnotes

1   Scott Crowe, global real estate strategist at UBS, speaking at the European Public Real Estate Association (EPRA) seminar in Barcelona in January 2005, quoted by Reuters: "Property equity growth to storm world markets," by Steve Hays, January 27, 2005.

2   Michael Smith, head of Asia property investment banking at UBS, quoted by Reuters: "Chinese buildings to spur Asia's property trusts," by Dominic Whiting, June 28, 2005.

3   Ibbotson and Associates analysis, quoted by National Association of Real Estate Investment Trusts (NAREIT) in "REITs: Building dividends and diversification," 2006.

4   *Ibid.*

5   Lehman Brothers global equity research: "J-REITs: Yield Rush" by Yoshihito Oshima, August 9, 2005.

6   UBS Global Real Estate Analyzer, June 13, 2005.

7   OECD estimates.

8   "Property trusts give ageing Asia safe home for cash," by Dominic Whiting and Mantik Kusjanto, Reuters, June 29, 2004.

9   "Urbanization in Asia: An overview," by Graeme Hugo, University of Adelaide, paper prepared in June 2003.

10 "ING starts up S. Korean property venture," Reuters, by Dominic Whiting, November 21, 2005.

11 "Investors want Asian property but risks remain-DTZ," Reuters, by Dominic Whiting, October 18, 2005.

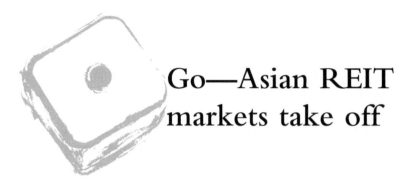

Go—Asian REIT markets take off

Rollercoaster in Hong Kong

There was a time when the name Lo Siu Lan could send shivers down the spines of the property investment bankers who worked for years trying to create a REIT market in Hong Kong.

Now, mention of the 67-year-old pensioner who scuppered the world's biggest initial public offering for a REIT in 2004, infuriating half a million Hong Kong residents who signed up to the deal and several big-name global property investors, would probably be greeted with a wry smile.

The $2.8 billion "Link REIT," an attempt by the cash-strapped Hong Kong Housing Authority to sell 151 shopping centers and 79,000 car park spaces, was finally launched in November 2005—a year late.

But the protracted legal struggle against the Link REIT by the public housing tenant, known in the media as "Madame Lo," is a lesson for any government trying to push through privatization, even if it ultimately failed.

More importantly for investors, it highlighted the fact that buying into REITs is not just about buildings but also about the people who use them.

The Link fiasco

The Link REIT saga began in late 2003, when the Hong Kong government hatched a plan to effectively kill two birds with one stone: kick-start a REIT market and raise much needed funds so that the Housing Authority could take its mind off running shopping centers it had built to serve public housing tenants and concentrate on building more subsidized apartments for the poor.

Although Hong Kong had just introduced a REIT code in July 2003, allowing property trusts to be created and list on the stock exchange, several factors prevented a market from blossoming.

Firstly, many landlords said they were reluctant to sell buildings in a city where land was so scarce, especially at a time when property values had slumped during the Asian economic crisis after reaching a heady peak in 1997. Then an outbreak of the SARS respiratory disease sent property prices into a tailspin.

For many, their buildings also had a strong psychological grip. Some of Hong Kong's biggest fortunes were made, or at least propagated, in the property business, including those of the former British colony's big trading houses, the Jardine Matheson group and John Swire & Sons. The dominant property developer in Hong Kong, Cheung Kong (Holdings), is controlled by the richest man in Asia, Li Ka-shing, who built an empire that also includes ports and telecoms from a plastic flower business.

Hong Kong also did not give the special tax benefits to REITs that other countries offered, so listed companies holding property assets lacked the extra incentive to spin them off into property trusts (see Chapter 2).

But many analysts and bankers believed it just needed someone to launch a trust to show there was enough investor enthusiasm to allow other property firms to follow suit. Developers could sell off their non-core assets to raise capital for new projects, but still keep a stake of say 30%, which they could see rise in value after a stock market listing.

If the REIT were large enough, it would also be useful in setting a price benchmark for the rest of the market—an indication of how much an investor would be willing to pay for a certain type of building.

The Hong Kong Housing Authority stepped in. It employed investment banks UBS, HSBC and Goldman Sachs as underwriters and JPMorgan as an adviser, and announced publicly for the first time in mid-2004 that it would spin off buildings into the Link REIT.

The initial public offering (IPO) was slated for the end of the year and investor anticipation of what would be Hong Kong's first REIT built up into a near frenzy, with people forming snaking queues in front of banks to subscribe for shares when they were offered in early December.

A lot of hot money was flowing into Hong Kong in general at the end of 2004 on expectations a revaluation of the Chinese yuan would lift the returns from Chinese companies listed on the Hong Kong exchange and that the Hong Kong dollar might be pressured to change its US dollar peg.

With so much money flowing in, Hong Kong interest rates fell to rock bottom, making the Link REIT's promises of a 6.65% annual yield look even more enticing. Half a million individual investors signed up for shares in the trust, putting in a then Hong Kong record $280 billion worth of orders. The Link REIT also promised share allocations to 10 big "cornerstone" institutional investors, including Henderson Global Investors, ING Clarion Real Estate, and Prudential Asset Management. Singapore developer CapitaLand Ltd., which pioneered REITs in the Southeast Asian island state, became a strategic investor and adviser to the Link REIT's management team.

Then Lo Siu Lan appeared on the scene. The bespectacled pensioner with short grey hair, who lived on $460 a month in one of the world's most expensive cities, filed a court case arguing that the government's sale of its shopping centers contravened the territory's Housing Ordinance—legislation governing the provision of public housing.

At first, few took Lo seriously. But when Hong Kong's High Court began hearing the case the week before the Link's planned market debut, what began as a murmur in the newspapers became a front-page story as people suddenly realized the whole deal could be scrapped.

Many people suspected government critics within Hong Kong's legislative council were pulling the strings behind Lo, but a connection was not proven. She and a small band of elderly supporters just said that they feared the cost of their fish and vegetables would climb if, as they suspected, the Link REIT began putting up rents at its shopping centers in order to please shareholders.

The court ruled on December 15, 2004, in front of a gallery packed with journalists, that the government did have the right to spin off its property through the Link REIT. The Housing Ordinance stipulated that the Housing Authority needed to ensure that essential facilities, such as shops and car parking lots, were provided, but it did not necessarily have to own them.

"I've waited two years to hear that," exclaimed one investment banker in the courtroom who had worked on the Link REIT. But his wait was not yet over.

Lo appealed the decision but it was rejected. But she then had the option to take the case to the Court of Final Appeal. Despite an effort by Housing Authority lawyers to persuade a judge to compress Lo's period of appeal, she retained the right to the usual three months to decide whether to proceed or not.

With a possible legal case still hovering over the Link REIT, the government scrapped the listing. A stream of angry investors, many of whom had borrowed money at high interest rates from brokerages to buy their shares, vented their frustration on radio call-ins. Most fumed at the government for failing to foresee and deal with the legal challenge.

The Link REIT offering was only revived a year later, after Lo's final appeal was rejected, but ultimately it was a successful launch.

Skeptics said the Link REIT could flop. Much public bad feeling lingered from its first failed attempt to list, but the trust's investment bankers decided that it had garnered so much demand the first time around that it could be sold more expensively, at a promised yield of 6% rather than the 6.5% offered originally.

Even though interest rates—as measured by 10-year government bonds— had risen 300 basis points in the intervening 12 months, making the yield relatively less attractive, the bankers were proven right.

The IPO attracted institutional investor orders worth $33 billion, or 18.5 times the portion initially earmarked for them, while individual investors placed $108 billion worth of orders, 19 times their original collective allotment.

Link REIT shares jumped 15% on the first day, but within a month they were trading 50% higher than their IPO price, at a yield of 4.1%, with institutional investors particularly keen. A British-based hedge fund called the Children's Investment Fund (because it built charitable donations into its fee structure) built up a stake of nearly 18% in the Link's first couple of weeks of trading.

Property so bad, it's good

Behind the Link REIT's popularity lay a concept that is important for any investor looking at REITs—the trust's potential for rental growth. The shopping centers owned by the Link were among the shabbiest in Hong Kong. But that was the trust's main selling point.

Fixing up the Link's "wet markets" of fish mongers and fresh meat and vegetable stalls and its shopping arcades would translate into big profits down the road, according to Paul Cheng, chairman of the Link's management firm.

"The Link is unique in the sense that it's a very large portfolio of underperforming assets. The potential is obvious," Cheng said on the eve of the IPO. "And Hong Kong property has more pizzazz than other locations in Asia."[1]

The Link's management team promised a complete overhaul of its shopping centers, including bringing in brand-name retailers, upgrading toilets, and especially cutting costs. Its cost to income ratio stood at 48%, compared with just 30% typical at privately run suburban Hong Kong shopping malls.

Cheng said he wanted to improve entrances and signage, bring in tenants such as coffee chain Starbucks, and review deals with contractors. He also planned to invite school choirs and rock bands to play to make the shopping centers more attractive to the local communities and to offer new outdoor billboards on 180 premises across Hong Kong to the likes of Coca-Cola.

But many analysts doubted that the Link's management team could deliver on its promises. Some said that as a publicly listed entity, the Link would need to adhere more strictly to environmental laws, such as on drainage and asbestos, than it had as a government concern. It could also face stern opposition from public housing tenants and shopkeepers if it tried to raise rents aggressively— Lo's court case had already shown how passionate some tenants could be on the issue.

For example, at the three-storey Oi Tung shopping center on the east of Hong Kong island, which houses a McDonald's, a pharmacy, a tutoring school for children and a hair salon, some retail tenants said, just days before the Link's listing, that they would not be able to afford any rent rises.

"If there's a rent rise we'll have to move," said Franky Ho, as he served salted plums to a customer in his Chinese medicine shop selling a range of dried sea horses and sea cucumbers.[2] Ho made a monthly profit of about HK$5,000 ($645) after paying HK$20,000 in rent. "Everyone's afraid," he said.

Hong Kong REIT fever

Hong Kong property trusts were like the proverbial London buses. A long wait, in this case almost two years since REIT legislation was passed, and then suddenly three came at once. Two weeks after the Link's market debut, the Prosperity REIT listed, and that was followed a week later by the first trust completely comprising mainland Chinese buildings, the GZI REIT.

Prosperity REIT was initially comprised of seven office and industrial buildings owned by Cheung Kong and another Li Ka-shing company, Hutchison Whampoa Ltd.. It raised $250 million in its IPO and its shares shot up 20% on their first day of trading thanks to the excitement around property trusts stirred up by the Link REIT, not to mention the reinvestment by some investors of the profits they made from the Link's strong debut.

Li Ka-shing and Cheung Kong were not new to property trusts, having created the Fortune REIT of suburban Hong Kong shopping centers in August 2003. But Fortune was listed in Singapore partly because the Southeast Asian country had legislated for REITs and promoted them faster than Hong Kong's authorities had. Li also created a trust with his Suntec City office and shopping mall complex, located and listed in Singapore.

But when it became clear that the Link REIT would go ahead, Li decided it was the moment to sell his own property trust in Hong Kong, and the deal proved much more popular than his previous REITs. The tranche reserved for individual investors, who ended up getting half of the shares offered, was 200 times subscribed, while the institutional portion was about 20 times covered.[3] The hot reception was in sharp contrast to Fortune REIT, which was less than four times subscribed when it floated.

Many fund managers were surprised by the response because Prosperity offered a yield of just 5.3% on its IPO price, compared with 6.0% for the Link REIT.

Hong Kong office rents were soaring as three-year leases dating from the property market slump during the 2003 SARS outbreak were renegotiated. But while rents in some of Prosperity's buildings were due to double in its first year as a publicly listed trust, analysts predicted an average of just 9% income growth from the REIT in its first two years because of some nifty financial engineering, which enabled it to pay a decent yield at the beginning of its life, before rent rises kicked in.

Prosperity signed up to interest-rate swaps, which allowed its payment on its debt to rise annually from a low base, with the interest rate lifting from 0.3% in 2006 to 2.58% in 2010. The idea was that as rents rose, the trust would be able to pay more interest to its lenders.

The strong demand from investors looking for a solid yield and the potential to tap into Hong Kong's rising property market obscured any worry that Prosperity might struggle if the predicted rent rises failed to materialize.

"The strong debut clearly shows a good market appetite for REITs," said Anthony Ryan, head of real estate investment banking at JPMorgan Chase & Co., which sponsored the IPO along with Merrill Lynch & Co.. Ryan predicted (over optimistically, as it turned out) that within 12 months the market value of Hong Kong property trusts would more than double to $9 billion.

Much of the skepticism Hong Kong landlords harbored about REITs was evaporating, with the likes of listed developers Sun Hung Kai Properties, Henderson Land Development and Kerry Properties starting to make noises about spinning off some of their assets. They were tempted by the example of Singapore's CapitaLand Ltd., which had switched from being a traditional property developer to an "asset light" model of selling some buildings and creating a new fee-based business on REIT and property management.

Crowded Hong Kong, where land for new development is scarce, has been a favorite for property investors as a capital gain play. But the market is notoriously volatile because speculation is often rife. Bubbles can grow in a year and be pricked in an even shorter time. Commercial property values rose nine-fold in the decade from 1983, dropped by nearly half in the mid-1990s, peaked again in 1997, and slumped between the Asian economic crisis and the SARS outbreak in 2003. But in just two years after the SARS outbreak subsided, office rents had jumped 80% and values had doubled. Retail landlords hiked their rents 55% and saw their assets gain 80% in value.[4]

The stutter

But the Hong Kong REIT market soon began to stutter—and it happened when Champion REIT, a spin-off of the Citibank Plaza building by landlord Great Eagle Holdings, sold its IPO.

The timing of Champion's launch in mid-May 2006 was far from perfect.

Investors were getting nervous about rising interest rates, so REITs seemed less attractive as pure yield investments (see Chapter 5). At the same time, investor interest and funds were being sucked away by the $11.2 billion Hong Kong share offering by China's second-largest lender, the Bank of China—in what would be the world's fourth-largest IPO ever. On top of that, global stock markets began to slide, with investors especially trying to avoid Asia, as the prospect of rising US interest rates could damp demand for the region's exports.

Hong Kong's notoriously faddish individual investors were also becoming aware that REITs were steady, long-term investments, not stocks you could buy in the morning and sell in the evening for a short-term bet.

With the memory of the furor around the Link REIT starting to fade, individual investors were getting suspicious about property trusts, and wondering why a landlord would sell a building if it was such a good investment.

"The perception among investors, rightly or wrongly, is that if developers are prepared to part with assets—there must be something I don't know," George Pavey, head of equity capital markets at HSBC in Hong Kong said at the time.[5]

The way Champion REIT was structured, with several elements of financial engineering, and the fact it only owned one asset rather than a whole portfolio, did nothing to allay the doubts of many investors.

Champion REIT needed financial engineering because of Hong Kong's unique circumstances. By May 2006, average property values in the city had shot up 70% since a slump during the 2003 SARS outbreak, but rents were only starting to catch up because most leases lasted for three years. So at the price Great Eagle wanted to sell its Citibank Plaza into the trust, the building was only really giving a net property yield, or capitalization rate, of under 3%. That would be too low for any REIT to try to sell to investors.

Several measures were employed to bring forward to 2006 the benefits of projected steep rent rises in 2007 and 2008. Champion REIT entered complex interest rate swap agreements, which meant its debt repayments started small but would increase. And Great Eagle, which retained a 43% share in the trust, waived its right to a dividend in the first year and would get gradually higher dividend payments in future years (see Chapter 5).

But some analysts believed Champion had overdone the financial tricks.

"All REIT markets have some degree of financial engineering, but the lesson from Champion is the degree of engineering is important," said Matt Nacard, analyst at Macquarie Securities.

Champion's $808 million IPO was not a complete flop though. Its institutional portion—90% of the deal—was about three times covered by orders, but its retail investor portion was only just covered. The REIT's debut was weak amid the general malaise in the region's stock markets, and the REIT's shares fell 28% in their first two months of trading. As a result, the trust's yield jumped to 7.7% from the 5.45% offered at its IPO.

That was an awkward benchmark for the whole REIT market. Sun Hung Kai Properties and Henderson Land Development both decided to postpone trusts that they were planning to launch because they did not want to sell at such a low price.

HSBC's George Pavey argued that Hong Kong's REIT market would revive fairly quickly though, with property companies deciding to lower their price expectations. Many were eager to raise funds to expand their development activities in mainland China and also keen to adopt the "asset light" model.

"The big issue is that people think developers are selling at the top of the cycle," Pavey said. "They need to sell before the top of the cycle and give something to investors."

"I think what's going to happen is the frothiness will go out of the market, REITs in Hong Kong will be driven by the institutional investor in the next couple of years," he said. "And when retail investors see institutional investors are oversubscribing by three or four times, they'll come back and oversubscribe 100 times."

By the end of 2006, Hong Kong's REIT market had begun to show signs of life, with Henderson Land relaunching an IPO for its Sunlight REIT and Regal Hotels International Holdings also planning to spin off five Hong Kong hotels into a trust. Sun Hung Kai Properties said it would revive its REIT in 2007, and another landlord, Wharf Holdings Ltd., part of property group Wheelock and Co., said it would package a trust from six of its buildings, including its Lane Crawford House, in a prime spot in the Central district.

But contrary to what many in the industry had said about complex REIT structuring, investment bankers were still prepared to use their financial engineering tool box to help Hong Kong's developers obtain a good price when selling their low yielding buildings to the public.

Compared to Champion REIT, Henderson Land's Sunlight REIT toned down the interest rate swaps, but it employed a similar dividend waiver. It also introduced a new feature: a rental guarantee to sweeten the initial yield. In effect, the trust promised to pay investors a certain rent and therefore a minimum dividend for nearly three years, which boosted its forecast yield to 8.5% from its 20 office and retail buildings, some of which were really giving a net property yield of as low as 3%.

As with Champion REIT, and Prosperity REIT before it, the idea was that rents would rise quickly during the three years following its IPO, so when Henderson Land's dividend waiver and the rental guarantee expired, Sunlight REIT's yield would hold up. The obvious danger was that rents would not rise as quickly as anticipated and the trust's yield would slump.

Whereas REITs are supposed to be a half-way house between stocks and bonds, giving a steady yield plus prospects for income growth, Sunlight could be regarded as more of a high-yield bond—fixed income, with a much lower scope for rent-driven capital growth than other REITs. IPO investors were offered 8.5% for three years, while 10-year bonds were yielding 3.8%. That difference, or yield spread, was enough to persuade enough retail investors to sign up for the $350 million IPO for their tranche to be 8.4 times covered. Institutional investor orders were equal to four times the number of units offered, and the shares were priced at the top end of an indicated range.

However, that was not enough momentum behind the IPO to prevent Sunlight REIT from falling 6.5% on its debut. Within a week, the trust was trading 9% below its IPO price, at a yield of 10.1%.

Once again, unpopular financial engineering and a debut trading flop threw the immediate future of Hong Kong's REIT market into doubt.

China—The great hope and the hype

Hong Kong was also expected to become a thriving market for mainland Chinese property trusts.

The city was a more natural hub for Chinese REITs than Singapore or Tokyo because of its geographical location on the southern tip of China, experience since the early 1990s of investment in property in major cities (such as Beijing, Shanghai and Guangzhou) and a close alignment of the Hong Kong dollar and the Chinese yuan.

Hong Kong's history as an international financial center with high standards of corporate governance would also elevate it above Shanghai as a center for REITs, although the potentially massive appetite for property investment from China's burgeoning insurance and pension funds industries is likely to cajole Chinese regulators to establish their own market at some point.

The thirst for Chinese property trusts will be difficult to satisfy. A global survey of 180 banks, property firms and funds by consultants DTZ at the end of 2004 showed China as the top pick in Asia for property investment. And this translated into real fund flows. In just the first quarter of 2006, some international funds announced a combined $9 billion of direct investment in Chinese property. That was treble what the country's property sector attracted in 2005, when the whole of Asia received only $20 billion of direct property investment.[6]

Investors were dazzled by an economy growing at about 9% a year; a country transformed by a switch from a centrally planned to a market economy; huge investment in manufacturing by foreign firms, and a new tide of local private companies targeting export markets around the world. They also had an eye on a domestic middle class emerging from a population of 1.3 billion.

The construction of new housing, schools, hospitals, offices and shopping malls needs to keep up with an urban population that more than doubled, from about 220 million to 520 million, in the two decades to 2004, and which is expected to reach 655 million by 2014.[7] Not only is there a $186 billion stock of buildings ready to be packaged into property trusts, the owners are keen to sell some of their assets to raise money for new construction projects.

International investors are particularly keen on China's shopping centers, given the staggering jump in consumerism in the country. In the mid 1990s retail sales were growing as much as 30% per year, albeit from a low base, and they expanded at between 10% and 20% annually between 2000 and 2005. The boom allowed landlords to hike rents and in mid 2005 shopping centers were giving yields of about 10% in Shanghai and 14% in Beijing, compared to just 4.4% in Hong Kong.[8]

First Steps

The first property trust comprising completely of mainland Chinese buildings listed on the Hong Kong stock exchange in December 2004. Spun off by

Guangzhou Investment Co. Ltd., the investment arm of the local government of the southern Chinese city of Guangzhou, GZI REIT raised $230 million in an IPO that sold four of its buildings to the investing public.

The institutional part of the deal was 81 times covered and the retail portion was 495 times subscribed—amazing for a trust that promised no rental growth for at least two years. GZI's main asset, the 10-storey White Horse garment wholesale building, had only just hiked its rents by around 50% to lift the trust's distributable income for investors by about 44% from what it would have been and would have to wait until the leases expired to raise them again.

Many investors were hoping GZI REIT would be able to buy more high-yielding buildings from Guangzhou Investment, and some were betting the Chinese government would revalue the yuan currency, which would increase the relative returns the Chinese trust would give in Hong Kong dollars. Units in the trust jumped nearly 14% on their first day of trading, bringing the yield offered down to about 5.7% from the original 6.5% on the IPO price.

Analysts attributed the success of GZI's launch purely to the fact that it was the first mainland Chinese property trust.

"Scarcity value here is the number-one strength," said Matt Nacard, regional REIT analyst at Macquarie Securities.[9] "If you want listed exposure to rental income in China, as opposed to more risky development, this is the only way."

Here, "listed" is the key word.

Big Western institutional investors have been scouring China to buy good quality buildings as a way of tapping into the country's soaring economic growth. But the list of risks is long in a private property market that has flourished only since the mid 1990s. As a result, the likes of US investment bank Morgan Stanley and the Netherlands' ING Groep tended to prefer hooking up with local Chinese developers to build apartments, getting their investments in and out of a project in a matter of just two or three years. And because few big investors were willing to make the leap into such an immature market, even if they were to buy a building, they would fret whether they would be able to sell later.

GZI, and the other Chinese REITs that would follow it, offered investors a "bite-sized" exposure to Chinese property that could be unloaded instantaneously if necessary. The emergence of a REIT market can also become a virtuous cycle by stimulating the commercial property market in a country. An established REIT market offers the buyer of a building a convenient exit—selling into a trust. That would reduce the risk, so more investors will be drawn to Chinese property. And that in turn would boost prices, benefiting REIT shareholders.

In November 2006, the second REIT of Chinese buildings was launched, but this time in Singapore. In fact, the CapitaRetail China Trust, a spin-off of seven shopping malls in five Chinese cities bought by developer CapitaLand, was to become the most popular IPO launched in the Southeast Asian country, with the US$163 million issue 196 times subscribed by institutional investors and 39 times subscribed by retail investors.

As expected, the REIT's unit price soared on its market debut on December 8, jumping 59% from the IPO price, leaving a forecast dividend yield for 2007 of only 3.46%. At the time, most Singapore REIT yields were between 4% and 4.5%, and Singapore's 10-year bond was trading at 3.03%.

The frenzy around CapitaRetail China was attributed to the same factors as GZI's strong IPO: it was one of the few proxies available for China's rapid retail sales growth and thriving commercial property market. But unlike GZI, the Singapore-listed trust also had the mark of CapitaLand's strong brand, and a link to US retail giant Wal-Mart Stores Inc., which was growing rapidly in China and was the anchor tenant for the seven stores.

"It's not just yield, they're buying into the medium- and long-term growth and the China play," Yeow Kip Peng, associate director of equity research at Standard & Poor's in Singapore said of the surge in investor interest.

China Risks

But amid all the hype, it is worth mentioning the risks peculiar to China. Some investment bankers working on Chinese REITs are afraid that just one failed trust could taint the whole market.

"The sector is embryonic enough that you don't want that one bad apple," said Anthony Green, head of property investment banking at Australia's Macquarie Bank.[10] "If you're going into China, you need a credible REIT manager, someone who understands the local market and strong tenant names you can feel comfortable with, and growth."

Although the Chinese Communist Party enshrined the right to own private property in the constitution in early 2004, the young private property market is still riddled with disputes about land rights and usage. The most fundamental danger for any investor in Chinese property, including in REITs, is that the buildings will be simply taken away by authorities because the land titles are inaccurate.

Investors have encountered titles falsified by corrupt officials, or plots of land with competing land-use rights, and even titles nullified by courts after previous owners were found to have obtained the land fraudulently.

Untangling lease titles, called land use rights, after property has changed hands several times can be confusing. In some cases authorities have confiscated property on the grounds that it was originally obtained corruptly, because the wrong agency issued the title, or because of fake documentation.

"It's more of a mystery than anything," said Wit Solberg, head of Asia structured finance at Fitch Ratings.[11] "If there has been some fraudulent exchange with officials and someone shines the spotlight on it one day, what happens?"

Insurers have lobbied regulators in Hong Kong to make title insurance mandatory for REITs as it is in the United States. But after consultations with property industry executives, Hong Kong's Securities and Futures Commission (SFC) decided not to change its REIT code, which stipulates that trusts should carry out thorough due diligence on titles. The general response the SFC received was that the cost of title insurance would be too onerous on the REITs and would eat into the returns that investors expected from China.

"Definitely, the risk is there but the question is, do you want to take it?" said Wen Kai Meng, who, as chief executive of the finance arm of CapitaLand, worked on the CapitaRetail China listing.[12]

The land title risk was one reason Chinese shopping malls could be bought by foreign investors for yields of 8% or 9%, Wen said: "By the time you insure everything away, you might as well stay in the United States."

The other "China risk" that is commonly mentioned is unpredictable government policy toward property, which can be interpreted in a myriad of ways by provincial and district authorities across the huge country. So far the government has targeted residential development in an effort to control perceived property bubbles in key cities, most notably in Shanghai. But the fear is that authorities could impose arbitrary rules at any time that would affect the functioning of commercial property business, for example concerning land use zoning, or even retail opening hours.

Many property experts operating in China say such fears are more perception than reality. A more serious potential problem in China is that the economy is just moving so fast that holding property is not going to be as stable as in most other countries in the world.

With the urban landscapes of even China's "secondary cities" such as Tianjin, Dalian and Chongqing mutating so fast, a district can become unfashionable overnight as a sparkling new shopping center opens up across the river and sucks tenants from buildings that were state-of-the-art only five years earlier.

China's retailers are also a young and mostly local bunch. Some will undoubtedly become national giants and even international brand names, but others will fall by the wayside. A property trust of shopping malls with a 50% turnover of tenants each year could deliver bonanza results in a one-off year, but is unlikely to guarantee the steady and rising incomes that investors expect.

Tried and Tested

The answer, according to the most likely pioneers of Chinese REITs, Macquarie Bank and CapitaLand, is to go with tried and tested brands that offer shopping centers with a strong and predictable anchor tenant—in their cases US retailer Wal-Mart.

CapitaRetail China Trust was set up as a convenient buyer of shopping centers that CapitaLand accumulates in China. By late 2006, the developer had a fund building 19 malls and another revamping existing malls, most of which would be anchored by Wal-Mart. Macquarie Bank preferred to package its shopping mall venture into a private fund for institutional investors, but did not rule out launching a publicly listed REIT with those properties later.

US retailer Wal-Mart and its competitors such as France's Carrefour are expanding rapidly across China as the country opens up to investment in the retail sector in compliance with World Trade Organization (WTO) rules. But they are happy to let property firms take the risks and sort out the arduous paperwork connected with owning the buildings where they locate stores. It is a model that brand-name foreign retailers are likely to follow as they look for a slice of the growing wealth of China's middle class, and this should help provide a healthy flow of Chinese shopping center REITs in the future.

"It's one thing if your anchor tenant is Wal-Mart, but it's completely different if it's a local retail outlet," said Frank Slevin, Citigroup's head of investment banking for Hong Kong.[13] "If you bought into a REIT and in six, 12 or 18 months there's a risk of a 50% turnover in tenants, it would be a legitimate concern."

On the other hand, some industry players have also said that Wal-Mart has such high bargaining power with its property partners that rent rises for the likes of CapitaRetail China will always fall below market rates. And because Wal-Mart has such a huge range of products at low prices, the US retailer often stifles business for any other retailer in a shopping mall it anchors.

Although investors were clamoring for Chinese buildings, a Chinese government decision in September 2006 requiring all property to be held in local companies rather than in "offshore companies" made it much more complicated to set up REITS to be listed outside mainland China.

The preferred structure for such REITs, and the one used by GZI, was to hold the properties in an offshore company, thereby bypassing China's strict capital controls, high taxes and allowing rental income to be packaged into dividends regularly. "Onshore" companies can only repatriate income once a year, and because they can only extract after-tax profit, money equal to the non-cash depreciation item on company statements gets trapped in the country rather than paid out as a dividend.

GZI REIT was in many ways unique because the sponsor was a local government body listed in Hong Kong that had already put its buildings into offshore companies before spinning them off into a trust

But the CapitaRetail China Trust managed to show that the obstacles put up by holding buildings "onshore" were not insurmountable. The REIT needed to make a loan to the on-shore company holding the buildings, which was repaid using the "trapped" cash—therefore, freeing up that money for payment to investors. The trust also needed to make provisions (set aside cash) each year to make up for the fact that rental income could only be taken out of China once a year.

Some analysts predicted China would start up its own domestic REIT market soon after Hong Kong's REIT market got underway, and others expected it to take five years or more.

Morgan Laughlin, managing director at Deutsche Bank's property investment arm, RREEF, before he joined Royal Bank of Scotland, was in the camp arguing that China would act quickly, saying that the securities would feed growing demand for yield-generating investments from fast-expanding pension and insurance funds.

Chinese pension funds and insurance funds were barred from investing directly in property because it was deemed too speculative, but they might be able to persuade Chinese authorities that REITs, with their liquid nature and diversified assets, would be sufficiently safe.

"The real game's going to be in China," Laughlin said in early 2006. "Chinese authorities are watching Hong Kong and Singapore closely and, whether it's 12 or 18 months, it definitely will happen."[14]

Laughlin said a domestic market would not require as high a risk premium as Chinese REITs listed abroad. That would allow Chinese landlords to get a better price for their buildings to offset high taxes, although authorities could decide to give tax breaks to promote a domestic REIT market.

Case study: Shanghai surprise

A nine-year saga of embezzlement and fraud at a luxury housing project called the "Shanghai Links Executive Community" came to epitomize the risks of investing in Chinese property. This is a cautionary tale for anyone interested in Chinese property investment, including in REITs, but events surrounding the project also suggest that the country's regulatory environment is improving.

The nightmare for private equity firm H&Q Asia Pacific began in 1997, when it led a $50 million investment group including Deutsche Bank, HSBC Holdings and New York Life Insurance Co.. in the Shanghai Links venture.

H&Q's managing director responsible for China, Chih Wang, said his firm soon began to discover "irregularities" in the project—which was to build 474 villas and 326 apartments around a golf course, aimed at expatriate residents, on the outskirts of Shanghai.

He said two Canadian brothers involved in the project, Barry and Stuart Hansen, were siphoning off money by claiming they had spent $33 million on land leases from the Shanghai government. In fact, the brothers had only paid $260,000.

A court in London upheld H&Q's claims for damages against the Hansens in late 2001, awarding damages of $66.5 million to the private equity investors, the *Financial Times* reported at the time.

H&Q won a series of court cases against the brothers in Britain, Hong Kong, the Turks and Caicos Islands and Canada, Wang said. But the result of a Shanghai government investigation into a falsified receipt for $33 million for the land use rights was never released, he said.

In June 2006, H&Q finally managed to extricate itself from Shanghai Links when it sold the project to state-owned Pudong Development Group.

Singapore—The government's hand

The Singapore government, with its long-standing nexus with the city-state's biggest companies, including major property firms, originally did more than any Asian government to foster a REIT market and set a benchmark for other countries to follow.

But the creation of a REIT market was far from smooth. Singapore drew up its first REIT guidelines in 1998 in the midst of the Asian economic crisis, but had to wait three years for the first attempt to create a trust, and that failed.

Developer CapitaLand Ltd., which is about 60% owned by the government, tried to launch its SingMall Property Trust in October 2001, but the US$300 million issue was only 80% subscribed and was scrapped a month later.

"We decided to have a go but unfortunately it didn't work," explained Wen Khai Meng, chief executive of CapitaLand's financial arm, which works

Nine years after the project began, only 66 villas and an international school had been built. The Hansens were forced to give up their ownership of the golf course, which had been transferred into a company they owned, for $1, Wang said.

Wang was grateful that the Chinese government finally intervened by buying the project, for an amount H&Q would only describe as "recovering not only our original cost basis, but also a small return on our investment plus reimbursement of legal expenses."

"During the Hansen era there were a tremendous amount of irregularities," Wang said.[15] "For any international investor to accept and undertake that situation would be very difficult. So the final outcome was a very good solution."

Wang said much had changed in China since the Shanghai Links project began.

"In order to attract foreign investment, irregular steps were allowed to be taken at the time," Wang said of the rush for Chinese property in the 1990s.

"By fighting through the cases and trying to recover investment in the last six years, we've seen a change in the government's attitude," he said. "I'd say we've found respect of regulations to be much, much higher."

Wang said he was undeterred by the experience, adding that H&Q planned a new fund to funnel as much as $500 million into Chinese property, mostly hotels and resorts.

"The legal system has drastically improved since the mid- and late-1990s, and we now know what to watch out for," Shanghai-based Wang said. "There are plenty of opportunities in China if you carry out your business prudently and do your due diligence. This has been a good learning experience for us."

on creating REITs. "The climate wasn't good—it was just two months after September 11—and there was still a lot of uncertainty about real estate in Singapore and Asia. People also didn't understand whether it was a bond or equity."

But just a year later, the three shopping malls were repackaged as CapitaMall Trust, offered at a 7.1% yield rather than the original 6.1%, and investors took the bait, heralding the start of a REIT market whose popularity would surpass all expectations in its first couple of years.

CapitaMall is a good example of how management can bring changes in existing buildings and buy new buildings to increase rental income for shareholders, which translates into share price gains. The trust expanded retail area in its malls by creating smaller shop units, moved food outlets to better locations to increase rent, and in its first year, bought the IMM Building in Singapore at a property yield of 8%.

The renovations and acquisitions received a firm thumbs up from investors. In 2003, CapitaMall units gave a distribution yield of 6.9% on its weighted average market price, but a jump in its unit price gave a capital gain of 41.6%, resulting in a total return of 48.5% for the year.

"We wanted to focus on growth, and the fact that we could articulate a specific plan impressed a lot of investors," Wen said of the second attempt at listing CapitaMall Trust. "In each of the three malls we laid out an asset enhancement plan."

The success of CapitaMall Trust soon persuaded a handful of other landlords to spin off their buildings. Industrial park operator Ascendas launched a trust, Ascendas REIT, in November 2002, offering investors the chance to buy into its warehouses, business park buildings, light industrial factories and buildings housing high-tech operations. The Fortune REIT of Hong Kong shopping malls followed with an IPO in October 2003 in Singapore, and CapitaLand created its second trust, the CapitaCommercial Trust of office buildings, the following year. Then Hong Kong tycoon Li Ka-shing formed another REIT with Singapore's Suntec City mall and office buildings.

Throughout this period, Singapore authorities were improving the climate for REITs with a series of regulatory changes, which fuelled more enthusiasm for these trusts, especially among individual investors.

The first step, in 2001, was to tax dividends at the individual shareholder's personal tax rate, but this was superseded in February 2004 with full tax exemption for local and foreign individual investors. Withholding tax paid by foreign institutional investors was cut to 10% from 20% for a period of five years from February 2005.

Regulatory changes also helped the trusts to make new acquisitions that would lift the yields on distributable income. The gearing limit (the maximum debt of a trust as a proportion of total assets) was lifted to 35% from 25% in February 2003, but raised even further to up to 60% in 2005, providing that the trust received a rating from a credit rating agency. By borrowing more, a trust needs fewer funds from shareholders to buy a new building, and if interest rates are lower than the yield received from the building, more rental income can be distributed to the shareholders. The government also waived, for five years from 2005, the stamp duty of 3% on property transactions, making it cheaper for trusts to buy buildings.

Words of warning

A three-year bull run by Singapore's REIT market came to an abrupt halt in July 2005, when the chief of the Singapore government investment agency,

Temasek, gave a speech about dubious fees, hidden debt and other risky practices by some REIT managers (see Chapter 5).

Unusually frank talk by Temasek Chief Executive Ho Ching, who is also the wife of Singapore Prime Minister Lee Hsien Loong, suggested nasty surprises could await unsuspecting individual investors who might not understand "financial engineering." Speaking at the launch of the Temasek-sponsored Mapletree REIT, she said some trust managers were getting into deals that were "charades to shore up short-term performance indicators at the expense of long-term pain."

Among the dangers Ho highlighted was a practice of partially paying for a building with new trust units, but delaying the issuance of those units, say for three years, so that existing shareholders will get a bigger share of the newly added rental stream for the interim period.

Paying in deferred units, as the practice is called, lifts yields for existing shareholders, but maybe only temporarily. The idea is that by the time the new units come alive, rents will have increased and existing shareholders will feel no drop in their income from the trust. But if rents do not rise, shareholders could be in for a nasty surprise once the new units are in circulation.

Ho also criticized deals in which owner–occupiers sold a building at inflated prices to a REIT in return for paying higher rents. Yields are unaffected unless a tenant leaves, but then it could be difficult to find someone to pay above-market rents.

She also suggested that REIT managers might make bad acquisitions just to increase their fees. "In any market, all it takes is one black sheep to taint the reputation of the other players and set the market back," she said.

Most analysts thought the comments were aimed at Suntec REIT and an acquisition it planned to make from Singapore property firm City Developments. The week after Ho's speech, ARA Group, the manager of Suntec REIT, said it would forego acquisition fees in future deals involving the trust. The planned acquisition was later scrapped.

But the effect of the speech was far wider, and the whole REIT market lost its luster for a few months. After such a strong and sustained rally—Singapore REITs gave an average total return of 35% in 2004 against a 17% gain in the wider stock market—it was time for investors to reexamine valuations for the trusts rather than simply to expect all REITs to do well. Many in the REIT business thought Ho's speech served as a much needed wake-up call, but some believed that she clumsily used a broad brush to tarnish the whole market.

"What she said has woken up the investor community to the tricks, if you like, that some managers use," said one fund manager in Singapore.[16]

"Previously, investors were so focused on yield income that they weren't really paying attention to much else."

New opportunities

But after the reality check, the rise of Singapore REITs continued in 2006, with several IPOs hitting the market, offering investors much more variety.

For instance, Keppel Land Ltd. launched in early 2006 a trust of four office blocks in the central business district at a time when Singapore office rents were predicted to take off. Consultants CB Richard Ellis predicted rents would rise another 30-40% in 2007 and 2008, after a jump of 20% in 2006.

New supply of office space was tight, with occupancy up to 92% from a trough of 83% in 2001, and the city-state's economy was starting to buzz, thanks to bidding for two US$2 billion "integrated resort" casino projects after the government decided to legalize gaming.

But in comparison with other major cities, Singapore was still cheap, and therefore attractive for companies looking to set up operations in Asia. In 2006, the annual cost of occupying a prime office in Singapore was $42 per square foot, compared with $101 in Hong Kong, $130 in Tokyo and $185 in London.

Singapore has successfully used tax incentives to establish itself as a location for the regional headquarters of multinational companies and to promote certain economic sectors, such as biotechnology and investment fund management.

Investment bank Credit Suisse, for example, was planning in 2006 to add up to 1,400 employees to its back-office operations, tripling its office space with 110,000 square feet in the swanky new city center office complex One Raffles Quay. Swiss competitor UBS was setting up a campus to train wealth managers in the Asia-Pacific region, offering courses lasting up to six weeks at a time in Singapore for about 5,000 students.

Because of the attractive tax incentives for holding property in a REIT, Singapore's market is likely to grow quickly, with a high proportion of major buildings in the city-state eventually ending up in trusts.

But in such a small country, with a population of just four million, Singapore's REIT market is destined to become a center for listing assets from across Asia, as trust managers look for new opportunities to expand their portfolios and create new ones.

In 2006, four cross-border REITs listed in Singapore: the CapitaRetail China Trust of Chinese shopping centers; Allco REIT, which owned half of a building in Perth, Australia; Ascott Residential Trust, with serviced apartments in China, Vietnam, the Philippines and Indonesia; and First REIT, which was backed by three hospitals and a hotel resort in Indonesia.

Given the overseas activities of developers such as CapitaLand Ltd., Keppel Land Corp., and Ascendas Pte, Singapore is likely to offer investors more trusts in the future with assets in China and India, as well as maybe smaller countries in the region such as Malaysia, Thailand, Vietnam, the Philippines and Indonesia.

CapitaLand goes "asset light"

Singapore developer CapitaLand Ltd. was arguably the first Asian property firm to ditch the traditional developer-landlord model and fully embrace an "asset light" strategy.

Since the Asian economic crisis, Singapore's residential market held out little hope for CapitaLand and the city state's other developers. Massive oversupply of housing—around 14,000 apartments were still empty in 2004—and an already high home ownership rate of around 80% meant developers could only hope to build and sell high-end niche apartment blocks.

One of CapitaLand's solutions was to look abroad, especially to China, to build new residential projects. But the biggest change in the firm's strategy was to take advantage of REITs to raise money for expansion.

By selling some of its buildings into REITs it can obtain a relatively high price, because REIT investors are generally willing to pay a premium to the market value for a property asset that is "liquid."

The company can still keep control of the buildings by retaining a stake, typically around 30% while building up two new sources of fee income: fees for managing the trusts and fees for managing the buildings.

Selling buildings in this way should please shareholders by lifting the return on assets recorded by the company. The following simplified example illustrates how this is done:

Imagine a developer has $100 of cash and $300 of property assets, which are together funded by debt of $300 and shareholders' equity of $100.

The developer uses the $100 cash to establish the (yet to be listed) REIT, which then borrows $200 to give a total $300 of funds for buying buildings. The developer now sells its $300 of property to the trust.

On its balance sheet, the developer now sees the original $100 of cash appear as an equity stake in the REIT. The $300 worth of property assets is now $300 of cash to fund further projects. And there are zero direct property assets, just the $100 equity stake in the trust.

The $300 of cash can be used to finance a higher returning development, to pay down debt or buy back equity.

If the money is funneled to development, return on assets should improve, assuming the new projects give better returns than the assets in the REIT. For example, developing housing in China can give internal rates of return of 20–30%, or building a shopping centre in Japan could give returns of 15%, while a building in Singapore might give a rental yield of just 5.5%.

The developer can then launch an IPO of the REIT, possibly raising more cash for itself if it decides to sell some of its stake. And it can set up a REIT management company and receive fees through that, as well as garnering fees for managing the property.

Once this structure has been established, the big business will be "incubating" buildings for the existing REIT or new REITs. The developer can build a new office block or a new shopping center, knowing both that there is a willing buyer (the REIT) and that the price will probably be good (slightly lower than the price implied by the current yield of the REIT).

The company can also decide to buy existing buildings at a low price, improve their marketability through renovations or changing the tenant mix, and then sell them on to the REIT at a hefty profit. This is exactly what CapitaLand was trying to do with shopping malls it bought in China from the beginning of 2005—buying them at a property yield of about 8.0% with the aim of selling them into a REIT. The CapitaRetail China Trust gave a yield of just 5.4% on its IPO price—so the difference of 2.6 percentage points would be CapitaLand's reward for buying the shopping malls, improving them, and setting up the trust.

If the buildings cost, for example, $500 million, an 8.0% yield would imply an income of $40 million a year. If that income was then capitalized at a yield of 5.4%, that would imply a new valuation for the buildings of $740 million. (740 million x 5.4/100 = 40 million). So the company would make a $240 million profit, or 48% of its initial investment possibly in the space of just under two years.

But CapitaLand's deals in China will be tough to mimic. The company has built a reputation for successful REITs, has more experience in China than most of its foreign rivals and has more shopping malls in the pipeline.

Investors have consistently shown their appreciation for developers who turn to an "asset light" model by driving up their share prices as REITs are spun off, as demonstrated in the charts below. CapitaLand's share price has soared since 2002, with noticeable uplift when it launched a new property trust. Guangzhou Investment saw a similar spike in its share price when it sold buildings into the Hong Kong–listed GZI REIT at the end of 2005 (see charts below).

As these examples show, buying stock in a company that is tipped to launch a REIT can be a legitimate investment tactic, but investors should be wary of firms that publicly say they are considering launching a REIT but may not be very serious about following through with the plan.

For example, Hong Kong regulators warned investors to be cautious after Chinese Estates said in February 2006 it wanted to launch a $500 million REIT, causing its share price to jump. Later in the month, the Lau family that controlled the Hong Kong retail property landlord twice sold stakes of around 10% stake to other investors. Just as shares can rise in a company planning a REIT, if the IPO is delayed for any reason, the stock can drop sharply. When Hong Kong's Regal Hotels International said at the end of December 2006 that it would wait for better market conditions to launch its REIT—following the debut flop by Henderson Land's Sunlight REIT—shares in the hotel landlord dropped 9% in one day.

Share Price Charts for CapitaLand, Guangzhou Investment and Regal Hotels

CapitaLand

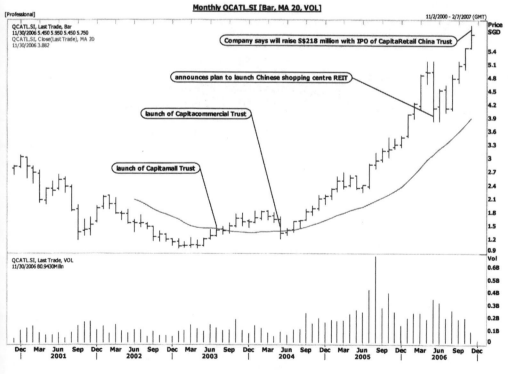

Source: Reuters

Guangzhou Investment

Source: Reuters

Regal Hotels International

Source: Reuters

Big in Japan

The Japanese REIT market had just as inauspicious a start as those in Hong Kong and Singapore, but it quickly shook off its troubles to truly become an important force in turning around the country's ailing property market. The Tokyo-listed REIT market is, and will continue to be, the biggest in Asia, simply because Japan has about half of the continent's investment grade property, worth about $1.27 trillion.

When Japan enacted its Investment Trust Law in 2000, allowing REITs to set up, the country had all the ingredients for a market to take off. A decade of stagnation punctuated by the Asian economic crisis had left an economy in urgent need of reform. A seemingly endless queue of unprofitable companies needed to deal with massive debts, and selling off property assets seemed a good way to start. Much property had already fallen into the hands of banks, struggling with non-performing loans, which had reached 41 trillion yen ($362 billion) by 2000, and peaked at 43.2 trillion yen in March 2002. But with land values falling as much as 70% in some areas since a heady peak at the end of the 1980s, buyers were scarce and nervous, while sellers were often not willing to cut their losses by quite as much as the property market suggested they should.

Property trusts were the perfect way to sell at a reasonable price to a willing buyer—the public. Because Japan's monetary policy aimed at kick-starting investment in the economy meant interest rates were almost zero, and the stock market was in the doldrums, anything offering a decent yield looked good. The county's first REITs offered 5% at a time when 10-year government bonds were at just 1.4%.

Unfortunately, the first two trusts, which were backed by $2 billion of property assets and set up by property firms Mitsui Fudosan and Mitsubishi Estate Co., were listed on September 10, 2001 and suffered as much as other stocks following the attacks, a day later, on the United States.

It took another 12 months for the sector to gain popularity, but the subsequent rush into REITs drove down yields to 3.5% from 5.0% by the beginning of 2006.

But Japanese REITs soon became victims of their own success.

In 2004, more than half of major property transactions in Tokyo were acquisitions by property trusts seeking to increase income for their shareholders. The burst of activity revived a moribund property market in the Japanese capital and a host of foreign property funds, private equity funds and local Japanese institutional investors such as insurance firms and pension funds started to buy in Tokyo.

On a nationwide basis, 2004 marked the first year in a decade and a half that national land prices did not fall, although the gain was miniscule. In Tokyo though, people were talking about a property bubble.

An expected oversupply of new office blocks did not result in a widely expected fall in prices. Dubbed the "2003 problem," the equivalent of the average yearly supply of new offices in the whole of the United States hit the Tokyo market in the space of a few months. But multinational corporations, banks and financial companies were keen to move into the new, plush surrounds. The premises where tenants left en masse were either refurbished or turned into something new, such as much sought after city center apartments, although there was still a temporary problem of high vacancy in old buildings.

Prices were rising quickly, but rents were not. Japanese landlords say they have a "special relationship" with their tenants, and many are in fact parts of conglomerates and their tenants are other companies within the same group. So when the property market was slumping in the 1990s, with Tokyo prices falling as far as 70% below their late 1980s peak, tenants often accepted that they would not get big discounts on rent. And when the property market began to flourish in 2004, landlords did not aggressively put up their rents. So yields on Tokyo buildings fell and REITs suddenly could not find acquisitions that would be yield-accretive for their shareholders, even though REIT yields had also fallen.

The REITs had to start getting inventive, and those with strong connections with Japan's biggest property developers were at an advantage.

Nippon Building Fund, for example, started looking beyond Tokyo to provincial buildings and to brand new developments that offered better yields at lower prices. In 2004, the trust made 12 acquisitions in Tokyo, where about two-thirds of its assets were located. The trust was set up by Mitsui Fudosan Co. and Sumitomo Life Insurance, with both companies using it to offload buildings that they did not want.

But with prices rising on the open market, the trust had to rely more on Mitsui Fudosan to sell buildings at the right price and to start developing new projects.

"The real estate market is getting better and better and many players have come in, especially for A-class buildings," said Satoru Yamanaka, an executive at Nippon Building Fund's management firm.[17] "We have to find a special route, cooperating with Mitsui Fudosan and other developers because on the open market, you have to win a bidding process."

While office yields in central Tokyo were down to 3.6% in 2006 from as high as 7% in 2003 and 2004, trusts could still find yields of 5.5%, or even 7%

in other provincial cities such as Nagoya and Osaka. That was partly because many areas of Japan were still in economic decline—a risk in itself for REITs that rely on stable tenancy.

Transparency jolt

As it became more difficult for REITs to source buildings, regulators did two things: they put forward new legislation, due to be passed in 2007, to allow trusts to buy buildings abroad; and they also started to examine the deals between trusts and their sponsors to make sure that they were above board.

In early June 2006, the Japanese REIT market was shaken when the Securities and Exchange Surveillance Commission (SESC) called for disciplinary action against the managers of Orix J-REIT and its parent company. The SESC said the trust had not conducted proper due diligence before acquiring properties from its parent, and had not held as many board meetings as it said it had.

Many analysts believed the SESC would keep a much closer eye on other REITs, but said investors overreacted to the Orix developments because earnings would not be hit and more scrutiny would improve the quality of acquisitions.

Orix J-REIT fell 13% in the first week after the SESC's announcement, but the Japanese REIT index quickly recovered from a 3% one-day fall, suggesting the country's REIT investors were fairly resilient.

"There is a lot of conflict of interest regarding companies which sell properties into their real estate investment trusts and people out there were quite nervous that Orix may be the tip of the iceberg," said Michael Coates, director of equity sales at KBC Financial Products in Tokyo. "But really, real estate in Japan, for me, should be leading the market higher, so just the concern there is holding us back."

Unhostile takeovers

After just five years, Japan's property trust market was tipped to see some takeover activity, with strong managers targeting rivals who were struggling to deliver income growth for their investors.

In the early days of the market, Japanese investors bought into REITs across the board, but by 2006 they had become much more discerning. Trusts with a good track record of delivering dividend growth were outperforming the market, while more than 10 of the 37 REITs in mid-2006 had slid to below their book values, making it difficult for them to buy new buildings.

A decision by the Financial Services Agency to introduce a rule requiring investors to disclose stakes of more than 5% in REITs suggests regulators expected a bout of mergers and acquisitions, said Matt Nacard, Asia REIT analyst at Macquarie Securities.

"Depending on what's occurring with property prices, it can be difficult for some REITs to buy property in an accretive way," said Nacard.[18] "When that happens, REITs will look to each other to achieve economies of scale to grow more effectively."

Analysts said that developers who set up REITs as a vehicle through which they could sell their buildings might lose interest if that option was no longer available. Residential REITs, such as Japan Single-Residence REIT Inc. were especially vulnerable. They are good defensive plays in an economic downturn but were underperforming at a time when Japan's economy was strengthening and rents at office REITs were rising. Other REITs trading below their book values in mid-2006 were Prospect Residential Investment Corp., FC Residential Investment Corp., and BLife Investment Corp..

But taking over a REIT is no easy matter. One barrier is that REITs will no longer receive the corporate tax waiver that makes them so attractive if three shareholders or fewer hold more than 50%, making hostile takeovers difficult. The best way to ring the changes at a REIT is through a switch of its management company.

REITs in Japan are managed externally, unlike in Australia, which saw a spate of mergers in the early 2000s that joined management firms with listed property trusts, partly to save on management fees.

If a majority of shareholders in a Japanese REIT vote in favor, they can ditch management and install a new firm. Or one REIT could buy out a rival, but that would also need the support of more than two-thirds of the shareholders of the target trust as well as the suitor's own shareholders. The new management could either try to improve operations or start actively trading buildings—all of which would be watched over by a trustee who looks after shareholder interests.

Some analysts said another likely scenario would be for a new management team to disband a REIT by selling assets to another trust and paying cash to investors.

In the only case of mergers and acquisitions (M&A) in the Japanese REIT market by mid-2006, consulting firm Business Bank Consulting Co. Ltd. bought the asset management company for REIT fund TGR Investment Inc.

Although a hostile takeover would be very difficult, analysts expected some attempts. Daisuke Seki, head of the real estate investment information department at private REIT research firm BRRI Inc., said the most likely scenario would be mid-sized REITs buying struggling REITs.

"I don't expect mergers among struggling REITs," he said.[19] "But REITs whose share prices are steady may think that M&A could be the fastest way to grow."

Earthquake risk

Despite a long history of devastating tremors in earthquake-prone Japan, property investors are only starting to seek protection from the risks of volatility in the earth's crust. Compared with other quake zones, such as San Francisco in the US, insurance and the risk metrics that guide investment are scarce in Japan, even as government surveys suggest it is a near certainty metropolitan Tokyo will be hit by a major quake sometime in the next half-century.

So REITs and rating agencies are trying to address investor concerns.

Nippon Building Fund, Japan's biggest property trust with about 50 buildings by mid-2005, issues a statement after earthquakes to reassure investors. Like many REITs, it has a policy to limit earthquake risk by limiting probable maximum loss (PML)—an estimate of how much of a property would be destroyed in a major quake. The trust will only buy a building if this level is 10% or less, according to Saturo Yamanaka, who helps manage the trust.

Even so, as the 1995 Kobe earthquake demonstrated, such estimates are often guesswork.

"We once asked the seller of a building to spend one billion yen strengthening it before we would buy it,"[20] Yamanaka said, referring to the Toranomon Building in Central Tokyo.

In the broader Tokyo area, home to 35 million people, studies suggest a quake similar to one that hit in 1923 would kill thousands of people and cause more than $1 trillion in damages today.

Property firms tout modern engineering, but collapsed buildings killed more than 6,000 people in the Kobe earthquake, causing $147 billion worth of damage, of which only $4.1 billion was insured.

Some insurers cover about half a building's value in Tokyo, up from only 15% before deregulation in the late 1990s. But many landlords think this insurance is too expensive—as much as 40 times the cost of coverage in some high-risk areas in the United States, where such insurance is required by law in certain cases. Without similar legal requirements to spread the insurance costs widely, any single earthquake insurance policy will cost more.

Sensing rising demand for quake-risk assessments from foreign investors, rating agencies are considering ways to calculate property exposure. Standard & Poor's and Moody's Investors Service put out notes after a strong earthquake near Fukuoka in March 2005 saying listed property trusts and their mortgage-backed securities were largely unaffected.

Shinsuke Tanimoto, senior analyst at Moody's in Tokyo, said his agency did not include "event risk" in assessments of property securities because it was so difficult to quantify. But earthquake risks were often discussed in its ratings committees.

"You have to look at diversification of assets and their geographical concentration, and assess potential support from banks and the government," Tanimoto said.[21]

By the time Japan's REIT market was five years old, the country's trusts had about 70% of their assets in Tokyo and tended to buy buildings not more than 15 years old. Established developers Mitsubishi Estate and Mitsui Fudosan hold older buildings and are more at risk from earthquakes than the property trusts, although both have set up REITs and will feed them more of their buildings in the future.

Many Tokyo offices coming up for sale were built before 1981, when the government raised construction standards following an earthquake in 1978 that killed 13 people and injured 9,300. But the opportunity to buy cheap, old buildings and fix them up to increase rents has been a major draw for property trusts. Some say there is no point fretting over an "act of God," such as an earthquake.

"If we have an eight magnitude right in Tokyo Bay it would be difficult to escape," said Chuck Larson, head of property investment in Japan for Australia's Macquarie Bank.[22] "But it's not a huge thing hanging over everyone's head. Maybe it should be, but it isn't."

Malaysia eyes the *sharia* oil dollar

Malaysia led the Asian move to embrace REITs in the early 1990s, but the fledgling market of three small "property trust funds" that listed at that time was marred by a lack of tax incentives for investors, relatively low yields and capital gains and asset overvaluation.

A property market crash during the 1997-98 Asian economic crisis, which still left vacancy rates of 18% at Kuala Lumpur offices and 16% at the city's shopping malls eight years later, worsened matters.

But with one look over the shoulder at neighboring Singapore, Malaysia decided in 2004 to try again to foster a REIT market, allowing local investors in trusts to be taxed on dividends at their personal tax rate rather than the previously uniform 28%. REITs were also allowed to buy buildings abroad to enhance returns.

Authorities hoped a rush of property trusts would draw money from the Middle East to the market. But analysts said Malaysia, which is trying to carve out a niche for Islamic finance, would have to do away with the 28% withholding tax it charged on dividends paid to foreign investors before that would happen.

"For Arabs, tax is taboo," said Fazlur Rahman Kamsani, head of regional Islamic finance at property consultants DTZ.[23] "They'll just come and say, 'I don't pay tax in my country.' They love Malaysia, but the tax regime would have to be tailor-made to be competitive."

In late 2006, the Malaysian government reconsidered the tax issue, and was proposing to cut withholding tax to 15% for individual investors and domestic institutions and to 20% for foreign institutional investors.

With oil profits and much investment pulled from the US in recent years, analysts were saying in 2005 that the Middle East had around $750 billion of private assets scouring the world for new ideas. The Institute of International Finance estimated that Saudi Arabia, the United Arab Emirates, Kuwait, Oman, Qatar and Bahrain would export at least $450 billion of capital just in 2006 and 2007.

REITs, because they essentially pay rent to investors, are an attractive option because the listed securities are a natural fit for *sharia*, or Islamic law, which shuns interest payments and speculation. Trusts that want to be *sharia* compliant cannot have tenants involved in manufacturing and handling pork products, banking and insurance, alcohol, tobacco, weapons or pornography. As a result, serviced apartments or industrial trusts tend to present fewer problems than shopping malls and offices.

In Malaysia, the first trust to list after the 2004 rule changes was Axis REIT, which originally owned five commercial industrial buildings in Petaling Jaya and Shah Alam, housing multinational companies such as Fuji Xerox, Johnson & Johnson and Electrolux. Unlike previous Malaysian trusts, Axis set out from the beginning to be an active REIT, promising to increase its assets rapidly after listing on the stock market by buying up warehouses yielding 7–8%.

By September 2006, Axis had seen its share price increase 42% from its IPO in early 2005, with the addition of four buildings to bring its net asset value to 400 million ringgit ($109 million). At that time, the trust was trading at a 7% yield, about 280 basis points above 10-year bonds.

Stewart LaBrooy, executive director of Axis REIT's management firm, said the trust planned to double its assets by the end of 2007 to about one billion ringgit.

"We've consistently bought below market prices, around 10% below," LaBrooy said. "Our directors are well linked and are always finding nuggets."

Axis would concentrate its acquisition efforts on Malaysia, where business and logistic park properties were yielding about 7%. But Indonesia, where some buildings are giving 15% yields, was also enticing, LaBrooy added.

"There are some nice properties in Jakarta and the yields are phenomenal," he said. "But there's a huge currency risk issue."

Although the Malaysian market is small, worth about $650 million in late 2006, it had some of the most interesting issuance.

The Al 'Aqar KPJ REIT owns hospitals and Boustead Holdings, and its property arm was planning in late 2006 to sell 500 million ringgit worth of palm oil plantation assets into an Islamic REIT. Hotel owner Tradewinds Corp. Bhd. and YTL Land, which owns shopping centers and the JW Marriot hotel, were both mulling spinning off trusts.

In December 2006, Singapore's CapitaLand also stepped into the fray, saying it planned to raise as much as $42.2 million in a Kuala Lumpur REIT listing of Malaysian commercial buildings. The developer had teamed up with Malaysian real estate firm Quill Group to form the Quill Capita Trust, which was expected to generate an initial distribution yield of 7.14%.

"It's getting to be a real potpourri," LaBrooy said.

Growing pains in Thailand and Taiwan

In the wake of the Asian economic crisis, sparked by the 1997 devaluation of the Thai baht, Thailand allowed REIT-like listed property funds to form in the hope that failed companies could use them to offload their property assets. The idea never really took hold, and just three small funds were created before 2005.

But when CPN Retail Growth Property Fund and Ticon Property Fund listed in 2005, they suggested a real REIT market would develop for the same reasons they did in other Asian countries—healthy and ambitious companies wanted to free up capital for investment in new projects.

Thai property funds are similar to REITs in other markets in that they do not pay corporate income tax if they pass on at least 90% of the net income from their property to investors in the form of dividends. But the Thai funds were not originally allowed to borrow or buy a new building before first raising funds from investors, which seriously hampered their chances of clinching deals and their potential for growth.

"It's still in its infancy," said James Pitchon, executive director at CB Richard Ellis in Bangkok.[24] "To develop the market more, it would be beneficial to see larger funds and see some of the current restrictions amended."

The two funds most likely to give investors income growth were the CPN Retail Growth Property Fund of two shopping centers and the Ticon Property Fund of 39 factories, because they both had a ready supply of buildings to acquire from the companies that set up the funds, Central Pattana PCL and Ticon, respectively.

Central Pattana, in particular, is shaping up to be a major issuer of property funds in an attempt to adopt an "asset light" growth model—selling assets into REITs, in which it kept a 30% stake, while garnering new fees for managing the properties and regenerating cash to build more shopping centers.

The IPO of Central Pattana's CPN Retail Growth Property Fund in 2005 was 4.5 times subscribed with strong interest from institutional investors in Singapore, Hong Kong and Australia, giving the impetus to create more funds. The company hatched plans to sell its sparkling new office block attached to the Central World shopping mall in one of Bangkok's busiest retail districts and two more office blocks attached to its Central Pinklao and Central Bang Na malls into a new fund.

"We will more or less be like Westfield and CapitaLand—fewer and fewer assets," Central Pattana chief financial officer Naris Cheyklin said, referring to the Australian and Singapore REIT pioneers. "This is a good mechanism to unlock asset value for expansion."

But hopes for a vibrant REIT market were dealt a blow in December 2006 when the government, installed by a bloodless coup three months earlier, imposed capital controls to try to halt appreciation of the baht currency and protect exporters.

Foreign investors were required to deposit 30% of non–trade-related capital flows with the central bank for a year, with no payment of interest.

With overseas investors obviously reluctant to tie their money up for such a long time, the stock market plummeted 15% the day after the new rule was announced, prompting partial backtracking by the government. Stocks were given an exemption, but foreign investors in bonds, mutual funds and REITs still had to comply.

Players in Thailand's small REIT industry implored authorities to rethink the capital controls and in February 2007 the central bank said it was considering lifting the measures. But the episode had served to highlight the potential risks of investing in emerging markets.

Taiwan

The Taiwan government approved a REIT law in July 2003, but similarly to Thailand, trusts were "close-end"—they were not allowed to sell new shares in order to raise funds to buy new buildings. However, the government set no limit to borrowing, so that gave REITs some limited scope for expansion. But they were not allowed to invest in any building without a solid rental stream, ruling out buying into development projects, or, for example, snapping up an old office block for renovation to bring in new tenants.

The island's first REIT, Fubon No.1 REIT, listed in March 2005 and was five times oversubscribed when initially offered. Sponsored by Fubon Financial Holding Co., the trust launched with four buildings in Taipei with an initial dividend yield of 4%. This was considerably more than the 1.79% deposit rates being offered at Taiwan's top five banks or the 1.15% offered by 10-year bonds. The trust was popular because it gave investors access to modern property—all the buildings were constructed after 1999—in good locations in prime business and residential areas in Taipei. It was also diversified across property sectors, with its two offices, one retail building and a serviced apartment.

The prospects for rents were looking up, as the island's sluggish property sector showed signs of renewed life—Taipei office rents rose about 10% in 2005. But some analysts said unfamiliarity with the new investment product and a lack of portfolio diversification could hamper development of the REIT market.

Nevertheless, the successful launch prompted a slew of financial groups to draw up plans for REITs, and Cathay Financial Holdings and Shin Kong Financial Holding were the first to follow. Because of the rule against selling new shares, Fubon was also planning to set up another REIT, Fubon No.2, rather than add buildings to Fubon No.1.

The Cathay No.1 REIT's portfolio was dominated by the Sheraton Taipei Hotel, which made up about 75% of the trust's asset value, but also included two buildings with offices and retail space.

The Shin Kong No.1 REIT was a favorite among many analysts, who believed it had the highest quality property, with solid lease contracts to reliable tenants, compared with its peers. It owned a serviced apartment building in a good location in suburban Taipei, which had managed to keep a low vacancy rate in the years prior to its inclusion in the trust—an average of just 5.2% between 2001 and 2004. The trust also owned a building in the south of Taiwan, leased to Shin Kong Mitsukoshi Department Store Co. Ltd., the island's largest department store chain with a market share of more than 30%.

South Korea—Designed for corporate restructuring

As in other Asian countries, the South Korean government introduced REITs primarily to help corporate restructuring efforts—to allow struggling companies to sell their property to the public at a good price. But unlike other countries, it created two types of REITs: Corporate restructuring REITs, or "CR-REITs," and the ordinary trust structure, called "K-REITs."

CR-REITs were unique in that they needed to source at least 70% of their assets from companies undergoing restructuring due to insolvency or companies that intended to use the proceeds to pay off debt. Because the incentives were more generous for CR-REITs, all early trusts created in South Korea chose that structure. CR-REITs received a waiver on acquisition taxes and were able to use dividends as deductions from corporate tax if the payout was more than 90% of profit. In comparison, K-REITs were given a 50% exemption from acquisitions tax and registration tax, but received no corporate tax benefits. Neither type of trust could borrow to fund new investment—a serious impediment to growth.

Another problem with the original rules was that they only allowed CR-REITs to exist for five years, raising concerns among investors about what would happen to the trusts once that period was over. Would they sell their buildings and dissolve themselves or would they convert to K-REITs? What would their tax treatment be?

The whole landscape shifted in 2004, when the government introduced a new structure for indirect property investment, the Real Estate Trust Fund (RETF), which had many advantages over the CR-REITs and K-REITs. For example, there was much less regulatory red tape for creating a RETF; the funds could borrow more and could start up with less capital; and there was no limit to their lifespan. Many expected RETFs to become the dominant form of listed property investment.

But with REIT markets flourishing in Singapore and Japan, South Korea finally changed its rules in April 2005 to extend the tax benefits of the CR-REITs to K-REITs. Authorities also allowed two types of general property trusts to be formed: a "self-managed" REIT and a "paper company" REIT, for which the management functions are delegated to a third-party asset manager.

Analysts said the changes made in 2005, which allowed the CR-REITs to continue indefinitely by converting into general REITs, were needed to keep foreign investment flowing into Korean property. Several pension funds and insurance companies, especially from Europe, bought Seoul office blocks cheaply in the wake of the Asian economic crisis, and a flourishing REIT market would offer them a good way of cashing in, if they wanted to sell. The REIT market was also tipped to become popular with a domestic population that was wary of an often volatile stock market.

"I think they will take off. It's a natural progression," said Scott Girard, head of research at consultants Jones Lang LaSalle.[25] "By history and tradition, Koreans are not keen on the share market, where there are transparency issues. The government wants to get liquidity into the market because money is in bank deposits or under beds, so it is trying to attract capital by offering more investment vehicles."

Korea's fading rental system

Sang-hyun Moon is a software programmer who did his master's degree in the U.K., but he could hardly afford to rent a one-bedroom suburban apartment he set his heart on in the South Korean capital Seoul. He blamed a traditional rental system unique to South Korea called *chonsei*, where a tenant pays a big down payment instead of regular rent payments, which the landlord invests, gambles, or leaves in a bank savings account.

"The landlady wanted to do things the old way," Moon, 32, said.[26] "It was 40 million won ($34,570), and although I've got a good, steady job, I just don't have that kind of money."

Because the *chonsei* is returned at the end of a contract, the tenant effectively only pays the opportunity cost of not having the money to spend for a period of time.

The system is popular with landlords who dabble in other businesses and with small-scale developers, who use *chonsei* payments to finance new projects. Those who can afford to pay it are happy because *chonsei* appears to be a rent-free deal. In contrast, tenants in Japan often pay two months' rent as "key money"—which is never returned—a legacy of bribes paid when housing was short after World War II.

But at $170,000 for a 100-square-meter (1,076 square feet), three-bedroom apartment in Seoul, *chonsei* is not easy for the average worker to raise.

Chonsei is also going out of fashion with landlords, partly because they find it hard to make money while interest rates are low. So both sides are edging toward wolsei, a mix of rent and *chonsei*.

Traditionally, South Koreans would take turns pooling funds among family and community members to stump up for *chonsei*. That system is breaking down as low interest rates make bank loans more attractive and extended family units fragment.

Chonsei is also fading in the commercial sector, partly because foreign investors were snapping up Seoul office buildings in the early 2000s for rental yields of as high as 8% and discarding the traditional system. The proliferation of REITs in Korea will also undermine the traditional system, because investors in trusts want a stable, long-term rental income. Landlords looking to set up a REIT will face problems if tenants insist on *chonsei*. But because the typical *chonsei* for a 400 square meter office in central Seoul can reach $1 million, a growing number of corporate tenants prefer landlords who ask for rent.

"It's becoming less common," said Jones Lang LaSalle's Girard. "Internationals can't do it in their buildings because they need cash flow. And because of lower interest rates, landlords are going to hybrids."

The *chonsei* system has endured partly because Korean banks only gave short-term loans, typically for five years, making it difficult for people to raise enough money to buy a home or for small companies to buy their own premises.

About 54% of Koreans live in their own homes, compared with 67% of people in the US, 71% in Australia and 92% in Singapore, according to the World Bank.

But with long-term mortgages available for the first time in 2004, for 70% of an apartment's value, Koreans are eager to withdraw their *chonsei* and supplement it with a mortgage to buy an apartment. Elsewhere in Asia, mortgages are typically offered for 80-90% of a home's value. A new state home-lender, the Korea Housing Finance Corporation, which started offering cheap 10 to 20 year mortgages in March 2004, lent more than 1 trillion won ($864.3 million) in its first two months.

Pakistan and Philippines jump on bandwagon

Of Pakistan's 160 million people, only three million own any kind of landed property. With this in mind, Pakistan's Finance Ministry was set to approve rules in late 2006 to allow the creation of REITs, which the government hoped would give a greater proportion of the country's population access to a rising property market.

Some property industry experts said Pakistan property prices had grown at a stunning average annual pace of 20% in two decades from the mid-1980s. Price rises were increasingly fuelled by money sent home by workers in the Middle East and the United States who wanted to buy new homes. Overseas remittances quadrupled to an annual $4 billion by 2005 from 2002, according to Pakistan's central bank.

But the property market has remained fairly immature, with developers restricted to asking for bank loans to fund their investments. Pakistan's government hoped that introducing a REIT market and opening up to foreign investment would change that.

Competing for investment with neighboring India, Pakistan brought in regulations that allowed full foreign ownership of property, free movement of capital and unrestricted repatriation of profits.

The Securities & Exchange Commission, which would regulate the new REIT market, expected around five REITs to list within one year of approval of the new rules and some $3 billion of foreign funds to flow into Pakistan's REIT market within five years.[27]

To curb speculation, the draft rules, drawn up by the Securities and Exchange Commission, said that land owned by the REITs would be forfeited to the government if it was not developed within four years of purchase.

The Commission also recommended lowering costs for REITs by capping property registration duties at 1% of the land value and eliminating stamp duties which differ by province and range from 3% to 5%.

A REIT management company would need a minimum equity of 50 million rupees and would have to distribute 90% of its net annual income. Each fund set up by a REIT manager would need a minimum size of 250 million rupees.

By early 2007, parliamentarians in the Philippines were also keen to present President Gloria Macapagal Arroyo with a REIT bill in order to attract more foreign capital to the country.

Philippines office rents and capital values had doubled in two years to the end of 2006, and retail rents were up 20% between 2002 and 2006, but foreign investors were still wary of political instability because of a recent history littered with coup attempts.

However, fearing a loss of income, the Bureau of Internal Revenue was a potential stumbling block to the creation of a REIT market as it was concerned about proposals to waive stamp duty and capital gains tax on transactions, as well as corporate tax.

To hedge their bets, property trust proponents were also trying to persuade the Board of Investment to grant REITs a corporate tax holiday for at least four years, which would allow a de facto market to set up if the REIT bill stalled.

If REITs were introduced, the market could grow to as big as $20 billion within five years, according to Melchor Guerrero, vice president for capital markets development at the Philippine Stock Exchange.

He pointed to the potential injection of some $12 billion worth of commercial buildings that an asset management firm had taken form non-performing loan portfolios that built up at banks during the Asian economic crisis.

"They're very supportive in the house and the senate," Guerrero said of parliamentary support for REITs. "Many are very pro-growth, and a lot want to be sponsors of the bill."

The biggest property firms in the Philippines were keen to spin off buildings into REITs. For example, the country's biggest developer, Ayala Land and rival SM Prime Holdings were both keen to package shopping malls and offices.

Ayala Land planned to build 400,000 square metres of office space for outsourcing activities, such as call centers, between 2007 and 2012, and would have 1 million square metres of shopping centre space by the end of 2008.

Philippines shopping centers and offices were giving much higher yields than in most countries in the region, at 10% to 12% in 2007. But REIT investors were likely to be satisfied with a lower yield—at the beginning of 2007, Philippines 10-year government bonds were trading at 6.9% yields.

"It's worth considering because of the low cost of capital and the chance to liquefy assets and redeploy funds," said Jaime Ysmael, Ayala Land's chief financial officer.

Jeffrey Lim, executive vice president at SM Prime Holdings, said his firm could spin off some of its 20 shopping centers into a REIT to help fund expansion. SM Prime was planning to build 12 more malls at the cost of about $300 million by 2010.

"We're definitely interested," Lim said. "Once the incentives are in place, we'd evaluate whether to go into a REIT structure."

Early days in India

After China, the next big frontier for international property investment is India, which eased rules on foreign investment in the construction industry in early 2005, unleashing a wave of excitement among local land owners and property developers as well as foreign funds.

Most analysts believe it is just a matter of time before a REIT market is established in India as a means for property companies to finance their activities, and in mid-2006, authorities took the first step by allowing the creation of real estate mutual funds—investment products that were very similar to REITs.

But the problem was that there were very few good quality buildings on the market that can be packaged into a trust. Of India's $300 billion of commercial buildings in 2006, only $83 billion worth can be considered investment-grade and could be considered for a REIT, compared with $1.27 trillion in Japan.

However, some industry experts believed rapid development would boost the value of the commercial market in India to $463 billion by 2010, and the new buildings would all be of investment grade.

The initial challenge was to build housing—the country faced an estimated shortfall of about 20 million homes in 2006. India also needed to overhaul the country's creaking infrastructure, and put up modern offices and shopping malls demanded by a booming economy partly spurred by the outsourcing of work by cost-cutting Western firms.

India's rule changes in 2005 made it easier for foreign investors to team up with local developers, who were eager to gain expertise in design, construction and marketing buildings as well as finance. Among the main changes in regulations, authorities lowered the hurdles for foreign investors. Previously India only permitted foreign investment in projects of more than 100 acres (40 hectares), with some exceptions in special economic zones. In 2005, the government cut the minimum to 25 acres (10 hectares) for housing development and 50,000 square meters for commercial space. To try to stop sharp movements of hot money, foreign investors were obliged to hold their Indian assets for a minimum of three years before repatriating capital.

Foreign investors itching to tap the country's thriving property industry needed to target small developers because the big players wanted to go it alone. With only a handful of property stocks to choose from, only direct investors were active.

They tended to be big names—US investment banks Morgan Stanley, JPMorgan, Lehman Brothers, Citigroup and Merrill Lynch—many of whom would eventually like to exit their investments by selling buildings into REITs or the real estate mutual funds.

Many of the private equity funds looking for deals in India complained that developers were sticking huge price tags on themselves and their projects to take advantage of the billions of dollars of promised investment. This was also potentially a problem for the planned real estate mutual funds.

Even though the economy was booming and property prices were jumping as much as 60% annually in some areas, developers were asking too much, said Nipun Sahni, India country head for the property arm of GE Commercial Finance, a unit of US conglomerate General Electric Co.. "There's a valuation mismatch," Sahni said.[28] "How much future growth can you price in today? Every Indian company can be worth billions of dollars."

Kurt Roeloffs, Asia chief executive of RREEF, the property asset management arm of Deutsche Bank, blamed high valuations on India's rigid procedures and rules for foreign direct investment. The market was skewed because many foreign funds had instead applied for approval for venture capital status, which is more flexible because it lets investors divest within three years.

"Now the window's too narrow and it's forcing a huge amount of money on certain developers, certain regions and creating imbalances," Roeloffs said.[29]

GE Commercial Finance signed a deal in 2005 to invest $63 million in a fund that invested in business parks with Singapore's Ascendas Pte. Ltd., a company considering packaging its Indian property into a REIT. Despite excessive valuations for deals in some areas, the firm still wanted to go on to partner with developers in fast growing Bangalore and Hyderabad, Sahni said.

"I have a hunch real estate will have bumps and cracks in micro-markets, but you're literally creating a new country," he said. "After the Moguls and the British there's been no building. You have to create places for people to work, live and shop."

India's property industry is hampered by poor foreclosure laws, tedious property registration processes, as well as tax and transaction laws that vary by state. Compounding the confusion, rapid land price appreciation in many major towns sparked frequent contests over property ownership, many dating back to the days of the British Raj and the years following India's independence in 1949.

But many investors are willing to take the risk because development can give internal rates of return of as high as 25%. US funds are especially keen on India as English is spoken widely and many feel comfortable because of the influx of so many Western companies outsourcing information technology and back-office work to the country. Several US property investors have made India their first call in Asia, despite the fact that it is much riskier than mature markets such as Japan, Singapore, Hong Kong and South Korea.

Lagging Indian banks

One of the main constraints on the property industry is India's banking system. Although they are starting to open their doors to developers, banks remain wary about the risks of a fast-growing but young property market, making loans expensive and difficult to obtain.

Industry professionals complain banks have been slow to adapt to the fast-changing landscape in India, and the huge demand for funds from up-and-coming developers. Prospective foreign investors, such as US shopping mall REIT Taubman Centers Inc., are also keen to borrow locally but balk at the personal and corporate guarantees on loans often required by Indian banks.

"The immaturity of India's debt markets is one of the most constraining conditions of investing there," said Taubman's Asia president, Morgan Parker.[30] "It's not only the requisite guarantees but the cost of debt and low leverage that make Indian sourced real estate debt generally unattractive."

Traditionally, the central bank has tried to steer banks away from lending too heavily to the property sector, wary that banking systems in other developing countries, such as Thailand, have nearly disintegrated because of property market crashes. Property project funding by Indian banks added up to $1.8 billion in mid-2006, about 1.5% of outstanding bank loans, according to the Reserve Bank of India. In comparison, Chinese bank exposure to developers in a private property market barely a decade old is worth $114.7 billion, 4.7% of total loans.

Banks are especially wary of murky land titles in a country lacking a centralized title registry, and also fear projects could get tied up in red tape for months or even years after they disburse a loan.

One of India's newest banks, Yes Bank Ltd., says it is leading the way in property project lending, together with ICICI Bank and UTI Bank.

About 12% of Yes Bank's loans have been to developers, and about a third of those are non-recourse loans, which are priced just on projected cash flows with the property as collateral and do not require personal guarantees. The bank, with outstanding loans of $750 million after two years, aims to double its business each year. Many of its property loan deals are syndicated to other banks.

"We're the active players, the rest are frankly followers," said Yes Bank's president for corporate finance, Samak Ghosh.[31] "They don't have the skills to do the loans on their own, the risk analysis. They trust us, and when we do a deal they come in on the back of that."

Yes Bank's non-recourse loans carry an interest rate of about 12.5%, and are typically given for residential projects promoted by local governments, where land titles tend to be more secure, Ghosh said. Tenors are 30-40 months for residential projects but seven to eight years for commercial projects.

Loans with personal guarantees are charged at a 10-10.5% rate, compared with an interbank rate of 6.1%. Chinese banks lend to small developers at about 6%, but offer much lower rates to listed developers. Loan to value (LTV)—total borrowings as a proportion of asset value—for a project in India is typically 65%, similar to emerging property markets such as China, but much lower than developed markets such as Japan or Hong Kong.

"In an emerging market one expects more volatility in property prices. LTV needs to be lower and interest rates (need to be) high," Ghosh said. "But after factoring in India risk, my belief is there is still enough value for everybody."

Foreign investors are lobbying for non-recourse loans from established banks, such as State Bank of India, Bank of Baroda and Union Bank of India, said Shobhit Agarwal, head of investment division at property services firm Trammell Crow Meghraj.

"It's a barrier, but the markets are opening up," he said.[32] "Non-recourse loans should be widely available in India sooner or later. It will allow foreign institutional investors to come in much more smoothly."

Real estate mutual funds (REMFs)

Faced with an investing public clamoring to get a piece of the booming property market, and developers hungry for funds, the Securities and Exchange Board of India (SEBI) announced in June 2006 that it would allow the creation of real estate mutual funds (REMFs), which were to be listed on the stock market.

Just like REITs in other countries, individuals could put their money into the funds, which would buy buildings for their rental returns and, hopefully, capital appreciation. But the funds were also much more flexible than REITs in many Asian countries as they could also buy property stocks and mortgage-backed securities, invest in development projects and even take stakes in unlisted property companies.

The REMFs had the potential to catalyze India's construction industry, streamline the opaque property market and lure millions of investors, but many experts wanted changes to the rules governing the schemes because they were unfeasible.

Fund managers said it would be difficult for funds to abide by some guidelines for REMFs, particularly the need to declare their net asset value (NAV) every day. It would be easy to gauge the value of a fund's investment in listed securities on a daily basis, but almost impossible for investments in shopping centers, office blocks, or townships, they said.

"It could lead to some teething problems," said A.K. Sridhar, chief investment officer at UTI Mutual Fund, the country's second-largest fund. "Only a limited section of the assets (traded shares) can be valued on a daily basis."

Globally, property funds declare the value of their assets in their annual reports, while real estate investment trusts and listed property companies report NAVs along with their earnings. All mutual funds were keen to launch a real estate scheme, but analysts said only mortgage leaders Housing Development Finance Corp. and ICICI Bank had enough expertise on property and access to a database. HDFC and ICICI also had mutual fund companies.

"The business of buying and selling property is completely different from buying and selling stocks or bonds," said Dhirendra Kumar, managing director at Value Research, a mutual fund tracking firm.[33] "HDFC has some expertise and a combination with the likes of DLF and Larsen & Toubro Ltd. could work," Kumar said. Larsen is India's largest engineering and construction firm and DLF is a major developer based in New Delhi.

The REMFs would also be close-ended, meaning that they would not be able to issue new shares to increase their investments. This is a vital difference from typical REITs, which can keep growing and making new acquisitions as long as investors are willing to buy new shares. The funds would therefore be prevented from growing past a certain size.

Industry experts predicted that the funds would accelerate a revolution taking place in Indian property, already started by foreign investors and domestic property funds that were pooling money from rich individuals. The whole industry was becoming more professional, with wider use of scientific project evaluation, more information flows and greater openness because investors were demanding it.

But there were also fears that too much money was flooding into property, fuelling rampant speculation and huge price hikes. Because the property market was still very immature, the country lacked experienced fund managers who could spot good deals and discard bad ones. And the funds would also have to make deals with people who were also often very new to the business.

The accidental developers—India's emerging elite

In a rush to build shops, offices and houses worthy of a thriving economy, a new elite is emerging in India—young people asked to turn plots of family land into a property business. These are the landlords of the future—the people who will be creating REITs.

The 30-something professionals have set their sights on capturing a piece of an estimated $12 billion of annual inward investment earmarked for property in India since the country eased rules on foreign financing of construction in early 2005.

They are inexperienced. But they are accumulating valuable land in a billion-person economy that grew more than 8% in 2006 and is suffering a shortage of good quality housing for its burgeoning middle-class.

Shrirang Sarda, 34, for example, describes himself as a "reluctant developer" whose 83-year-old family business, Sarda Group, employs 16,000 workers making *bidis*, cigarettes rolled in dry leaves that are hugely popular in India.

When his once-serene ancestral house in Nashik, between booming Mumbai and Pune, found itself on the main street of a horn-honking city of one million people, Sarda pulled it down and built the city's first modern cinema complex.

He sold the cinema and was moving on to develop a shopping center and a township (a housing estate with amenities such as schools and shops) with a group of foreign investors.

"There's a huge change happening in India, with a wave of consumption," Sarda said.[34] "And if you enter the property business at a chaotic time, you've got a good chance of making it."

Some of Asia's biggest fortunes were made that way.

Hong Kong tycoon Li Ka-shing snapped up land in Hong Kong four decades ago, when riots inspired by China's Cultural Revolution sparked a property slump. Now only a small club of developers have the clout to compete in the cutthroat Hong Kong market.

And Li's empire has grown to include property developer Cheung Kong (Holdings) and ports-to-telecoms conglomerate Hutchison Whampoa Ltd..

China's private property market, barely a decade old but booming, has also spawned a group of mega-rich businessmen in their 30s, leading companies such as Shanghai Forte Co. Ltd. and China Vanke Co. Ltd.. Many owe their beginnings to close links with local Communist party officials.

In India, success is more haphazard and often begins with the good fortune of owning prime plots of land.

Daleep Akoi's great, great-grandfather was a contractor during the British Raj who built a forest research institute and a military academy in Dehradun in northern India and picked up land across the country along the way.

Now Akoi, 30, is giving up journalism and 11 years of living abroad to turn a former British officer's mess in central New Delhi into a boutique hotel before developing other parcels of family land.

India, which will host the Commonwealth Games in 2010, had just 12,000 high-quality hotel rooms in 2006, while tiny Singapore has 70,000.

"I'm excited," Akoi said.[35] "There's liberalization of foreign capital coming in, confidence in the economy—you really feel it now—and the government is more open to new ideas."

He said young developers are also more open-minded.

"They've been abroad and have seen what value-added stuff you can do with property," Akoi said. "And the younger generation has no barriers of culture, caste and language. You can shed that baggage and go to Mumbai, Kolkata, anywhere to do projects."

The property sector, with only a couple of listed firms, has few billionaires because a tangle of red tape and poor finance prevented firms from expanding beyond their local bases. The industry is hampered by poor foreclosure laws, tedious property registration processes, tax and transaction laws that vary by state and frequent contests over property ownership.

In a *Forbes* magazine list of India's top 40 richest people, dominated by pharmaceutical and technology magnates, the only top-placed developer is Kushal Pal Singh, chairman of DLF Universal Ltd., who comes in fifth.

DLF, which turned a sleepy New Delhi suburb into a bustling zone of malls and offices, was planning to raise $3.5 billion in 2006 in what was expected to be India's biggest share offering, but the deal was shelved because of a volatile stock market and doubts about land valuations. The company expected to revive the IPO in 2007.

Sarda and Akoi hoped foreign capital can someday help them achieve the same as DLF and are encouraged by recent deals.

In 2006, US bank Morgan Stanley invested $68 million in Mantri Developers Private Ltd., compatriot developer Tishman Speyer tied up with India's ICICI Bank to pour more than $1 billion into the country and US pension fund CalPERS has put $100 million in an Indian property fund.

Private equity arms of JPMorgan, Lehman Brothers and Merrill Lynch were all hunting similar deals.

Sarda said old-style wheeler dealers were losing out to businessmen like him, who attract foreign partners because they understand concepts such as cash flow predictions and internal rates of return.

"Two years ago there was no market—it was just very traditional, handshake-driven," said Sarda, who travels to conferences in the region to network and learn more.

"Because the funds are coming in, there's a lot more transparency now. But they're also being very flexible because they're not willing to miss the India bus."

REIT players—Valuers and brokers

Savills is one of several property services firms that are employed by REIT sponsors to help in the preparation work for an IPO. The firm values properties and can also carry out market and structural studies for the sponsors. After an IPO, the company offers property management services such as security and cleaning, as well as tenancy management services, which would include collecting rental payments and fees, and conducting lease negotiations on behalf of the REIT. Firms such as Savills also act as brokers, introducing properties as potential acquisitions to REIT managers.

Charles Chan, managing director of Savills valuation services in Hong Kong, worked on Hong Kong's first REITs. He carried out market studies for Link REIT, Prosperity REIT and Fortune REIT and was the independent valuer and conditions surveyor for Champion REIT. Robert McKellar heads Savills in the Asia-Pacific region and is overseeing the fast growth of the company's business in servicing REITs.

Here they talk about how the types of buildings they expect will be packaged into REITs in Hong Kong and the imminent advent of cross-border REITs.

Few prime Hong Kong properties will be packaged into REITs because their yields are too low, Chan said. The poor response to Champion REIT in 2006 meant that financial engineering to lift yields had become unfashionable.

"I don't think you'll be able to get grade A REITs in the future," Chan said. "Fundamentally, property yields are too low, especially in prime areas—just 2% or 3%. Investors are only willing to accept 5%, so there's a need for some complex financial structuring. But financial engineering hasn't been very well received."

Chan expects industrial and warehouse properties near Hong Kong's ports to be prominent among future IPOs in the city.

"Sponsors may be more interested in selling buildings in fringe areas that yield at least 5%," he said. "Look at industrial buildings. Funds are purchasing these at 6% yields. If they're investing in these properties, I can't see why they can't be marketable as a REIT."

Traditionally, Hong Kong investors have been more interested in capital gain, which can be very sharp because the property market is one of the world's most volatile. But REIT investors, especially outside Asia, are more focused on yield, Chan said.

Chan had valued the Champion REIT's Citibank Plaza shortly before its May 2006 IPO, and just three months later grade A market rents were about 50% higher on average.

"Investors in Europe or the US have no idea of the Hong Kong property market and they just look at the yield," he said. "They don't look at the historical capital gains."

"It's amazing that REITs with low-quality property like the Link are preferred by foreign investors."

Chan said property yields are falling fast across the region because of an influx of foreign investors who are pushing up prices.

"We have to reshape the traditional thinking," he said. "In the past, five or 10 years ago, property investors were very sensitive to yield. There was a big gap between industrial and residential and retail and office. And there was a gap between good and poor offices. But there's been too much money chasing property and the range of yields has converged. Industrial property in Tuen Muen, for example, is selling at just a 6% yield. Historically, it hasn't been less than 8%."

REIT players—The Australians are coming

Driven from their mature home market by slowing business, Australian property bankers, fund managers and analysts are popping up in Asian cities, lured by the region's new REIT industry and an influx of investment.

"We could see our client base dwindling every day," said Philip Levinson, who worked on property trust finance at Westpac Banking Corp. in Sydney.[36]

Now Levinson lives in Singapore and is head of client services for Asia at LaSalle Investment Management, which advises investors looking to buy in Asia. The company raised a property fund last year with $3 billion to $4 billion of spending power for Asian markets.

"When Australians come through the door they're highly regarded," Levinson said. "We're getting lots of e-mails and calls from people in Australia saying, 'What's going on up there and how can we become part of it?'"

Japan, Singapore and Hong Kong have been abuzz with REIT talk from the early 2000s, while Australia's listed property trust sector had its heyday in the 1990s, growing through purchases of buildings and value-adding renovations, and then buying assets abroad, especially in the US.

Mergers and acquisitions in 2003 and 2004 among the trusts have cut numbers, even after a few new IPOs, to about 30. Purely Australian property deals became scarce, because about 60% of the country's $103 billion of investment-grade buildings were already held by the trusts and the rest were unlikely to change hands.

Property professionals say lower income tax, especially in Singapore and Hong Kong, mean they are generally better off in Asia than in Australia. Hong Kong is a popular destination because of its nascent REIT market and a flurry of deals in mainland China, where developers squeezed by a clampdown on bank lending are desperate for finance from foreign funds or from the capital markets.

Australian bankers Anthony Ryan at JPMorgan Chase & Co. and Michael Smith, firstly at UBS AG before moving to Goldman Sachs, helped launch the world's biggest REIT IPO, Hong Kong's $2.8 billion Link REIT, in November 2005, kick-starting the city's REITs market.

Australians Peter Barge and Rob Blain are chief executives for Asia-Pacific at property consultants Jones Lang LaSalle Inc. and CB Richard Ellis Group Inc., respectively. And former Lend Lease employee and Morgan Stanley banker, Brisbane-born Morgan Parker, is Asia head for US shopping mall REIT Taubman Centers Inc., which hopes to expand into China, Japan, South Korea and Singapore.

Ryan, head of Asia property investment banking at JPMorgan, moved to Hong Kong from Sydney in 2003 and has expanded his team to 10 from three, including an Australian, an Indian, a Korean and an Indonesian, as well as Chinese staff.

"It's still a challenge up here to find people with strong relevant experience," Ryan said.[37] "Lots of our competitors have general bankers trying to do real estate deals."

However, it's not just the Asian REIT business the Australians are after, cash-rich Australian property funds are also snapping up assets, particularly in Japan, and listing them back at home.

The Australian hunger for overseas property is being driven hard by abundant capital from superannuation funds and attractive yields uplift from currency arbitrage. Australia has more managed funds per capita than any other country. Superannuation funds, Australia's compulsory pension scheme, are expected to grow to $1.7 trillion in 2020 from $587 billion in 2006.

In 2005, 8% of superannuation funds were allocated to property, according to the Australian Prudential Regulation Authority, and some bankers estimate about $5 billion of investment a year will flow from Australia to the rest of the world.

"The Australian market is very competitive and securitized but enjoys very strong capital flows," said Craig Dunstan, managing director and chief investment officer at MacarthurCook.[38] "We'll look at the Japanese market, and if we find the right opportunities, we'll package up the assets as a REIT."

Australian listed property trusts (LPTs) began accumulating overseas property in the late 1990s, particularly in the US, in a drive to give their investors more diversification. By 2006, foreign buildings had made up about 48% of total assets held by LPTs, with almost all in the US. To offer superannuation funds more diversification, it makes sense to make LPTs look more representative of global property markets, and Japan is home to about 11% of the world's investment-grade buildings.

By the end of 2006, three Australian funds had already packaged Japanese real estate and listed them in Australia. The first was Babcock & Brown's Japan Property Trust, which was followed by Rubicon Japan Trust and Galileo Funds Management Ltd.

In a reversal of Japanese property investment in Australia during the 1980s, which made the Gold Coast skyline soar, Australian funds now see a lot to offer in Japan. For one, it is the world's biggest office market with about 840 million square feet of office space. Another attraction is the yield spread in Japan. At the end of 2006, the difference between yields on top-grade Tokyo office blocks and 10-year bond yield was about two percentage points, while rental yields in London and Australia were actually below finance costs.

Australian funds have also been locking in favorable currency exchange rates to lift the final yield for their investors by about two percentage points. This was first done by Babcock and Brown through currency swaps and was only possible because of the big differential between Australian and Japanese interest rates. A Japanese bank would be willing to forego lower-than-market currency exchange rates because relatively high Australian interest rates would make up the difference.

This meant that Tokyo buildings giving a net property yield of 6% could give a yield of 8% in an Australian listed property trust.

However, venturing into a foreign market is no picnic, and Australian firms may struggle to source deals in Japan, where competition for assets began getting intense in 2005.

In many cases, yields in risky countries such as China have fallen the fastest.

"And it's amazing that yields in China are getting close to Hong Kong yields," Chan said. "Two years ago they were 8 or 9% and now it's 6 or 7%. Investors have forgotten the (differences in) country risk between China and Hong Kong. It used to be 2 or 3 percentage points difference."

Chan uses two ways to value buildings. One looks at cash flow and yields for similar buildings to derive a capital value—a method that is generally preferred by professionals in developed REIT markets. The other way is to compare transaction prices for similar buildings—a method Chan said was still popular among landlords in Asia.

"In Hong Kong almost all property owners put more weight on unit price, how much per square foot," Chan said. "It's similar in Singapore. Because there are also a lot of active transactions in these markets, it can work well."

Robert McKellar, Savills' Asia-Pacific chief executive officer, said he expected bankers to start marketing cross-border REITs to investors as a way of delivering high yields.

"People will be trying to sell sexy types of REITs to Joe public," McKellar said. "You could get a REIT with Bangkok apartments, hotels in Japan, retail in Hong Kong for example, marketed together. They are going to offer different asset classes to spice it up; the psyche is moving that way at the moment."

McKellar suggested some of the motivation behind cross-border REITs is a thirst among investment bankers for fees for arranging IPOs.

"You could be a bit cynical and think it's a way for banks to get more fees," he said. "But you can't stop securitization of real estate. In the US it's moved on to toll roads and infrastructure.

"If you listen to the financial advisers in Australia, they're pushing forward other avenues for fees, such as these cross-border REITS. But the tax, accounting and foreign ownership regulations are hampering their ability to deliver."

McKellar also predicted much more cross-border investment in property, including REITs, especially by Japanese investors who could borrow domestically at rock-bottom interest rates.

"It would make sense for investors to borrow in Japan and invest in Australia, for example," McKellar said. "It's only recently that banks have allowed it again, letting foreign properties be the collateral for a loan. I'd expect a lot of Japanese investors to start investing abroad. But many Japanese were stung in the U.K. and elsewhere (in the late 1980s) and they have pretty long memories," he said.

McKellar said servicing REITs is a rapidly growing but still relatively small part of Savills' business. But if REIT markets in Singapore, Hong Kong and Japan grew to the size of that in Australia, the company would profit handsomely.

"Once the number of REITs has increased, it will become a substantial part of our business," he said. "We'll do valuations every six months or a year, and then there are research and consultancy fees, source stock for brokerage fees. It's a growing part and very lucrative, but not as lucrative as it is for the merchant banks."

The crystal ball—What lies ahead for Asia's REITs?

Analysts at Australia's Macquarie Bank have developed a useful model to understand the probable evolution of Asian REIT markets, which they call theEvolution and Cycle of Listed Property Securities (ECLIPSE) analysis. The model is based on the development of Australia's listed property trust market since the early 1970s, so it gives a roadmap for Asia's nascent REIT markets, but only up to where Australia stands at present. Any prospective investor should be aware of the possible wider developments in property trust markets as they can have a large bearing on share movements of individual REITs.

Macquarie's ECLIPSE analysis

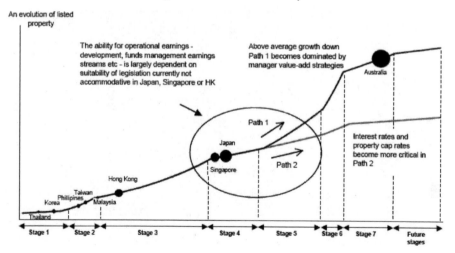

Source: Macquarie

Stage 1—The first attempt

The initial stage represents the first attempt to establish a listed REIT market in a country. The listed vehicles can be lowly geared (low borrowing), illiquid, single-asset REITs that are not owned by institutional investors and don't have a competitive cost of capital. In 2006, Thailand and Malaysia were ranked in this first stage, although more trusts were being planned in both countries, suggesting that REITs were gaining more acceptance among investors.

Stage 2—Legislative change drives sector growth

As governments recognize the benefits of a healthy REIT market (as a serious alternative for investors to stocks, bonds and bank deposits and as a way of invigorating physical property markets) they bring in regulatory changes to encourage REITs. These changes themselves can provoke strong share price gains by property trusts. The waiver of dividend taxes for individual investors in Singapore, for example, spurred a new wave of enthusiasm for REITs. By raising the limit on how much a trust could borrow, the government also made it easier for trusts to cheaply fund new acquisitions that would lift income for shareholders.

Stage 3—Acquisition-driven growth

Once legislation is in place and REITs are established, a phase of acquisition-driven growth can follow. The market provides the listed vehicle with a cost of capital low enough to acquire buildings that are yield-accretive. Early REITs gain first-mover advantage and have limited competition in the acquisition market relative to mature markets. Large earnings-per-share and dividends-per-share revisions are also possible in Stage 3.

What marks the end of this stage? In the view of Macquarie analysts, it is important to keep a close eye on the yield given in the direct property market and the cost of capital of the listed REIT market (the REIT market yield). When they converge, it will be difficult for trusts to make yield-accretive acquisitions and it will be time for them to look to buy abroad. In Australia, trusts began to buy in the United States in the mid-1990s. Singapore REITs were starting to look beyond their home market in 2005, and one, Mapletree REIT, bought a warehouse in China.

Stage 4—Growth plateaus

One factor that is absent from stage 3 but becomes more important in stage four is a focus on underlying property performance. Clearly acquisitions will usually bring a bigger jump in income than lifting occupancy in a building, say to 96% from 94%. So while good purchases are possible, REIT managers will focus on those. But once suitable buildings are scarce, and if a REIT decides it wants to focus on its core market rather than look abroad, it will put more effort into creating operational improvements such as more effective leasing, a more aggressive development program and internal organizational restructures. In Australia, when many REITs decided to go offshore, notably Westfield Group's venture into the United States, Gandel focused on Australia. By late 2005, it had a property development pipeline of $1.1 billion from which it expected to earn an average yield of 8%. Its buildings were 99.9% occupied.

Stage 5

Path one—A move up the risk curve—operational earnings enter the sector

In the late 1980s, Australian listed property trusts started to take on a "stapled securities" structure: property trusts that owned buildings and distributed income as dividends in the traditional sense were "stapled" together with a company that could be dedicated to property development. A shareholder would own units in the trust and shares in the company attached to it. This structure allowed investors in the stapled security to be exposed to construction at a time when listed property trusts were running out of acquisition targets in Australia. This obviously brought its own risks, but in the period between 1999 and 2003 total returns from the stapled securities outstripped the broader listed property trust market by 6.7 percentage points. Residential developers were particularly healthy in that period because of an upturn in Australia's housing market.

It is quite possible that Asian authorities will not go down the stapled securities road, wishing not to add too much risk associated with development to REITs in their jurisdictions. Macquarie analysts believe that some countries will allow their trusts limited exposure to property development by stipulating a maximum level of income that can be earned in that way. Otherwise, trusts will have to look abroad for buildings once options in their home property market dry up.

Path two

In a second scenario, regulators do not allow Asia REITs to take on riskier activities, and they remain pure investments in rental income. With diminishing prospects of income growth through acquisitions and improving operations, property trusts become more susceptible to moves in interest rates and rental yields in the physical property market. They remain steady sources of income but REITs become largely inert investment products.

Stage 6—Sector consolidation

Because good buildings become scarce on the open market, REIT managers would embark on a strategy of mergers and acquisitions—strong REIT managers bid for weaker managers with good assets. In Australia, REIT management companies merged with the REIT itself, so that the management fees did not "leak"—allowing the REIT shareholder not only to have a stake in the rental income of the REIT but the management fees too. This also helped to allay suspicions of conflicts of interest between the REIT managers and shareholders—for example, over fees that managers receive for arranging an acquisition of a building. Many believe that managers should be given incentives to search for new acquisitions, but shareholders could get upset if they thought the managers were getting overpaid.

Stage 7—Growth plateaus again

As Stage 6 ends and Stage 7 began in Australia, there was a period of lower growth and price gains by the listed property trusts. Stapled securities dominated the listed property trust market, so there were simply fewer externally managed trusts for them to target. However, the sector kept growing with new, smaller property trusts listing on the stock market, including trusts with foreign assets such as one sponsored by Babcock and Brown with Japanese buildings.

REIT players—The analyst

REIT analysts are a new breed in Asia because the markets are so young. Most have researched and written about the region's traditional property development companies, and then made the switch to cover REITs.

Employed by stock brokerages and investment banks to supply research so that clients can make investment decisions, analysts are a vital component to Asia's growing REIT market. The more trusts that are listed, the more demand there will be among investors for tips on who are the REIT managers delivering on their promises, which shares are overvalued or undervalued, how results match up to expectations, and the state of REIT finances.

A good analyst will also give you an opinion of the development of REIT markets, which can be useful for long-term investment strategies.

Matt Nacard, Asia REIT analyst at Macquarie Securities, for example, has designed the Macquarie ECLIPSE analysis to try to help investors understand the likely development of REIT markets in the region.

Nacard, who researched Australian-listed property trusts before moving to Hong Kong in 2005, explains why it is important to keep abreast of regulatory changes and gives a few extra pointers on what to expect from Asian REITs.

"We recognized that there are very distinct characteristics as REITs develop over time, and we looked at how to break them up to determine what are the drivers of the lifecycle of REIT markets," Nacard said of the thinking behind the ECLIPSE analysis.

"If you look at the early stages, one and two, the drivers there are legislation. If one doesn't recognize the relevant pieces of legislation, an investor could buy on the basis of the internal element of REITS and might not be satisfied with the outcome."

Nacard said that since he drew up the original Macquarie ECLIPSE analysis in 2004, Asian REIT markets had pretty much developed as expected.

"The smaller countries have gone according to plan," he said. "Legislative changes came through, but markets have not performed and grown if legislation wasn't appropriate. The first stages (of the ECLIPSE analysis) are fairly predictable."

But Hong Kong's REIT market has surprised, with its investor frenzy for property trusts at the end of 2005 followed by a sudden waning of enthusiasm in early 2006. Hong Kong individual investors were particularly susceptible to fads, and REITs had not escaped, Nacard said.

"In stage three, Hong Kong has been a little more volatile than we anticipated," Nacard said. "It's not earnings driven, more sentiment driven, and there are also the vagaries of IPOs in Hong Kong. It's very binary, either zero or one. IPOs are either hundreds of times subscribed or three times subscribed."

"I think REITs have surprised on the upside and the downside because it's a volatile market. What's hot or not can change depending on lots of things."

But the Singapore market is much more predictable.

"Singapore is what we thought would occur," Nacard said. In "a mature market, acquisitions become not so important, and REITs rely more on organic growth. It's less spectacular but there's less risk associated."

Nacard's original ECLIPSE analysis assumed that Asian REITs would follow the Australian model, with regulators gradually easing rules on the activities of property trusts so that they would be able to give their shareholders more income by getting into fund management and property development. But

Nacard redrew the analysis to take into account a possible reluctance on behalf of Asian regulators to allow REITs to take on more risk. Many countries will probably prefer property trusts to stay relatively simple.

"There's a fork in the road approaching, though Asia has not gone that far yet," he said. "Either you take the path of Australian listed property trusts (LPTs), and legislation will have to change to allow development and fund management, or you take the New Zealand path where legislation does not allow it."

"Our feeling is that Singapore will go down path one, but it will take time yet," Nacard said. "Singapore authorities are keen to develop a market and encourage IPOs. When a market has fewer options, and runs out of acquisitions, to encourage IPOs you have to open up."

"Instead of 100% rental income, you could have 70%, with 30% from real estate-related development or funds management. Then it's a whole different ball game. REITs become a different style of vehicle. It takes REITs up the risk curve a bit, but there's a chance of good returns as well."

But Hong Kong regulators will probably go down the other path, according to Nacard, and are even unlikely to give the same sort of tax breaks that Singapore has offered.

"In Hong Kong there will probably be no tax changes," he said. "Hong Kong guidelines are evolving and are very much at a preliminary stage. It very much revolves around interpretation of the REIT code. Authorities are only just becoming comfortable and I can't see any changes."

Meanwhile, Japanese REITs could become targets for mergers and acquisitions as the property market recovers from a near 15-year decline that began around 1989. As stiff competition makes it difficult for traditional property investors to buy buildings on the open market, property trusts with a long list of assets would start to look attractive, according to Nacard.

"In Japan, the most interesting element that I've noticed is that they've just changed legislation (in 2006) so that a REIT must disclose if a shareholder has a 5% stake, whereas it used to be 10%," Nacard said. "They're aware of M&A activity in REITs, especially as property prices firm up. If physical property is more expensive than the REIT markets, REITs will be privatized, essentially bought out by pension funds and opportunity funds."

Nacard expects India and China to both eventually create REIT markets, but the property sector in both countries, although booming, will take time to settle and mature. He thinks China will not have a viable REIT market until about 2010, with India following maybe five years later, once it has built a good stock of new buildings.

"There's a general maturing of the market, but authorities will really want to sort out the main physical property markets first. REIT legislation is way down the list," Nacard said of China.

And what about the far right side of the ECLIPSE analysis—the "future stages" part? Nacard predicts the end of REITs as we know them, because they will become more and more dependent on property development, and then the rebirth of a new REIT market.

"Australia will move into a phase where REITS become almost property companies, they will go a full circle. These things become property companies, and start spinning off assets into REITs," he said.

Endnotes

1 "Hong Kong's Link REIT: Property so bad, it's good," by Dominic Whiting, Reuters, November 24, 2005.
2 *Ibid.*
3 "Hong Kong's Prosperity REIT IPO price at top end," by Daisy Ku, Reuters, December 8, 2005.
4 Jones Lang LaSalle and Macquarie Research, June 2005.
5 "Investors demand more from Asia's property trusts," by Dominic Whiting and Sebastian Tong, Reuters, June 27, 2006.
6 Jones Lang LaSalle data.
7 Asian Demographics and ING Real Estate, September 2003.
8 Jones Lang LaSalle and Macquarie Research, June 2005.
9 "Best in a class of one: Scarcity boosts China REIT," by Dominic Whiting and Daisy Ku, Reuters, December 13, 2005.
10 "Bankers fear a China REIT flop could taint new market," by Dominic Whiting, Reuters, January 12, 2006.
11 "False titles a risk to property investors in China," by Dominic Whiting, Reuters, October 31, 2005.
12 *Ibid.*
13 "Bankers fear a China REIT flop could taint new market," by Dominic Whiting, Reuters, January 12, 2006.
14 *Ibid.*
15 "Private equity firm learns from Shanghai nightmare," by Dominic Whiting, Reuters, June 23, 2006.
16 "Questions about risk slow Singapore REIT bandwagon," by Dominic Whiting and Sebastian Tong, Reuters, September 15, 2005.
17 "Japanese property trust looks beyond expensive Tokyo," by Dominic Whiting, Reuters, May 20, 2005
18 "Japan REIT market set to enter M&A phase," by Eriko Amaha and Dominic Whiting, Reuters, August 2, 2006.
19 *Ibid.*
20 "Quake fears rattle Japanese property investors," by Dominic Whiting, Reuters, May 26, 2005.

21 *Ibid.*

22 *Ibid.*

23 "Tax snags Malaysia REIT hopes for Mideast money," by Dominic Whiting, Reuters, July 1, 2005.

24 "Teething pains for Thailand's property funds," by Chawadee Nualkhair and Orathai Sriring, Reuters, August 26, 2005.

25 "South Korea leads as property trusts catch on in Asia," by Dominic Whiting and Yoo Choonsik, Reuters, January 16, 2004.

26 "Koreans frustrated by traditional rental system," by Dominic Whiting and Rhee So-eui, Reuters, June 21, 2004.

27 SEC commissioner Salman Ali Shaikh quoted in "Pakistan ready to allow REITs - It aims to draw $3 billion from overseas investors in 5 years," by Naweed A. Mangi, Bloomberg News, June 21 2006.

28 *Ibid.*

29 "Private equity bemoans price of Indian developers," by Dominic Whiting, Reuters, June 29, 2006.

30 "Wary Indian banks open doors to property firms," by Dominic Whiting, Reuters, August 1, 2006.

31 *Ibid.*

32 *Ibid.*

33 "Valuation rule seen hindering Indian property funds," by M.C. Govardhana Rangan and Dominic Whiting, Reuters, July 26, 2006.

34 "Accidental developers—India's new elite," by Dominic Whiting, Reuters, June 28, 2006.

35 *Ibid.*

36 "Oztracized property professionals head for Asia," by Dominic Whiting, Reuters, February 9, 2006.

37 *Ibid.*

38 "Cashed-up Australian property firms raid Japan," By Alison Tudor and Eriko Amaha, Reuters, December 4, 2006

Community chest—
Tax and regulations

REITs owe their very existence to authorities creating new guidelines and granting special privileges. The taxation regimes for investors and the trusts, and the rules governing trusts, are therefore central to the scope and nature of a REIT's activities and ultimately to its performance. Regulatory changes introduced after a market has been created can have a massive and immediate effect on share prices.

Governments have introduced REITs for a variety of reasons. The major motive is to offer a much-needed alternative investment vehicle to investors (both individuals as well as institutions such as pension funds) whose choices have mostly been limited to stocks and bonds. A vibrant REIT market also improves the transparency of property markets because trusts are obliged to supply a flow of information about rents and capital values to their investors. REITs also tend to be active purchasers of buildings, so they can help revive property markets.

Landlords are often keen to sell their buildings in order to raise funds for new projects, and REIT markets can give them a good price. But in most cases, for a REIT market to take off, a government needs to provide special corporate tax incentives to persuade owners of buildings that it is more advantageous for them to hold a stake in a publicly traded trust than to own the whole building privately.

Typically, governments will waive corporate income tax on REITs. That can present a landlord with the following choices: Keep the building and receive all of the net income, after tax; or sell into a REIT, but by keeping a stake, still enjoy a share of the gross income before tax, as well as the proceeds from selling a majority stake in the building.

For example, a landlord sells a building worth $10,000 into a REIT but keeps a 30% stake of the trust. The annual rent is $500, and corporate income tax is 30%. The landlord would receive $7,000 on the sale of 70% of the building and would then collect $150 of annual income (tax free).

By keeping the whole building, the landlord would just collect $350 of income each year, having paid the corporate tax.

The relative return from the REIT is higher for the landlord. An income of $150 for a share worth $3,000, gives a 5% yield. That compares with $350 for the whole $10,000 worth of ownership, which gives 3%.

The 30% stake in the trust could also rise in value if the REIT units trade higher on the stock market. It would be much more difficult to gauge any rise of value if the building were held privately, and probably much more difficult to sell it than it would be to sell shares in the REIT.

The basic example above assumes a 100% payment of income. In reality, it would probably be slightly less as most Asian governments have stipulated a 90% minimum dividend pay out, with the remainder allowed to be reinvested in the business. That is still a very high proportion compared with dividends distributed by other types of publicly listed companies, and is another of the typical characteristics of a REIT designed to lure investors.

A fundamental result of the corporate income tax waiver, together with tax breaks for investors, is that property trusts are usually valued higher than other types of property companies.

REITs in general tend to trade at much more than their buildings are actually worth on the open property market (a premium to their net asset value, or NAV) whereas other property companies listed on stock markets tend to trade at a discount.

This is partly because trust units are valued more than physical property since they are easily traded, and they are more predictable and less risky than property firms that construct buildings but also might dabble in any business ranging from a limousine service to a budget airline.

But in a majority of cases, the premium is also largely due to the tax breaks for REITs. Because more of the rental income flows to the owners of the buildings, the buildings are more highly valued. This difference in valuing property held by trusts exists for almost all REITs in Asia, and over a much longer period, has been the case for the established REIT markets in the US and Australia. Trusts in Japan have traded at as much as 80% premiums to net asset value, whereas 30-50% premiums are common in Australia.

If a REIT trades at below its net asset value it becomes a prime takeover target for bargain hunters wanting to take advantage of the price gap between the stock market price of the buildings and their value on the open market. The biggest US pension fund, the California Public Employee Retirement System, or CalPERS, has said, for instance, that one of its strategies for expanding its portfolio of investment properties is looking for REITs around the world that are worth taking private.

Buyouts of listed property companies trading at below NAV would be much more cumbersome because, unlike REITs, most have a raft of small business interests that would have to be dealt with as well as their buildings.

Experience has already shown that regulatory changes after a REIT market has been introduced can have a major bearing on the way REITs operate and the returns they can give investors.

Obviously any reductions on tax, either at the corporate or REIT level or on investors, will immediately improve returns.

In Asia, Singapore has been the most generous with its tax incentives for REITs, and has gone furthest in easing rules on the activities of trusts. Some analysts say there is no better way of owning property on the island, and investors are starting to realize it. For example, when the Singapore government waived withholding tax for local individuals and cut it for foreigners, REIT share prices jumped.

On the other hand, Hong Kong decided that its tax breaks for investors in any kind of stock were already good enough, and it offered nothing special for property trusts. The REIT market there took a long time to start up, because there was no big tax incentive to persuade cash-rich property companies to sell their buildings unless the property market was approaching its peak.

Investors in Hong Kong REITs got no special tax benefit, so some would argue that units in a trust were little different than shares in a company such as Hongkong Land Holdings, which owns a large chunk of Central, the main business area.

The main differences are in their businesses rather than the regulatory and tax treatment. A REIT guarantees a certain share of its profit as a dividend, while Hongkong Land can change its dividend policy at any time. Hongkong Land can be seen as more aggressive, but also more risky, because it builds housing in China, Hong Kong and Macau and gets into joint ventures to build giant commercial complexes in Singapore. Meanwhile a Hong Kong REIT's virtues are that it has a simple business model and gives a relatively reliable flow of income.

Another tool regulators can wield to make REITs more attractive is raising the amount a trust can borrow, which makes it easier for trusts to expand by buying new buildings. Higher debt can give a REIT the opportunity to improve returns for investors from buildings that have relatively low yields on the open property market. Here's a simple example of how using borrowing to "leverage" can work to deliver a higher yield.

A building costs $500 and generates $25 in rent a year, or a 5% yield. But an investor is demanding a 6% yield. So the trust borrows $250 at a 4% annual interest rate and only asks the investor for $250 to finance the deal. (The "gearing," the proportion of debt to assets, is therefore 50%.) The interest payment on the loan for the first year of ownership of the building is $10. So when the $25 annual rent is paid, $10 is siphoned off for paying interest and $15 is paid to the shareholder. This represents a yield on the initial shareholder investment of 15/250, or 6%.

Regulators in Asia have limited the amount of debt REITs can take on in order to protect investors from excessive risk. Obviously, when interest rates rise, trusts can get into trouble if their debt is high, although managers usually try to fix their interest rates by issuing long-term mortgage-backed securities or through interest rate swaps. Australia has no limit on borrowing, but listed property trusts there have tended to keep to around a 40% gearing rate, with investors going cold on trusts that have overshot that level.

Singapore and Hong Kong have both raised their limits on borrowing since they introduced their original REIT codes. Singapore has gone the farthest, with trusts allowed to borrow as much as 60% of their asset value as long as they obtain a debt rating from a credit ratings agency. Hong Kong lifted its gearing limit to 45% in 2005 from 35%.

Asian governments have on the whole chosen to prevent REITs from developing property, or at least they have restricted it to a small part of their business, in order to limit the risks for investors.

But as Macquarie's ECLIPSE analysis in Chapter 1 suggests, this stance could well change over time as it becomes more difficult for trusts to acquire suitable buildings. Constructing new buildings and leasing them would give trusts far greater opportunities to improve income for shareholders.

But at the same time, it carries risks. Can the costs be controlled? Will a project be finished on schedule? Will the market turn in the meantime, and will the REIT be able to find enough new tenants?

Development also tends to make income flows more uneven. From inception to opening, a large office building could take five years to complete during which the trust will incur expenses. Then, suddenly, it will reap a new inflow of rental income.

For a large REIT, the risks involved in developing one project can be small in proportion to its overall cash flow, and distributable income can still be relatively smooth. The smaller the REIT, the more magnified the risks and the more unpredictable the income stream.

Below is an outline of the tax and regulatory environments in the major Asian REIT markets of Japan, Singapore and Hong Kong as they stood in 2006. For these markets, which were tipped to be the main REIT hubs in Asia, few major regulatory changes were expected. Other markets such as South Korea, Thailand, Taiwan and Malaysia were expected to bring in changes over time to bring their rules and tax incentives in line with those in Japan and Singapore.

Japan

The Japanese REIT market has its roots in the collapse of the country's "bubble" economy in the 1990s. Throughout that decade the government passed a series of reforms to protect investors and allow the securitization of property assets, culminating in the Investment Trust and Investment Corporation Law in 2000, which allowed property trusts to set up.

The rules governing Japanese REITs were modeled on the US market and many analysts believe so many trusts subsequently listed in a short time because Japan "got it right the first time." In the first six years, the market had grown to about $45 billion with 40 REITs, including offices, shopping centers, warehouses and apartments, traded on the stock market.

REITs are highly regulated in Japan and can take as long as a year to set up, because of a complex process of having to form an asset management company and vehicles to buy properties before a trust can be launched.

But the tax incentives are very generous.[1] If a trust complies with certain criteria, the dividends it pays are tax deductible, meaning that it will pay almost zero tax, whereas the effective rate on other types of companies is 42%. The conditions REITs must meet to receive this benefit are not overly arduous: The shares of the trust must be publicly traded and valued at more than 100 million yen, or shares must be held by 50 or more people or by institutional investors. Shares must be offered mainly in Japan, more than 90% of distributable income must be paid as a dividend, and the trust cannot control or own 50% of any other company.

The tax treatment of dividends for investors depends on whether they hold more or less than 5% of the total issued shares in a trust.

If an individual investor, either Japanese or a non-resident, holds 5% or more, the dividend income is subject to a 20% withholding tax, and should be included in the investor's aggregate taxable base, which is subject to progressive income taxes.

For a shareholding of less than 5%, Japanese individual investors are charged a 10% withholding tax but a non-resident is charged 7%, and no further tax is paid in either case.

Capital gains tax on the sale of shares is charged at a 10% rate for all individual Japanese investors, regardless of the percentage of shares held. A non-resident individual would pay 15% capital gains tax for a shareholding of more than 5%, but would be exempt from the tax if the shareholding were less than 5%.

Japanese corporate investors are charged full corporate tax rates for dividends from REITs and capital gains, and a 7% withholding tax on dividends. Non-resident corporate investors are just subject to the 7% withholding tax and no capital gains tax if the shareholding is less than 5%. If the shareholding is more than that, a 30% rate is charged on capital gain from the sale of shares.

In a country with almost zero interest rates in the early 2000s, designed to reflate the economy, Japanese REITs were unrestricted in the amount they could borrow as long as they did so from qualified institutions. That allowed them to compete in the property market with Japanese and foreign private equity funds, which typically borrowed up to 70% or even 80% of the value of the assets they were buying.

General rules governing Japanese REITs include the following: At least 75% of a trust's assets must be invested in property and at least 50% of a REIT's total assets must be invested in income generating assets, while non-property assets must be limited to cash and cash equivalents.

Trusts have sometimes needed to be creative in order to stay within these rules. For example, a Japanese trust can choose to buy an old building with tenants (therefore income generating), then sell it to a construction company, which refurbishes it or even tears it down and builds a better building before selling it back to the REIT with new tenants.

Singapore

REITs in Singapore were not created by any single act. They owe their existence partly to a set of guidelines on property funds issued by the Monetary Authority of Singapore (MAS) in 1999, which now broadly govern the scope of a property trust's activities. The guidelines are non-statutory, so failure to comply will not result in criminal proceedings.

Those MAS guidelines, however, did not address the issue of tax privileges. Singapore's first REIT, CapitaMall Trust, negotiated a "tax ruling" in 2002 which provided for tax transparency—no tax was charged at the REIT level, but investors were taxed at their own rate of income tax. (About 60% of Singapore's workers do not qualify to pay personal income tax.)

This tax ruling has been extended to other REITs that list on the Singapore stock exchange. And Singapore's government went further in its 2004 budget, by bringing in full tax exemption for individual investors, irrespective of their nationality, and cutting withholding tax on foreign non-individual investors to 10% from 20% for a period of five years to February 2010. Singapore does not charge capital gains tax on the disposal of units.

In an effort to boost the activity of REITs in the property market, Singapore also waived stamp duty on acquisitions of buildings, also effective for five years from 2005. And as previously mentioned, the 35% cap on gearing was raised to 60%, provided that the borrowing received a rating from a ratings agency such as Standard and Poor's, Fitch or Moody's.

There is no prescribed application form for a REIT to attain the tax ruling, but it would need to outline its investment focus and state that it had a policy of paying at least 90% of its distributable income to investors as dividends. Because it would need to list on the stock exchange to attain the tax privileges, a trust also must have a minimum asset size of S$20 million and at least 25% of its units must be held by at least 500 public shareholders.

Singapore REITs are allowed to invest in property abroad, and because of the small size of Singapore and its property market, many trusts are expected to venture into neighboring countries in Southeast Asia as well as further afield, in particular China and India.

The MAS guidelines on property funds prevented REITs from participating in property development, either on their own or in a joint venture, but many analysts expected the rules to be changed to allow trusts to be allowed to have 10% of their asset value invested in development.

Hong Kong

Unlike in Singapore and Japan, Hong Kong does not provide any outstanding incentives to either investors in REITs or to companies that want to set up REITs. Hong Kong does not levy tax on dividends or capital gains on stock investments, and authorities felt it would be too much of a concession to waive taxes on REIT companies completely.

In fact, although Hong Kong's tax regime in general is simpler than in most countries, the situation for REITs has become slightly complicated by the trusts themselves.

Trusts are not subject to a profit tax but pay a property tax if they hold their buildings directly. This is actually less of an advantage, because deductions, which reduce the amount of income that is subject to tax, are limited to 20% of the income.

So trusts are much more likely to use "special purpose vehicles" (SPVs)—subsidiary companies set up especially to own the buildings—to cut the tax bill. The SPVs pay profit tax, but there is no limit on the deductions they can claim to reduce the tax burden. For example, an SPV can mark costs, such as external interest payments against its income, and avoid paying tax on that portion of income. The dividends that the SPVs pay to the REIT are exempt from tax.

This SPV structure can be used by any Hong Kong property company, so REITs do not hold any special advantage.

While Hong Kong's government decided against cutting tax for property trusts, the REIT code, introduced by the Securities and Futures Commission in July 2003 and amended in mid-2005, concentrated on setting the remit for trusts' activities and ensuring they paid a high dividend.

In line with other jurisdictions in Asia, Hong Kong trusts must distribute at least 90% of their audited annual net income after tax to investors in the form of a regular dividend. In fact, the city's first property trust, the government-backed Link REIT, took a unilateral decision to adopt a policy of paying a dividend of 100% of its income.

The code stipulates that REITs must be domiciled in Hong Kong, and listed on the Stock Exchange of Hong Kong. A trust should have a transparent investment policy and can only invest in real estate for long-term purposes—a building must be held for at least two years.

A majority of a REIT's income must be derived from rent. (Other sources of income could include selling advertising space, for example.) But the property can be freehold or leasehold, and can include assets such as car parks, recreation parks, hotels and serviced apartments, as long as they are income generating. Hong Kong REITs cannot buy vacant land or engage in property development activities, although they can carry out refurbishments, retrofitting and renovations of buildings.

Trusts are allowed to acquire uncompleted units in a building that is unoccupied and not producing income, or in the course of substantial development or redevelopment, but the aggregate contract value of such property must not exceed 10% of the total net asset value of the REIT.

A geographical restriction limiting REITs to only Hong Kong property was lifted as part of the changes to the code in 2005, mostly because of the massive potential for packaging mainland Chinese property into trusts.

A maximum borrowing limit was originally set at 35% of assets, but regulators increased the limit to 45% in 2005, a change that was vital for the launch of a REIT market. This made it easier for trusts to buy property that would deliver the yields of more than 5%, as expected by investors, from a property market where rental yields for offices had dropped as low as 3%.

Summary

	Japan	Singapore	Hong Kong
Tax on REITs	Distributions are deductible so corporate tax almost zero	Exempt from corporate tax	REITs subject to property tax if buildings held directly; if buildings held by SPV, SPV pays profits tax but dividends paid to REIT are tax-free
Tax on dividends, paid by investors	Withholding tax of 10% for domestic individual investors, 7% for non-resident individuals. Normal corporate tax rates on Japanese corporate investors plus 7% withholding tax; 7% withholding tax on overseas corporates with less than 5% stake	All individual investors exempt. Foreign non-individual investors' withholding tax rate cut to 10%, from 20% until 2010	None
Capital gains tax on investors	10% for Japanese individual and normal corporate tax rate for corporate investors. None for non-resident investors	None	None
Debt restrictions on REITs (as proportion of assets)	None	60%, with a debt rating	45%
Profit distribution obligations	At least 90% of distributable income	At least 90% of distributable income	At least 90% of distributable income

Hong Kong's stock market regulators generally require high standards of corporate governance, and REITs, as a new asset class, were especially closely watched. For example, any transaction involving a trust and any connected party, such as the management company, the property valuer, the trustee or a shareholder with more than a 10% stake, must be subject to a vote by unit holders. Unit holders who have a material interest in the transaction tabled for approval, and whose interest is different from that of all the unit holders, must abstain from voting.

The code also requires the management company and the trustee to be independent of each other and to not have common directors. Neither can be a subsidiary of the other.

REITs are not allowed to redeem units from time to time. There are no restrictions on the number of units a trust can issue or the number of unit holders, but the REIT code does try to protect the interests of existing unit holders when a REIT wants to raise capital by issuing new shares. Shareholder approval is needed if new units are not offered on a pro-rata basis to existing shareholders and the market capitalization will increase by 20%. Such approval is also needed if the units are distributed on a pro-rata basis but the market capitalization rises by 50% or more.

REIT players—The regulator

To give some insight into the thinking behind REIT regulations in Asia, Alexa Lam, Member and Executive Director of Hong Kong's Securities and Futures Commission (SFC), discusses here the Commission's role in drawing up Hong Kong's REIT code and the beginnings of the city's property trust market.

Lam explains that the introduction of REITs was a natural progression for one of Asia's major financial centers, already with one of the widest choices of investment products on offer, especially because the securities were starting to gain popularity around the world.

"There were lots of representations made to us, from market players, industry people, prospective issuers and economists," Lam said in an interview in the SFC's offices in Central, Hong Kong's main business district.

She said the main argument put to the SFC was that Hong Kong, where property investment was arguably more popular among average citizens than anywhere else on earth, needed a "middle ground" between direct investment in apartments and investment in property company stocks.

"Direct investment comes with its own hassles because you have to manage the property, you have to let it out, to maintain it and everything else," Lam said. "So it comes at a cost, and that cost is not just dollars and cents, you need a certain type of management. Alternatively, you can invest in shares…We are probably unique in that we have so many listed companies that are property developers or property investment companies. Shares would be a proxy to direct investment in property. But they're a very poor proxy. The companies may change their core business overnight, and companies may not distribute dividends. They may want to build up a war chest. But clearly, you as a minority shareholder, there's not a lot you can do."

"Between the two, REITs actually provide the middle ground," she said. "It's more akin to a direct investment, in a sense that you have a bit of control, that that the investment is safe, it won't turn into a dot-com company. And a certain percentage of the income will be distributed to you as profits. Yet you don't have to physically go in and manage the property, some professionals will do it for you. The Hong Kong property market has always been an interesting market, but for the market to develop that depth and maturity we needed that mezzanine product."

Lam was confident that Hong Kong would blossom as a REIT market because of the massive investor interest in Hong Kong and mainland Chinese property. "Once we had the platform, the players would come in, the supply would come in to meet demand. And quite naturally, we are the hub, particularly since we are the natural center for capital formation for Chinese companies and Chinese assets. The scope for growth is massive."

Although Hong Kong does not grant special tax incentives, it can still compete strongly for REIT listings with other new markets, Lam said.

"There's no need for any special tax advantage because the Hong Kong tax structure is very simple and very low, just 16%," she said. "Dividends in the hands of recipients are not taxed, and we don't have capital gains tax."

"Singapore has been very aggressive," she said. "But the most important factor about Hong Kong is the market, the depth of the market, the liquidity of the market. The ability to place supply and demand together, on a huge scale, which other markets in Asia, ex-Japan, can't do. Everyone can race to the bottom in terms of tax. But for someone to provide this market, it's not doable overnight."

"We also have a critical mass of professionals here who follow the market," Lam said. "After an IPO you need analysts who follow the stock, and we have that depth."

When drawing up its REIT code, Hong Kong's SFC firstly took the view that it was dealing with a fund-type vehicle and borrowed from its framework for investment funds—notably, separating the management of a trust from the custodial role carried out by a trustee. But the SFC also wanted all REITs to be listed on the stock exchange, so another layer of rules regarding corporate governance was added.

"We saw that one of the problems Australia had in the 1970s, was that REITs did not have sufficient liquidity," Lam said. "So when there was an exodus out, the REITs were in real difficulty because the underlying assets were not liquid and were not fungible."

To make sure REITs had liquidity, the SFC decided they should be listed on the Hong Kong exchange.

"With the REITs we felt it was very important, given that the underlying assets were not liquid, that the superstructure, i.e. the units themselves, be listed and have their own liquidity," Lam said.

"Now as soon as we came to that it was very obvious we should try to imbibe as much of our listing rules for companies as was applicable," she said. "We have imbibed principles like connected-party transactions, like major shareholders' conflicts of interests. Basically, we would like a REIT to behave in a corporate governance model that is every bit as good as a listed company."

"The inherent conflicts could be there, but you need to build a structure to manage those conflicts and to reduce them," she said. "In the listing rules, you see the way to do it is to make sure you have the concept of a major shareholder, you have the concept that on certain types of transaction you need an independent shareholders' vote. So that has been replicated in this code."

Some analysts have suggested that the initial mania surrounding REITs at the end of 2005 was due to a misunderstanding of the product among Hong Kong's individual investors—that they saw the first REITs as any other stock, with the potential of big capital gains, rather than an investment that gave stable income with only modest growth. Lam said one of the SFC's main roles was to promote transparency and plain disclosure of information so that investors were well informed.

"Hong Kong retail investors are pretty savvy," she said. "I don't know if I could pass a judgment on whether they understand the product. We have always told them that this is a product which you should examine both from a point of view of a stable yield and also from the point of view of the quality of assets, and therefore potential for growth.

"It's very important to look at the assets, the quality of the management," Lam said. "For the assets, look at what type of asset it is, in which sector, the quality of those assets, and the existing arrangements for those assets, i.e. the existing tenancies. It's very important that you have good quality tenants, and a good tenant mix, both in terms of their nature and also in the terms of the tenancies, because you don't want everyone's lease to expire on the same day."

Lam said that for the initial public offering of Hong Kong's Champion REIT in May 2006, the SFC ensured that the trust's promoters clearly described the financial engineering features.

Champion REIT, and Prosperity REIT before it, employed an interest rate swap arrangement that increased interest costs over time, so future rent rises would not translate fully into increased dividend payments. And Champion's major shareholder, Great Eagle Holdings Ltd., initially waived its dividend payments, but its share of those payments would gradually increase, diluting future dividend payments for other shareholders (for more on financial engineering, see Chapter 4).

"We've been told that maybe retail investors may not understand the features if they are written in legalese, and often they are," Lam said. "The features are very complex, so the explanation itself is very complex.

"For the Champion REIT, what we did was rather than just explain the features, which could leave a lot of investors behind, we wanted them to explain the effects, which are quite simple. Immediately, the newspapers caught on and they warned investors. It tells you that prominent disclosure in clear layman's language is useful. Once you understand the features and you understand the effects they could have, you can make your own judgment."

Lam said the SFC would probably need to modify its regulations governing REITs in the future as the market matures. One set of changes were already introduced in 2005—to lift a ban on non-Hong Kong properties and to raise the borrowing limit for trusts. Both steps encouraged the creation of more REITs.

"Depending on the development, we may need to tweak the platform to ensure that it remains efficient and can accommodate various needs: the need for investor protection, the need for enough room for the market to grow, the need for confidence in the market, the need for certain flexibility," she said.

"These needs could conflict with each other and we have to ensure that there is a healthy balance."

Cross-border REITs

Both Hong Kong and Singapore see themselves as future regional centers for property trusts, and authorities in the two financial centers spend much time touting their stock markets to potential REIT issuers.

Hong Kong changed its REIT code in mid-2005 to allow property outside the territory to be owned by Hong Kong-listed trusts, a move designed to open the door to mainland Chinese property trusts. At the end of the year, the GZI REIT of shopping centers in the southern Chinese city of Guangzhou launched its IPO.

Japan was expected to allow its REITs to buy overseas assets from 2007, and given the low interest rate environment in Japan at the time, higher-yielding assets from the United States, Europe, Australia and the rest of Asia were likely to be popular.

Singapore on the other hand, is likely to become a hub for Southeast Asian REITs, possibly a natural center for trusts with Indonesian, Malaysian, Thai and even Indian properties.

The first property trust of Hong Kong buildings, Fortune REIT, actually chose to list in Singapore in 2003, rather than wait for Hong Kong's REIT code to be finalized. Singapore government-backed Mapletree REIT began life with Singapore property, but quickly added logistics buildings in Malaysia and China. Then 2006 saw the listing of four cross-border REITs in Singapore, by domestic firms Ascott Group and CapitaLand, as well as by Indonesia's Lippo Group and Australia's Allco Finance.

Singapore is probably more likely to offer a greater range of cross-border REITs than Hong Kong or Japan in the foreseeable future. The domestic property market is relatively small, so existing trusts will look abroad for expansion. Singapore property firms have also shown themselves to be keen on launching REITs and have tended to be more adventurous than their Asian peers, with the likes of CapitaLand and Keppel Land undertaking projects in China, Vietnam, Thailand, Indonesia and India.

REIT players—The lawyer

Joan Janssen, a partner at Clifford Chance in Singapore, worked on the Allco REIT—a cross-border REIT which acquired at IPO a 15% stake in an Australian property fund, a 50% stake in a Perth office tower and a Singapore retail and office complex.

Janssen, a Singaporean, also worked on the launch of CapitaMall Trust and Fortune REIT. Clifford Chance's Singapore office tends to work with the underwriters on REIT offerings, primarily because of its relationships with the investment banks.

The role of lawyers such as Janssen is to assist the underwriters in directing and overseeing the various aspects of due diligence (legal, financial, valuation, market reports, etc.) and in the preparation of the prospectus and drafting and negotiating the underwriting agreements.

"We tend to come on board at the start of the preparation for the IPO," Janssen said. "Counsel for the REIT managers however would typically come on board sooner. They would help with licenses and regulatory issues and also on the acquisition work, particularly if the REIT is buying property from third-party vendors."

Once acquisition agreements are done, then work starts on the IPO.

"We work with local counsel," she said. "On REITs, a very small number of Singapore firms dominate the market. Our role is to assist the underwriters to execute the deal with international sales in mind."

Where international sales are contemplated, the securities regulations of overseas jurisdictions become relevant and need to be complied with. Where the REIT invests in property outside Singapore, there are also issues of foreign law in the relevant jurisdiction.

Cross-border REITs are much more complicated to structure than pure Singapore trusts, Janssen said.

"The tax analysis and structuring on cross border REITs is complex," she said. "This was true of Allco REIT and also for Fortune REIT. This is self-evident since instead of just having one tax jurisdiction to think about, you need also to consider a second or many jurisdictions.

"Domestic REITs often hold Singapore property directly, in the name of the REIT trustee, which is very tax efficient since the REIT is tax transparent," Janssen said. "Once property is overseas, the REIT will often need to hold the property through a local vehicle, whether a special purpose company or another trust. There may be local tax imposed on this vehicle. You need to structure to avoid tax leakage, or suffer tax twice on the same revenue."

To encourage cross-border REITs to list in Singapore, the government introduced a tax exemption for foreign-sourced interest and foreign trust distributions, which to some extent mitigates the tax leakage.

A cross-border REIT is also more likely to borrow in a different currency than where it is listed, and will therefore shop around for the best interest rates, while taking into account possible currency fluctuations. Such a trust will need to carefully manage its foreign exchange exposure, employing hedging techniques to ensure that dividend payments do not fluctuate wildly.

"It will have net income coming to it in the foreign currency, and it will also have expenses such as management fees and possibly interest expenses in that currency, but will make distributions, in Singapore dollars," Janssen explained.

As a foreign owner of property overseas, the REIT may also be subject to restrictions on foreign ownership of property. Sometimes foreign ownership is permitted only if consents from overseas authorities are obtained. Such approval may take time and may have an impact on a REIT's IPO schedule.

Only a few local law firms in Singapore have REIT experience, Janssen said, but they have become popular because of their lower costs. However, cross-border REITs prefer international counsel with experience of different jurisdictions and global offerings.

"I think Singapore will be a hub for Asian REITs," she said. "As the market gets used to investing in overseas assets, and becomes more mature, the pricing should get better. Chinese assets are one potential source of growth for REITs and many people have their eye on India."

REIT players—The trustee

The broad role of the trustee is to ensure that a REIT is structured, and its management team carries out its activities, in accordance with the REIT code or legislation of the jurisdiction where the trust is listed.

C.G. Lim, vice president for REITs at the institutional fund services unit of HSBC Securities Services, speaks here about the role of a trustee and how she works with REIT managers. HSBC is the trustee for Hong Kong's first four REITs: The Link, Prosperity, GZI and Champion.

Lim said her role starts at the very early stages of the formation of a REIT, long before a trust launches its initial public offering.

"From a trustee perspective, our involvement starts before the IPO, looking at the documents and guarantees by the sponsors. It's a really intense time," she said. "The most important thing is compliance with the REIT code and we work closely with the managers to ensure that. Our core role is to safeguard the assets of the trust. Things like making sure the rental income is paid into the bank."

Lim described the trustee's role as a protector of investor interests, but she is careful to point out that this does not extend to taking any kind of view at all on whether the investment decisions of a REIT are good. A trustee just ensures that they are in accordance with regulations.

"From our perspective, we don't want to interfere with operations, it's at a higher level than that—safeguarding the assets and making sure investment decisions comply with the REIT code and what is promised to investors," she said. "If a manager says we'll only invest in office buildings but then wants to change, we would say it might be best to consult unit holders."

Lim said she had regular meetings with each REIT manager, and especially often if new issues arose. She keeps an eye on matters such as a trust's debt levels, to see if they are reaching the limit of 45% of total assets set by Hong Kong's regulators.

"In terms of borrowing, the REIT code says it can go up to 45%," she said. "If it's up to 40%, we would monitor the ratio closely with the managers. It's very much a partnership with the managers. We don't sit on the side and wait until the code is breached."

Acquisitions are also something for trustees to look out for, especially to make sure that deals involving the REIT's sponsor, which usually owns the REIT manager, are above board.

"If a transaction is with connected persons, especially if the manager is connected with the vendor, the trustee plays an active role to make sure that it is on commercial terms and at arm's length," Lim said.

In Hong Kong, both the trustee and the REIT manager can be removed by unit holders, if they are dissatisfied by their performance, in a vote in an extraordinary general meeting. If unit holders choose to remove the REIT manager, the trustee has the final power to do so and will act on their behalf.

Endnote

1   Details on Japan's tax regime taken from "Development and Taxation of Real Estate Investment Trusts," by Ken Takahashi, Asia-Pacific Tax Bulletin 2005.

Mayfair or Old Kent Road—What makes a good REIT?

Because REITs are so new to Asia, market regulators have been particularly cautious about them, keeping a close watch on the quality of trust managers and their buildings as well as maintaining a tight rein on the scope of activities that these trusts can carry out. But as investors in the region become more accustomed to the securities, and countries encourage the creation of more REITs, many of the rules are likely to be gradually loosened.

For example, Singapore and Hong Kong both raised the limits on borrowing to make it easier for REITs to be created and for them to make more acquisitions, and regulators lifted a ban on non-Hong Kong properties to be packaged into trusts listed on the city's stock market in order to promote a market in mainland Chinese REITs. Japanese regulators were expected to follow suit in 2007 because trusts there were keen on higher-yielding foreign properties.

The trend toward more flexibility should result in a wider choice of REITs for investors. Whereas Asia's first REITs needed to be sponsored by well-known companies to engender investor confidence, smaller and less prominent companies began launching trusts once investors were comfortable with the investment product.

While the first REITs needed to be well capitalized and had to attract equity investors with favorable yields, later they started to become less reliant on raising equity because they were allowed to borrow more money. By being able to borrow more at low interest rates, REIT managers can also use "gearing" to boost a REIT's yield. As a result, they would be under less pressure to seek out acquisitions of relatively higher-yielding buildings. Although this is a legitimate tactic, it also has the potential to land a REIT in trouble if interest rates rise sharply and a trust cannot find enough free cash flow to cover debt repayments.

So with more REITs operating in a more relaxed regulatory environment, investors will need to become more discriminating than in the early years of REIT market development in Asia. Here are the main issues an investor needs to explore when assessing a REIT:

- the property sector on offer
- the quality of the buildings and its tenants
- the location of the buildings
- the management team and its strategy
- fees paid by the REIT
- whether buying into the REIT is good value for money

None of these issues should be looked at in isolation when picking a REIT; an investor generally needs to balance up all the information from different REITs before coming to a decision. For example, it might be better to pick low-quality buildings in good locations and a strong management team than a top-notch building that offers a very low yield.

Which property sector?

"If it generates income, securitize it." This has become the rallying call of investment bankers around the globe.

In the property world, the people who structure REITs say they can work their magic on anything that can be rented out to a tenant—nursing homes, hospitals, casinos, car parks, telephone exchanges and even igloos. But the most common types of buildings that will be packaged into trusts in Asia are shopping malls, office blocks, warehouses and industrial buildings, simply because these are the most common commercial buildings and their steady rents make them good material for REITs.

Each of these three major sectors has slightly different characteristics.

Shopping Malls

Shopping malls are in many ways the best type of building to package into a REIT, and for the average person in the street, they are the easiest to assess. Just walk into a shopping center being offered by a property trust and you can get a quick impression of whether it is a good asset or not. Are people crowding in on a Saturday afternoon, or are the shop assistants staring into space or talking to a friend on the phone? Are people delving into their pockets for a credit card or just window shopping? Is the building bright and airy and easy to walk in or full of dark passageways? Are most shops occupied or are their workers dismantling display cabinets? Are the toilets clean? Are fashion outlets grouped together and easily found? Or is a luxury handbag store squeezed between a toy shop and a butcher's? Can you find tasty food?

Investors should look at the general direction of the economy, and the latest retail sales figures, but a brisk walk through a shopping mall will probably tell you much more. It is far harder to check out a logistics building in a warren of warehouses and containers in one of the world's busiest ports or to snoop around the corridors of a gleaming high-rise office in Tokyo's main business districts. It tends to be easier to sell a shopping center REIT to the general public and explain its business plans.

For a creative manager, shopping malls are also the best materials with which to mold a successful REIT—one which produces rent increases and therefore more income for investors. Managers talk of "repositioning" their shopping centers, which usually means bringing in changes to make a building more modern so they can raise rents. This can be done in many ways, but often involves a mix of refurbishment, moving tenants around to maximize the floor area actively used for retailing, pushing low-rent tenants out and inviting in higher-paying tenants while including more high-end restaurants. Offices, and certainly warehouses, offer much less scope for improvements that could lift income.

Some landlords also say shopping center rents are much more resistant to economic downturns than office rents. When the economy turns sour, all companies will look to cut costs, mostly from areas which are not vital to their main businesses. One of the first areas usually targeted are office occupancy costs. Firms will firstly try to renegotiate rents, and then downsize, maybe taking three floors of a building instead of four, and squeezing their workers more tightly together. As a last resort, they might even move to another, cheaper, building altogether. This process can quickly translate into a fall in rent at any particular building.

Shopping malls are slightly different. Although tenants will also try to cut their occupancy costs, they have relatively lower bargaining power than office tenants because their main business—retailing—depends on being in the shopping center. Moving premises would disrupt business. Customers might not follow, and a lower-grade shopping center might not offer clientele with the same level of spending power.

The graphs below, illustrating Hong Kong office and retail rents in the early 2000s, show how the two sectors fared differently during the sharp shock to the whole economy during an outbreak of the SARS respiratory disease in 2003.

Office rents were on a downward trend from a peak in the mid-1990s as the market was inundated with new office blocks even as the economy grew bleaker, especially after the 1997-98 Asian economic crisis. This is a common phenomenon in all property markets. Because buildings typically take three or four years to conceive and construct, the supply of property lags the economic demand. The already volatile Hong Kong office market was hit hard during the Asian economic crisis, and then the bursting of the dot-com bubble in 2000, and again during the SARS outbreak in 2003, with vacancies peaking in those periods and rents dipping.

Meanwhile, retail sales closely tracked the path of the economy, slumping in 2003 when the streets of Hong Kong emptied because of fear of SARS. But retail rents hardly budged, and then began climbing steeply as the city's property market recovered and the threat of SARS receded.

Supply, Take-up and Vacancy of Prime Hong Kong Office Properties

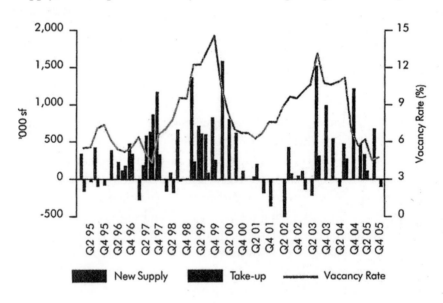

Source: CB Richard Ellis

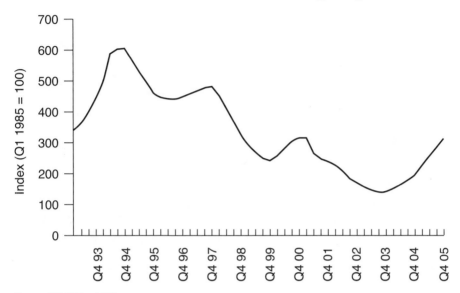

Prime Office Rental Index for Hong Kong

Source: CB Richard Ellis

Monthly Retail Sales in Hong Kong

Total Retail Sales   Year-on-year Change

Source: CB Richard Ellis

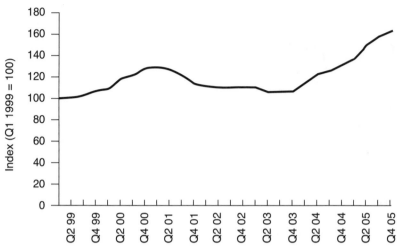

Source: *CB Richard Ellis*

Office Blocks

Although office blocks offer fewer opportunities for improvements than shopping malls, they can still be upgraded to conjure up big jumps in value. In Japan, for example, many investors have bought up second- and third-grade buildings cheaply and carried out renovations, such as smartening up lobby areas, installing new elevators, and knocking down walls to increase space. The changes can elevate a building's status in the market, and if they are in top locations, can result in as much as 15-20% increases in rent.

Buying into an office REIT can also be the best way of tapping directly into the economic fortunes of a country. Because leases tend to be fairly short, typically two or three years, landlords are in a position to try to raise rents often and aggressively if they want. As mentioned above, supply of new offices often lags an economic upturn, so in the early stages of an economic cycle there is often a shortage of space when a landlord has higher bargaining power than a tenant.

Industrial Buildings

Industrial buildings, including warehouses and factories, offer slower rent rises than shopping malls and offices, but more safety in times of economic uncertainty. Leases last longer, often for 10 years or more, and can include limits on rent changes allowed at periodic rental reviews. Such contracts limit the potential for income growth from an industrial REIT but provide stability in an economic downturn.

To compensate for a lack of income growth, industrial REITs will usually offer investors a higher yield than other types of REITs. They will also find it much easier to expand and lift investor returns through acquisitions. Whereas landlords are often reluctant to sell an office block or shopping center, which they may have spent years conceiving and building and can be status symbols, few have the same sentimental attachment to a warehouse or a factory.

Many manufacturers or logistics companies who built their own property are very willing to enter a "sale-leaseback" agreement, freeing up a chunk of capital while agreeing to rent a building for a certain number of years after selling to a REIT.

Singapore Snapshot

To illustrate the yields demanded by investors for different types of REITs, below is a snapshot at the end of 2005 of the property market conditions and the yields offered by three trusts listed in Singapore: Ascendas REIT, CapitaMall Trust and CapitaCommercial Trust.

Distribution Per Unit Growth Forecasts 2005-2007 (%)

	2005 forecast	2006 forecast	2007 forecast
Ascendas REIT	21.8	7.0	1.8
CapitaCommercial Trust	8.4	0.6	5.5
CapitaMall Trust	15.6	1.5	4.8

Source: Macquarie Research

At the time, Ascendas had just over 40 warehouses, business park buildings, high-tech factories and light-industrial plants, while CapitaMall owned five shopping malls and CapitaCommercial had eight office blocks.

A strengthening export economy in 2005 led to a general pick-up of Singapore's property market, which had been in the doldrums since the Asian economic crisis. Analysts predicted that it was the beginning of the "recovery" period of the typical four-part property cycle, which would subsequently involve a span of "growth" followed by "deterioration" and "decline."

Property cycles track general economic cycles but with a lag, and although each country at any point in time can experience anomalies, a cycle typically lasts six to eight years. In an economy with sustained growth, and in property markets where supply of new buildings struggles to keep up with demand for several years, the "deterioration" and "decline" periods of the cycle can actually end up as just a slowdown in growth rather than a drop in property prices and rent.

However, that was not the case in Singapore. The island-state's trade driven economy was hit hard by the Asian economic crisis, which dragged down demand for goods across the region, and then again by the bursting of the dot-com bubble, which depressed technology industries across Asia, including in Singapore. It was only in 2004 and 2005 that the economy and its property sector began to show signs of a strong recovery.

Singapore property sub-sectors—how they are placed

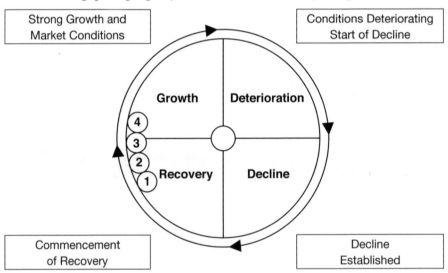

Key:
1. Singapore Industrial
2. Singapore Residential
3. Singapore Office
4. Singapore Retail

Source: Macquarie Research, June 2005.

Average rents for warehouses dropped from about S$19 per square meter at the end of 1998 to just above S$13 at the end of 2003, but then stayed flat for the next year and a half before rising slightly, giving hope that a recovery was underway. Average factory rents fell from S$16 per square meter to S$11.5 between 1998 and 2003, but then rose to more than S$12 in 2005.

Prime office rents dropped from about S$45 per square meter in a peak in 1996 to S$36 in 2004, when they started to increase slightly. Occupancy over the period fell from about 88% to 82%. Retail rents fell at a slower pace, however they still dropped 25% from 1996 to 2000, but in the next four years they stayed put, with occupancy rates steady at 92%, before rents perked up in 2005.

In 2005, all the signs pointed to a brighter future for Singapore's property market and the REITs operating in it. Analysts predicted the trusts would notch up strong growth in rental income, and therefore dividends, for the 2005 financial year followed by more modest rises in subsequent years. Although rents were rising, the steep initial rise in income was largely a result of yield-accretive acquisitions made by the REITs, which were predicted to taper off because of a lack of available buildings left in the small Singapore property market.

The forecasts for future dividend growth were reflected in the yields that investors demanded from the REITs—the higher the expected growth, the lower the yield that will satisfy an investor. The correlation was not perfect, with Ascendas REIT offering a relatively high yield and predicted to give the highest dividend growth in 2005, but the longer-term dividend growth expectations were lower than for CapitaMall and CapitaCommercial.

Singapore REITs – Yield and Performance – end 2005

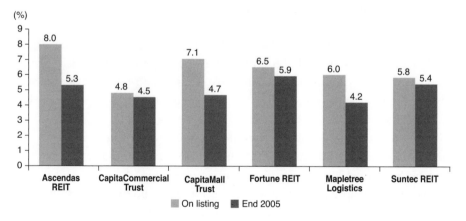

Demand for Hotels

Hoteliers are also lining up to sell buildings into property trusts to raise money for expansion. Many need funds to take part in the 10% annual growth experienced by Asia's hotel industry, worth $115 billion in revenue a year in 2006. The Beijing Olympics in 2008 spurred new construction in China, where a burgeoning middle class is eager to travel more within the country, as well as abroad.

Because of the nature of the industry, hotel firms are much less likely to trade buildings than other types of landlord and they also want to maintain control of their brand. These objectives are fulfilled through a REIT, as hotel firms can retain a controlling stake and play the role of manager.

A prime example of this thinking was Regal Hotels International, which was planning to launch a $760 million IPO of Hong Kong's first hotel REIT in early 2007.

The company believed that the stock market was hugely undervaluing its shares, partly because of the risks of the tourism industry, but that a REIT would trade at much nearer the worth of the buildings. Regal said its five Hong Kong hotels, based on replacement cost, were worth about HK$16 billion or HK$1.70 for each of the hotel group's shares. But the stock was trading at only around HK$0.80 at the end of October, just as the new REIT was being readied for an IPO.

Spinning off the hotels into a REIT would raise relatively more money than selling more shares to the public in Regal Hotels International. The company planned to use the proceeds to build more hotels in Chinese cities, such as Shanghai, Guangzhou and Shenyang in the northeast, which would later be injected into the REIT.

"By launching a REIT, Regal will end up with a fairly good amount of cash for expansion in Greater China," Regal International's executive director, Poman Lo, said.[1]

"We want Regal Hotels and the REIT to grow together," she said.

For investors, hotel REITS represent a good opportunity to tap directly into the region's thriving tourism industry. Daily room rates in 2005 jumped about 26% in Hong Kong, nearly 30% in Beijing, 16% in Singapore, and 12% in Bangkok.

However, the inherent uncertainties in the tourism industry mean that hotels can make an uncomfortable fit for REITs, which should be giving steady returns. So a hotel REIT must be structured carefully.

As room occupancy fluctuates seasonally and can be hit by anything from air traffic control strikes to disease outbreaks, hospitality REITs are set up through a sale-leaseback agreement where the hotel operator pays a stable rent to the trust.

But a fixed rent structure alone would prevent investors from feeling the real benefit of a tourist industry boom, so some hotel REITs introduced a variable element to provide the potential for income growth.

For example, Singapore's CDL Hospitality Trusts, set up by property firm City Developments, receives 20% of revenues and 20% of gross operating profit from its five hotels run by Millennium & Copthorne Hotels, with a base guarantee of S$26.4 million in rent per year.

CDL Hospitality was trading at a 5% yield at the end of 2006, around the middle of the range for Singapore REITs, suggesting that investors did not feel that the REIT was any more risky than other asset classes.

However, Japanese hotel REITs showed that the business was not all plain sailing. Japan Hotel and Resort REIT Inc., set up by Goldman Sachs and Oxford Advisory and Investment Group, receives about 40% of its income as a variable component, which relies heavily on its wedding business. But revenue from weddings, around 20% of total income, came under serious threat from competition from restaurants and stand-alone chapels, which were pushing immensely popular "house" theme weddings.

"We have to do creative things, like build an extra chapel in the lobbies of our hotels, or do western style weddings," said Rob Kline, president of Oxford Advisory. "We even do house theme weddings ourselves, with a fireplace and fake windows in our banquet halls."

Kline predicted in 2006 that about 12 to 15 new hotel REITs would be created in Japan over the following two or three years, partly because foreign funds were keen to cash in on their investments and because big hotel operators such as ANA and Tokyu had realized the advantages of holding their hotels in trusts. But he warned investors earnings would be more volatile than they would expect from other REITs.

Hotel REITs can also be much riskier than shopping malls or offices because they tend to rely on a single tenant. A sudden slump in tourism could endanger the rent paid to the trust, so the financial strength of the hotel operator, rather than the REIT itself, is the main issue for investors.

"Hotels are cyclical and volatile, so it could be a shock," Kline said.

Building quality

If you purchase a house to inhabit yourself, you will want the best your money can buy. You would look at how many bedrooms it has and how big they are, the state of the roof, signs of mold, the layout and spaciousness, the decoration and paintwork, and you would ask a surveyor to check the foundations. But if the house were purchased as an investment, and someone else would live in it, the quality of the building may not be the most pressing issue—if you were sure someone would rent it from you.

Eric Wong, an analyst at UBS bank in Hong Kong, uses the same analogy when looking at REITs. He compares a multi-million dollar luxury house in the Peak area, looking from a mountain over Hong Kong's famous skyscraper offices, with a shabby apartment block across the harbor in Mongkok, where massage parlors and stalls selling fake handbags cram into the world's most densely populated area.

"You could have a house on the Peak and a wealthy family comes in, but then for three months you can't rent it out," Wong said. "Or you can have a bunch of cages in Mongkok and rent them out bed by bed. Quality-wise, they're heaven and earth. But income-wise, the building in Mongkok is potentially as stable or even more so."

For office and retail REITs, analysts will come to a conclusion on building quality by looking at the grade of construction materials, how much outstanding maintenance work needs to be done, how well maintained the common areas are, and generally how well a building retains its tenants. For industrial property, such as a warehouse or a factory, access to the premises is important, as are ceiling height, the capacity of surrounding roads to accommodate large vehicles and the durability of improvements made to the buildings.

While Asia's REIT markets are in the first stages of development, landlords will probably want to keep hold of their best, "trophy" buildings, because they are still considered status symbols and good for long-term investments, especially in cities where prime land is scarce. Therefore, many REITs will be created with second- and third-grade buildings, which, as Wong suggests, is not necessarily a bad thing.

Hong Kong's Link REIT sold itself to investors as a "turnaround story," with management promising to upgrade badly run, low-grade, formerly government-run shopping centers, in order to bring about strong rental growth. Investors bought the idea, sending the share price soaring 70% within just a couple of months. The Link's shopping malls were located in government housing estates, with a captive audience of hundreds of thousands of residents wanting to buy their daily supplies. So there was an argument that the shopping centers were largely recession-proof—customers would still need their toothpaste in an economic downturn.

But just as you would expect when buying lower quality housing, the costs can build up at low-grade commercial property. If the roof needs to be repaired every year, the building needs repainting, and walls need strengthening, planned rent increases might be swallowed up by urgent expenditure rather than be passed on to investors. If the buildings are in a very bad state, a REIT could find it difficult to retain tenants and might have to offer cut-price rents.

High-quality buildings tend to retain tenants well during an economic downturn because their tenants are usually financially stronger than tenants in lower-grade property. But there is some evidence that second-grade property can also do well, as companies look to move to cheaper buildings that are still in reasonable condition. During the 2003 outbreak of the SARS respiratory disease in Hong Kong, for example, there was a shift away from the most expensive business district, Central, to the east of the island, prompting a steep fall in rents at top-tier office blocks while rents at second-tier buildings experienced a milder drop. Some companies used the lower rents in Central to upgrade their premises, but were then forced out again three years later when rents were hiked to reflect a 70% recovery in property prices after the SARS outbreak abated.

An analyst will also look at tenants and lease agreements. The more tenants a REIT has, the more the risk of rent defaults is spread. And bigger names usually inspire more confidence. The world's biggest banking firm, Citigroup, is less likely to go out of business than a small Japanese clothing manufacturer. It is also important to watch the annual turnover of lease agreements. If all the leases are up for renewal at the same time, this increases the risk to economic downturns—tenants could threaten to move out en masse, and therefore have more collective bargaining power.

Location

Location is often characterized as the defining factor in a building's success, and can sometimes completely override any concerns about matters such as construction quality and state of repair.

A good example is the first REIT of mainland Chinese buildings, GZI REIT, listed in Hong Kong and, in particular, its White Horse building in the southern city of Guangzhou. Fitch Ratings agency, which analyzes credit risk for listed companies, described the trust's asset quality in early 2006 as "average to below average" and said the White Horse had only "average standard retail facilities."

But what the REIT lacked in building quality, it made up for in location. "The location of the assets is considered to be strong to average," Fitch said. "The largest asset by revenue, the White Horse, is at the center of the garment district and is directly opposite the Guangzhou train station. Of the remaining properties, the majority are located in the Tian He area of the central business district."

At almost any time of day, Guangzhou train station is seething with people arriving or leaving the most prosperous city in southern China, which is also a hub for the textile and garment industry. The White Horse building houses thousands of retailers, mostly wholesale garment traders.

For shopping centers, analysts will base their judgments of a REIT's location on foot traffic—how well buildings attract pedestrian shoppers—as well as access for people traveling by car or other means of transport. For an office, public transport links are the main consideration, while industrial assets are judged on their proximity to major ports, roads, and on whether they enjoy any tax and other benefits within a free trade zone.

For any REIT, investors should also look at how geographically concentrated its buildings are, because the danger of an event affecting business diminishes if a trust's buildings are spread out. Similarly, risk is also reduced if a trust's income sources are evenly spread out across its property portfolio, and as many tenants as possible.

A REIT would be hit hard if it had two retail properties in one street which had to close for six months for new underground pipes to be laid. In an extreme example, if its buildings were all in one city, they could be wiped out completely if they were at the epicenter of an earthquake. Almost all of Asia's REITs are country-specific, which puts them at the mercy of national economic fortunes, although there are signs that more trusts, particularly in Singapore, will diversify by buying buildings abroad, as Mapletree REIT was doing in 2006. Over-reliance on a few tenants also cuts a REIT's bargaining power over rent and makes it a hostage to the fortunes of those companies.

Hong Kong's Link REIT is a good example of a "low-concentration" property trust, with 151 shopping centers and 79,000 car parking spaces spread across the city. At its launch in late 2005, its top three properties contributed only 8.4% of total revenue. The top three tenants contributed 21.9% of total revenue—a relatively high amount—but they were spread over several shopping malls.

In contrast, Singapore's CapitaCommercial Trust garnered 73.8% of its income from just three of its eight buildings, and its top three tenants contributed 30.5% of total revenue.

Management

As Asia's REIT markets mature and acquisitions start to dry up because of a lack of suitable buildings for sale, the quality of a trust's management team will become one of the most decisive factors for success.

In the first years of the Japanese and Singapore REIT markets, most of the income growth delivered to investors was driven by acquisitions of yield-accretive property. Almost all trusts were active in buying buildings, and they all saw their share prices rise as a consequence. But as investors drove REIT share prices higher, and therefore yields lower, landlords started to catch on that they could sell buildings to trusts at a yield only marginally higher than the REIT market's prevailing yield.

For example, if shopping mall REITs were trading at 4.1%, sellers of retail premises on the open market might charge a price that translated into just 4.2% rental yield each year instead of the 5% they would have been satisfied with earlier. Put simply, the proliferation of REITs eager to buy property pushed prices up to such an extent that it became very difficult to buy anything that would lift the trust's yield noticeably.

By 2005 the Tokyo property market was getting particularly expensive as the Japanese economy recovered and REITs had to start competing for assets with private equity firms and other investors. In Singapore, the small size of the island put a limit on how far a strategy of domestic acquisitions could go.

REITs would have to start squeezing more income from the buildings that they already owned, or buy buildings that they could improve. Investors would become more discerning, analysts predicted, rewarding only those trusts with management teams that had a good track record, set out a clear strategy of improving buildings for income growth, and delivered on their promises.

Management case studies

Singapore's CapitaMall Trust—Growth by repositioning

Singapore's first property trust, CapitaMall Trust, is a good example of how a REIT can make good acquisitions and improvements to shopping malls to increase dividends for shareholders. By the end of 2005, the trust had a market capitalization of about S$3.1 billion (US$2 billion) and an asset size of S$3.4 billion. It owned nine shopping malls in Singapore, which had a combined 1,200 leases.

When the REIT listed in July 2002 it forecast an annual dividend payment of 6.78 Singapore cents per unit each year, but by 2005 the trust had increased the annual dividend to 11.02 Singapore cents—an increase of 62.5% in three years. This was at a time when prime retail rental rates were hardly budging in Singapore. Retail rents in 2005, for example, rose 3.1%—roughly the same as the previous two years.

The increase in dividend helped drive CapitaMall Trust's share price up 157% in the three years after its IPO. The share price gain and the dividend gain, meant that an investor who bought a share in the REIT's IPO and kept it for three years would have made a total return of 193%—nearly three times the original investment.

CapitaMall Trust attributed 49% of its dividend growth in its first three years to yield-accretive acquisitions, and 21% to asset enhancement—improvements to shopping centers that led directly to higher rents.

Its Junction 8 shopping mall managed to increase its average rent by 47.8% in a little over two years, from S$8 per square foot (S$73.60 per square meter) per month in July 2002 to S$11.80 at the end of December 2004, thanks to a raft of asset enhancement measures.

The REIT converted a car parking area at Junction 8 into food kiosks. Then it transformed nearly 50,000 square feet (4,645 square meters) of office space in a block attached to the shopping mall into retail space—a process known as "decanting"—to bring in much higher rent. The remaining upper floors of the office block, about 70,000 square feet, were handed over to the National Council of Social Service, taking advantage of an incentive introduced by the Singapore government.

Under previous rules on decanting, a developer needed to demolish a certain amount of office space if the firm wanted to add more retail space to the premises, and pay a development charge. Under the new rules, a developer could keep the decanted office standing, as long as it gave the space to not-for-profit organizations, and the development charge was substantially reduced. Some industry experts believe the new rules saved CapitaMall Trust S$1.5 million.

Many new retailers set up shop at Junction 8, including several jewelers and fashion outlets. The shopping mall also turned its third floor into an area for exhibitions and shows to try to attract more customers, including events such as a "most beautiful mom" contest and a competition called "Wacky Waggy Fashion Fun," in which dogs and their owners paraded in their respective latest fashions.

The managers of CapitaMall Trust forecast that return on investment at the shopping center jumped to 17.7% from 14.1%, and the capital value of the property climbed to S$70 million from S$55.7 million. Even after losing rental income from the offices, its gross annual revenue grew to S$7 million from S$5.5 million before the transformation work began.

At its Bugis Junction shopping mall in the heart of Singapore, CapitaMall Trust employed a different tactic—turning to its main tenant, Japanese retailer Seiyu, to help it increase rental revenue.

Seiyu had been renting 57% of the shopping mall but only contributed 30% of its rental income. Four other big tenants also paid proportionally less rent than their space. Meanwhile, restaurants and other small tenants were renting about 32% of the space but paying 62.5% of the rent.

Even before CapitaMall Trust had completed its acquisition of Bugis Junction, the REIT's management signed an agreement with Seiyu in October 2005 to pay S$25 million for the retailer to surrender nearly a third of its rented space, about 75,000 square feet. It subsequently revamped the basement floor, which had been occupied by Seiyu for about S$5 per square foot per month, to boost rental yield. Almost half the space was taken up by a food court, where stalls selling Singapore's mainstay of steamed chicken and rice and spicy Indonesian beef *rendang* started to pay between S$8 and S$10 per square foot. Another large section was rented to a supermarket for about S$8. Specialty kiosks in the area were charged between S$30 and S$40 per square foot each month.

The changes helped increase the rental yield at Bugis Junction to 5.6% in 2006 from a projected 5.3% without the conversion agreement. CapitaMall Trust expected to earn an additional S$3.16 million in net income from the shopping mall annually.

At the beginning of 2006, Bugis Junction was still performing worse than other shopping centers in Singapore, with average monthly rental rates per square foot around the S$8 mark, while Junction 8 was getting about S$12. The management planned to improve the tenant mix and marketing activities, create new retail units and kiosks in open common areas and convert ancillary areas into productive retail space.

But by reducing the area leased to Seiyu, CapitaMall was also protecting itself—softening the potential shock from any decision by the retailer to move premises or unilaterally scale down, and spreading the termination of major leases over a wider timeframe. Before the Seiyu agreement, about 77% of the net lettable area was due for rent renegotiation in 2007, but after the deal, that dropped to only 26.8% of the shopping center's space.

Hopes were high that customer traffic through the shopping center would increase thanks to its location in an area that the Singapore government was promoting as an arts and entertainment hub. The national library was to open nearby, as were a new campus for the Singapore Management University and an arts college.

CapitaMall Trust Stock Price Movement Compared to Singapore Stock Market and Property Stock Index

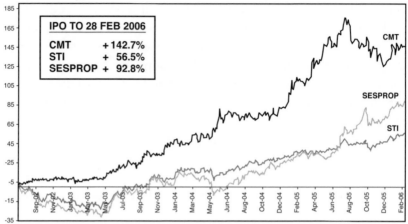

% change in unit price/index value

IPO TO 28 FEB 2006

CMT	+142.7%
STI	+ 56.5%
SESPROP	+ 92.8%

Japan's Nippon Building Fund—Growth through acquisitions

Japan's first REIT, Nippon Building Fund, had an inauspicious start, making its debut on the Tokyo stock market on September 10, 2001, a day before suicide plane attacks on the US, including on New York's World Trade Center buildings, rocked financial markets.

But in its early years, the trust grew quickly, snapping up office buildings in Tokyo and beyond that would help deliver higher dividend yields and, as a consequence, drive up its share price.

After an initial dip, the trust's units almost doubled in price in its first three years, from just under 500,000 yen in October 2001 to 900,000 yen in November 2004.

In 2004, Nippon Building Fund went on a big shopping spree, buying 18 buildings for just over 110 billion yen, mainly from its sponsor, leading property developer Mitsui Fudosan. The trust's total rented area rose to 460,901 square meters at the end of the year from 277,000 at the time of its stock market listing.

The acquisitions in that year had a big impact on the REIT's business. Net income grew 47.9% in the second half of 2004 from the first half, and distribution per unit rose 13.9%.

The jump was not only due to higher rental income, because revenues from property leasing only climbed 28.4% between the two periods. The increased size of the property portfolio also brought better economies of scale, with investors benefiting from a reduction in management fees relative to the number of buildings the trust owned. Outsourcing agreements, for work such as repairs and renovation, would also be relatively cheaper for a bigger package of buildings.

In Tokyo, buildings such as the S-ino Omiya North Wing were bought at a property yield of about 6%, whereas the L-Plaza in the provincial city of Sapporo gave an 8.5% yield.

Catching the market at just the right time, as the Japanese economy was showing signs of a sustained upturn after more than a decade of stagnation, Nippon Building fund saw its vacant space taken up quickly. In September 2004, just five months after it bought the Aqua Dojima Daiwa Dojima building in Osaka, the occupancy rate at the building had jumped to 93.1% from just 78.2%.

The result of the quick-fire acquisitions was a huge decrease in risk for the entire portfolio. For example, tenant risk was cut, with the top 10 tenants accounting for about 40% of total office space owned by Nippon Building Fund at the beginning of 2005, compared with 54% at the end of 2001. The economic activities of the tenants became more diverse, including steel, pharmaceuticals, retail, construction, transport and finance.

Unit Price Movement of Nippon Building Fund

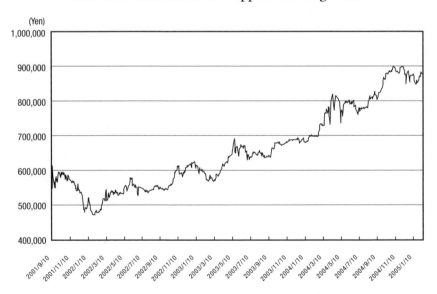

Source: Nippon Building Fund

Property risk also declined. With more buildings under the trust's umbrella, the purchase price of the three largest properties accounted for 33% of the total value of the portfolio, compared with 54% three years earlier. And the newly added buildings tended to be more contemporary, bringing down the average age of property in the portfolio to 16.8 years from 17.72 years. Nippon Building Fund was also judged to be more earthquake-resistant than before, resulting in a reduction of 70 million yen in annual insurance costs.

REIT players—The manager

Interview with Riichi Morihiro, chief operating officer of Nippon Building Fund

After its 2004 acquisition spree, Nippon Building Fund (NBF) started to find it more difficult to buy buildings on the open market because of fierce competition from other REITs, as well as from Japanese and foreign private equity funds and institutional investors.

But the trust was fortunate to have Mitsui Fudosan, the country's biggest property company, as its sponsor. The developer was keen to sell off buildings in order to raise funds to build more, and Nippon Building Fund (NBF) was the perfect conduit.

"There is no change in NBF's policy of investing in rigorously selected high-quality buildings," Nippon Building Fund's chief executive Riichi Morihiro said.

"The market for property acquisitions is overheated but to avoid getting involved in excessive competition, we intend to continue our policy of exploiting diversified investment channels such as the pipeline between NBF and Mitsui Fudosan."

In mid-2006 NBF was so popular with investors that it traded at a high share price, and therefore a low yield. At the beginning of June 2006, it traded at a dividend yield of only 3.17%—the lowest yield of any Japanese REIT. Japan Retail Fund, for example, was trading at a 3.4% yield, while some residential REITs were trading at nearly 5%.

That was a sweet spot for Mitsui Fudosan. The company could sell buildings to its REIT spin-off for a relatively high price, but the trust's investors would still be satisfied as long as the acquisition was yield-accretive.

But whereas yield-accretive acquisitions were driving growth in the REIT's first few years of development, by 2006 the Japanese economy was growing steadily, albeit at a low rate, and rent rises were starting to be the main factor to lift dividends.

"Rent levels for new contracts for space in first-class buildings located in Tokyo (central business districts) have dramatically increased during 2006," Morihiro said. "As far as NBF is concerned, for example the net operating income return with respect to the Yamato Seimei Building as of the time of its acquisition in October 2005 was 3.5%, but has since increased and is expected to be up to 3.8% in 2006."

In July 2006, the Bank of Japan raised interest rates for the first time in six years, increasing its key benchmark rate to 0.25% from zero. But Morihiro expected investors to still be drawn to REITs, despite a narrowing of the spread between borrowing rates, measured by 10-year government bond yields and REIT yields.

"If one thinks of J-REITs as simple, interest-bearing products, you might be right to think there would be a downturn in investor interest," Morihiro said. "However, moderate increases in interest rates are inextricably linked to the recovery of Japan's economy. J-REITs are the same as real properties, and we consider it important to see how the markets will evaluate increases in the prices of real properties."

Mitsui Fudosan also launched a residential REIT, the Nippon Accommodations Fund, in 2006 and was planning a trust of commercial property in 2007 that it wanted to expand three-fold to around 200 billion yen of assets within three or four years.

Morihiro said one of the key strengths of NBF was its close relationship with Mitsui Fudosan. A prime example of this was a deal sealed in 2006 in which NBF sold its JFE building to Mitsui Fudosan in return for buying five buildings from its sponsor.

JFE Steel, the sole tenant of JFE building, had decided to vacate the building it had used as its headquarters, leaving NBF facing a huge problem: a probable sizeable drop in income that would go down badly with investors and an old office block that would be difficult to fill considering the number of plush new options arriving on the Tokyo property market.

But Mitsui Fudosan came to the rescue. The company bought the JFE building for 91 billion yen ($830 million), 19.2 billion yen higher than its book value when the asset was originally transferred to NBF, and a profit that the REIT could record. Mitsui Fudosan's intention was to redevelop the building to make it attractive enough to attract new tenants.

In return, NBF agreed to buy the Toranomon Kotohira Tower, Gate City Ohsaki, Nishishinjuku Mitsui Building, Parale Mitsui Building and Shinanobashi

Mitsui Building for a combined purchase price of 110.1 billion yen. In an accountancy sleight of hand, NBF booked advanced depreciation of 18.5 billion yen on the five properties in order to limit future fluctuation in dividends. And by offsetting that depreciation against the profit from selling the JFE Building, the REIT recorded a profit from the transaction of around 700 million yen.

Nippon Building Fund Property Exchange with Mitsui Fudosan

JFE Building transfer price	91.0 billion yen
JFE Building book value	71.8 billion yen
Profit on transfer	19.2 billion yen
Purchase price of five properties	110.1 billion yen
Advanced depreciation on five properties	−18.5 billion yen
Book value after depreciation	91.6 billion yen
Transaction profit for Nippon Building Fund	19.2 billion yen profit from JFE Building −18.5 billion yen depreciation of five properties = 700 million yen

Source: Nomura Securities research

REIT players—The manager

Interview with Victor So, chief executive of Link REIT Management

As the first CEO of The Link Management Limited, manager of Hong Kong's The Link REIT, Victor So was put on the spot. He has come under much more public scrutiny than the average property trust manager.

The Link, a privatization of 151 retail facilities and about 79,000 car parking spaces formerly owned by the Hong Kong Housing Authority, first had to overcome a legal challenge from a pensioner to launch its share offering. Then, as a private entity, the REIT still came under attack from some politicians and tenants disgruntled that rents were rising.

When a hedge fund called The Children's Investment Fund (TCI) bought a stake and took a seat on the REIT's board, many analysts predicted pressure would be heaped on The Link REIT's management to fulfill its promises to overhaul its shopping centers and increase income. TCI had previously changed the management of Deutsche Borse, the German stock exchange operator, and had built up a reputation as an active and often aggressive player in shaping the companies it owned.

Here, So speaks about some of The Link Management's early successes, the relationship with TCI and expansion plans.

"From day one, and during the IPO, we said there were a number of shopping centers with upside potential, where you could carry out major asset enhancement and modernize outdated design," said So, whose office is hidden away in one of The Link's car park buildings several underground train stops from central Hong Kong.

"We identified eight projects that would give the most potential for yield accretion and brand building, and we've done quite well on the first three of those."

So and his team had worked hard to convince big brand name retailers such as coffee outlet Starbucks, perfume and accessories firm SaSa and sportswear retailer Marathon to move into shopping malls owned by The Link.

To draw these names, major renovation work needed to be carried out to spruce up the shopping centers. But the move has paid off, with income from one shopping center rising by more than HK$500,000 a month—about 75% more rent for the area that was modified—mostly as a result of putting tenants in unused space. For example, Starbucks was allowed to set up shop in space under an escalator.

The coffee outlet has become popular with Chinese mainland tourists who often pass through the Hau Tak shopping center on their way to a famous nearby temple.

"At first people treated us with suspicion," So said. "They didn't know if they could do good business. But since their openings, they've been paying turnover rents, so we can see that their business is good. Now it's much less effort to get brands like that in."

Another example of a successful catch for The Link was Kee Wah, a chain of shops usually found in luxury shopping malls, such as the gleaming IFC mall on Hong Kong's famous harborfront.

"In the good old days when I was young, Kee Wah was famous," So said. "In the 1960s girls getting married used to dish out wedding cakes bought from there. But the tradition has disappeared now, but the shop has become a brand name for gift items in Hong Kong."

The Hau Tak shopping center was one of the eight that The Link earmarked for renovation. When the work at the building and the other seven was completed, their valuation would increase, allowing The Link REIT to take out bigger bank loans to carry out work on other shopping centers, So said.

"Investors would like us to do more," he said. "After these eight malls we can do more, but probably not faster. You can't disrupt the daily visits of shoppers."

The Link wanted to bring in more new tenants, and saw an opportunity from urban renewal work in a district called Kwung Tong, where many retailers would be evicted. The REIT was also converting failed shopping centers for new uses.

"Because of design, all housing estates had a shopping center, so you could find two across the road from each other," So explained. "They weren't just competing but were cannibalizing each other. One was deserted, so we changed it into a household goods and appliances center. If you're stuck with old designs, you've got to be creative. In another place, we turned a shopping center into a gardening center. People can do their daily shopping and then on the other side of the road they can stop over to buy tools and plants."

So said improvements had allowed The Link to raise rents at one shopping center to the market rate of HK$40 ($5.10) per square foot (HK$368 per square meter) per month from HK$9 before the shopping centers were privatized. He defended these kinds of rent hikes, which had drawn criticism from some tenants and politicians.

"We tell politicians and our tenants that you can't stay with the mode of operations as if it were the 1960s or 1970s still," So said. "Our critics are starting to realize that, especially when they see our renovated mall, and they compare the new and old parts. Tenants can't accuse us of not creating more traffic in general. But it's also a matter of if their products are attractive enough for people to spend money."

"We say we give value for rent," So said. "For example, we've done up the toilets and put in a kids' washbasin. And now a lot of tenants are coming up with plans to upgrade their shops. If there are low rents at the end of the day either the landlord or the tenant comes to the end of the road."

So was equally unperturbed by the sudden appearance in late 2005 of TCI, which bought a 18.35% stake and clinched a non-executive seat on The Link's board.

"It's a very natural thing," he said. "If you own close to one-fifth of a company you would like to take a closer look at what's going on. I believe they're making a good contribution. We know we should look at investor sentiment and they understand the difficulties we face. We're talking about a privatization project."

Although The Link management has its hands full improving its existing shopping centers, So still has an eye on future acquisitions. He believes that as The Link builds a brand name for good shopping centers in Hong Kong, it will be able to find good deals elsewhere.

"We've got first right of refusal to buy malls either under construction or existing (malls) from the Housing Authority," So said. "The initiative is on their side. They have already made it known that running shopping centers is not their core business. We have some imminent and yield-accretive targets."

"We are also allowed to invest outside Hong Kong," So said. "We might look to Macau or across the border in Shenzhen in the long run. Brand name is very important and it would be good for us in the long term."

Fees—A matter of trust

Of course, managers only stay in business if they are paid, and investors in REITs need to be aware of the fees that they are in effect forking out of their pockets, and whether they are getting value for money.

The base management fee can vary widely between different REITs, but it is usually measured by a percentage of the assets under management. The managers will also probably receive a fee based on the financial performance of the REIT, a pre-agreed cut of the portfolio's net property income. On top of

---

Example of typical fees—Singapore's Allco REIT

(Source: Credit Suisse)

Fees payable to the manager:
- An annual base fee of 0.5% of value of the real estate assets
- An annual performance fee of 3.5% of the performance fee amount (net property income of buildings minus the base fee)
- An acquisition fee of not more than 1% of the acquisition price of any real estate assets purchased by the trustee for Allco REIT
- A divestment fee of not more than 0.5% of the sale price of any real estate assets sold or divested by the trustee
- A termination payment of S$20 million if the manager is removed by unit holders

Fees payable to the property manager:
- an annual management fee of 3% of revenue from real estate assets

Fees payable to the trustee:
- a fee of 0.03% of the gross asset value subject to a minimum of S$36,000 per annum
- acquisition fee of 0.2% of the acquisition price of any real estate assets purchased by the trustee
- divestment fee of 0.1% of the sale price of any real estate assets sold or divested by the trustee

those, managers will take a fee for any acquisitions and divestments the REIT makes, usually expressed as a percentage of the size of the deal.

The argument against paying just a simple base fee to the manager is that performance and special fees for acquisitions will give the manager an extra incentive to buy new buildings and keep costs down and profits high, rather than just sit on a static portfolio.

But doubts about the motives of managers can arise. In Asia, the sponsor usually owns the REIT management company, and the REIT will also buy buildings from the sponsor. So it is conceivable that a manager and a REIT sponsor could connive to bring unnecessary or bad deals before investors—just so that the manager will collect a fat fee.

Comparison of Singapore REIT Management Fees as a Percentage of Forecast 2006 Revenue[2]

REIT	Property management fees (%)	Base trust management fees	Management performance fees	Other management fees	Total
Allco	2.8	6.6	2.5	–	9.1
Ascendas	2.7	5.0	2.3	2.7	10.0
CapitaCommercial	1.8	1.9	3.9	–	5.8
CapitaMall	3.5	2.9	2.9	0.2	5.9
Fortune	2.0	4.2	2.2	–	6.4
Mapletree	n.a.	5.9	2.9	0.2	8.9
MM Prime	3.0	7.4	0.1	–	7.5
Suntec	2.8	4.7	3.2	0.6	8.5

Source: Credit Suisse Research

Value for money—Yields, NAV and DCF

When buying anything, a shopper will look for value for money, whether bargain hunting or preferring to pay more for better quality. And investing in a REIT is no different. The only problem is that coming up with an appropriate measure of a REIT's value can sometimes be hit or miss. Analysts, who often say valuation is more of an art than a science, tend to concentrate on three measures: the yield, the value of the buildings a trust owns, and projected cash flow (and therefore dividends). But the conclusions drawn from each method can vary for the same REIT, and are based on assumptions that can sometimes skew the whole calculation if they turn out to be just slightly awry.

Comparison of REIT Management Fees as a Percentage of Forecast 2006 Assets Under MSanagement[3]

REIT	Property management fees (%)	Base trust management fees	Management performance fees	Other management fees	Total
Allco	0.2	0.5	0.2	–	0.7
Ascendas	0.2	0.4	0.2	0.2	0.9
CapitaCommercial	0.1	0.1	0.2	–	0.3
CapitaMall	0.3	0.3	0.2	–	0.5
Fortune	0.1	0.3	0.2	–	0.4
Mapletree	n.a	0.5	0.2	–	0.8
MM Prime	0.2	0.5	0.0	–	0.5
Suntec	0.2	0.3	0.2	–	0.5

Source: Credit Suisse Research

Nevertheless, an analyst will still try to come up with a "fair value" for a REIT's unit price, and a recommendation that takes into account the current stock market price: "buy," "accumulate" or "overweight" if the market price undervalues the trust, "hold" or "equal-weight" if the price is about right, and "sell" or "underweight" if the stock market price is higher than the firm is seen to be worth.

Yield

Just as when browsing in a supermarket, the first instinct when window shopping for a REIT is to compare prices for similar products, and looking at yields is the easiest way. After all, the dividend is the major attraction of a REIT.

But it is important to compare apples to apples.

REITs that are more likely to increase rental income in the future tend to trade at relatively lower yields. That potential for growth may come from a skilful management team that has performed well in the past, or it may be derived from exposure to assets that are seeing strong rental growth at that point in time. For example, offices and shopping centers tend to perform well during economic upturns.

Trusts that are likely to see slow rental growth, thanks to uninspiring management or maybe because they are invested in assets such as warehouses and factories that have long leases, would trade at a relatively high yield to compensate.

Anatomy of a yield

Although the dividend, or distribution, yield is what will concern an investor most, it is important to know what the actual property behind a REIT is yielding. Because if the dividend yield is far below the property yield, the trust's business or financing structure might be inefficient, with high operating costs or debt repayments eating in to money that maybe should be paid out in dividends. On the positive, that difference could be attributable to how highly investors regard management of the REIT and expectations for strong growth.

But if the trust's dividend yield is much higher than the property yield, the REIT is probably engaging in some kind of financial engineering to boost the dividend yield.

It is often worth examining closely yields at various levels to see how well run a REIT is, and to compare different trusts using these property yields.

Here are the different yield levels:

Property-level yields
1) Gross rental yield: This is the top-line yield, calculated by dividing the gross rental revenue by the gross asset value of the REIT's buildings. This is the most basic yield, and it fails to take into account items such as tax, or using debt leverage. It is affected by market rents, the tenant mix in a building, and the quality and types of leases signed, and can be distorted by incentives to attract tenants or rental guarantees given by tenants to the landlord.
2) Net property yield: This is calculated by dividing the net property income by the gross asset value of the buildings. The net property income, and therefore the net property yield, is derived after adjustments for non-rental

Yields should also be judged against a wider investing environment. They are, therefore, often quoted in comparison to the "risk-free" rate of interest, usually 10-year government bonds.

For example, a Japanese trust of prime offices trading at a 3.5% yield would on the surface appear to give lower returns than a similar Singapore REIT trading at 6%. But within the parameters of each market, that would not necessarily be the case.

If Japanese 10-year bonds were trading at a 1.5% yield and the equivalent Singapore bonds were trading at 4.25%, the "spread" over the risk-free rate for the Japanese trust would be 200 basis points (or 2 percentage points), whereas the spread for the Singapore trust would be 175 basis points.

Because government bond yields are indicative of the level of bank deposit rates and more indirectly the health and profitability of the whole economy, it property income, such as from advertising hoardings, as well as costs such as building management costs, property management fees, government rates and utilities. But the net property yield does not account for using debt leverage.

REIT-level yields

3) EBITDA/EV yield: This is calculated by dividing EBITDA (earnings before interest, tax, depreciation and amortization) of a REIT by its enterprise value (equity plus debt minus cash). This yield gives an indication of how much of the net property income might be consumed by REIT management fees, trustee fees and administration costs.

4) Earnings yield: This is an equity yield, calculated by dividing a REIT's earnings, or net income, by the equity market capitalization (or earnings per share divided by the unit price). At this level, the yield takes into account debt, interest costs, taxation and any extraordinary gains or losses. At this stage, the yield will reflect use of heavy borrowing to boost returns, and the use of interest rate swaps to ensure low interest rates in the short-term.

5) Dividend, or distribution, yield: This final yield is dictated by a REIT's dividend policy (what percentage of earnings it pays out to investors) and the cash available for distribution. The cash available is derived from net income by adjusting for non-cash items that management deems appropriate. These typically include the reversing of property revaluations and depreciations, fees paid in units, and any distribution guarantee. This yield will also be affected by any dividend waiver that a REIT's sponsor-shareholder grants as part of a strategy to boost dividend yields.

(For an example of how yields vary at different stages for a financially engineered REIT and a "clean," non-financially engineered, REIT, see Chapter 5.)

is possible to conclude that a REIT is relatively more attractive to the Japanese investor than the Singapore investor.

Net Asset Value (NAV)

Another way to look at a REIT is to see how the unit price compares with the perceived market value of the trust's assets, what is called book value or net asset value (NAV).

In the physical market, property appraisers usually employ three different methods to come up with a building's value. The first is the "replacement cost" approach, which involves calculating the cost to construct the building again, and includes elements such as the land price, and labor and construction material costs. But it is difficult to quantify a monetary equivalent of the time and effort starting from scratch would entail.

A second approach is to look at transactions for similar buildings in the area and compare. In a market where there are many similar buildings changing hands very frequently, it would be relatively easy to benchmark. Prices in housing markets are usually derived in that way. But for commercial buildings, which are more unique and seldom traded, relevant comparisons are much harder to find.

Appraisers will then turn to a method using a capitalization rate—the net operating income (after expenses are deducted) of a building as a percentage of the building's value.[4]

If it is possible to find an appropriate capitalization rate for the type of building in question, then it can be applied to the current net operating income to find the value. Obviously an appraiser will look for capitalization rates for similar buildings. But if we were talking about a 15 year-old city center office block for example, it would also be wise to look at capitalization rates for a range of offices, such as 10-year-old blocks in the same location and 15-year-old blocks in more suburban areas, and try to place the building somewhere in that range.

A better measure might be to take the average capitalization rate for that type of building over a longer period of time, say 10 or 15 years. Sometimes rent rises will outstrip rises in a building's capital value and sometimes they will lag, but over a long period, rents and values should move in tandem. That long-term capitalization rate can then be checked against recent one-off deals in the market or against rates for other asset types.

Once the appropriate capitalization rate is found, it can unlock the equation.

For example, a shopping center in Kuala Lumpur is bringing in a net operating income of $10 million a year, while shopping malls in the city have changed hands over the last 10 years at an average capitalization rate of 6.5%. The NAV of this particular shopping center would be $10 million divided by 6.5%, or $153.8 million. (capitalization rate = NOI/capital value, so capital value = NOI/capitalization rate).

REIT analysts typically use this capitalization rate method to find a trust's NAV, but few would bother employing the method on every building because it is time consuming and it is not always possible to find out the current net operating income of each building. The analyst will instead try to conjure up a capitalization rate that reflects the whole REIT portfolio, introducing potential for inaccuracy, especially if the buildings are very different and spread out geographically. And that rate will be applied to the REIT's overall net operating income. The analyst will then fall back on similar market transactions, and maybe even replacement cost to check the NAV calculation is in the right ballpark.

Once NAV per share has been calculated, it can be compared with the current share price. Although property companies tend to trade at a discount to NAV because of risks associated with development, REITs tend to trade at a premium because they are relatively straightforward low-risk investments, and they usually do not have to pay the taxes that other landlords do. REITs are deemed to be intrinsically worth more than the sum of the buildings they own because their units are easily traded, whereas whole buildings are not.

US REITs have historically traded anywhere between a 30% discount to NAV to a 30% premium, but on average they have traded at just a single-digit premium. Japanese REITs in mid-2005 were trading at premiums of as much as 80% to NAV. Some analysts believed the premium would grow even further because the Japanese investing public had become so used to rock-bottom interest rates that they were prepared to buy a REIT for a yield of 3-4%. In addition, many analysts in Japan did not apply their own NAV calculations, instead taking on the NAV given by REITs when they acquired a building. These valuations easily became outdated in a physical property market that was starting to boom.

This model for four hypothetical Japanese REITs, operating under the same interest rate environment, with the same return on assets and debt, shows how unit price/NAV changes as a REIT trades at a lower yield.

	REIT A	REIT B	REIT C	REIT D
REIT dividend yield	3.8 %	3.3 %	2.8 %	2.3%
Implied unit price	79	91	107	130
Implied price/NAV	1.58	1.82	2.14	2.61

Source: Lehman Brothers Research

Discounted Cash Flow (DCF)

A common way to value companies in industries across the economy is to look at projected future cash flows and try to work out how much they are worth today—an analysis called discounted cash flow (DCF).

This model is particularly useful for investors in property trusts because the company earnings are relatively predictable. And because REIT codes set out a minimum proportion of distributable income that must be paid in dividends, for example 90%, projected profits will hopefully flow straight back to the investor in the form of cash. This is not the case for other types of company. Many choose to pay very low dividends, or none at all, preferring to plough the money back into company investment.

The first step to valuing any stock with a DCF model is estimating the future earnings the underlying company is going to generate. Many variables go into estimating those cash flows, but among the most important are the company's future income growth and profit margins. Projecting such variables does not involve simply extrapolating present trends into the future. In fact, doing so can often lead to conclusions that a stock is worth a lot more or a lot less than it really is.

When predicting a company's revenue growth, it is important to consider a variety of factors, including industry trends, economic data, a company's competitive advantages, and the trend of its expenses. But looking at a REIT's future earnings is much easier than looking at other types of company because they are so simple, in effect just a collection of buildings. So the main issue for analysts is the rental trend, including demand and supply of the property type, and acquisition plans, rather than much less predictable factors such as future market share and innovation.

Once future income has been projected, an analyst will have to discount those cash flows back to the present day to account for the time value of money. After all, a dollar today is worth more than a dollar 10 years from now, because it can be invested to earn a return over the next decade. An assumed expected rate of return on capital, or cost of capital, is often used by analysts to calculate how much a dollar will be worth at some point in the future. And putting the process in reverse, this is used as the "discount rate" to calculate how much cash in the future is worth today.

For example, if the cost of equity is 5.0%, $20 today would be worth 105% of $20, or $21, in one year's time (20x 1.05) and $32.58 in 10 years' time (20×1.05^{10}).

Looking at it in reverse, $32.58 in 10 years' time is worth $20 today ($32.58/1.05^{10}$). So for any given year in the future, the following equation can be used to calculate the present value of the cash flow:

Present Value of Cash Flow in Year
Present Value = CF at Year $N/(1 + R)^N$
CF = Cash Flow
R = Required Return (Discount Rate)
N = Number of Years in the Future

Because it is not feasible to project a company's future cash flows out to infinity, year by year, an analyst will estimate a company's future cash flows for a certain period, say five or 10 years, and then estimate the value of all cash flows after that in one lump sum. This lump sum is the perpetuity value.

The most common way to do this is to take the last cash flow estimated, increase it by the rate at which cash flows are expected to grow over the long term, and divide the result by the cost of equity minus the estimated growth rate.

Perpetuity Value $= (CFn \times (1+ g))/R - g$
CFn = Cash Flow in the Last Individual Year Estimated
g = Long-Term Growth Rate
R = Discount Rate, or cost of capital

The Discounted Dividend Model (DDM)

As REIT earnings are relatively predictable—with dividend policy set by regulators and borrowing levels held fairly steady—analysts often take a jump to forecasting future dividends rather than cash flow, in order to give investors a better idea of the returns they will receive.

The calculation in a DDM model are on the same lines as in a DCF model, except that the discount rate used is the cost of equity, rather than the cost of capital (which includes debt, as well as equity). This is because the distribution from a REIT has already taken into account debt and interest costs, to leave just the distribution available to equity unit holders.

In this example of a discounted dividend valuation for a hypothetical Hong Kong REIT listed during the 2006 financial year, the analyst first notes the distributable income already announced for 2006. Then a projection of distributable income is made for 2007 and the subsequent four years assuming a 5% rate of growth and discounted to present value using the cost of equity. Then a 3.5% rate of long-term income growth is used to calculate the perpetuity value. The perpetuity value is added to the value for the five years from 2007 and the earnings for 2006 to give the total net present value.

This particular REIT has 2.14 billion units, so the net present value (NPV) per unit is HK$14.15. That can be used as an indication of whether the current share price is fair, or whether it is overvaluing the trust or undervaluing the trust.

Distribution Projections (Millions of Hong Kong Dollars)

2006	Forecast for 2007	Forecast for 2008	Forecast for 2009	Forecast for 2010	Forecast for 2011	Terminal growth rate
466.2	1,500.0	1,575.0	1,653,8	1,736.4	1,823.3	
		+5%	+5%	+5%	+5%	+3.5%

Discount Rate = Cost of Equity

Risk-free rate = 10-year bond yield	4.8%
Equity risk premium = long-term market return of Hang Seng index (9.8%) − risk free rate	5.0%
Equity beta = risk factor of stock	0.8
Cost of equity = (beta × equity risk premium) + risk free rate	8.8%

Net Present Value Calculation (Millions of Hong Kong Dollars)

a. 2006 income	466
b. Income for 2007-2011 discounted to present value	6,428
c. Perpetuity value assuming long-term income growth rate of 3.5% per year, discounted to present value	23,354
Total net present value (NPV) = a+b+c	30,248

NAV versus DCF

NAV is a popular way of valuing property companies in Asia, but many analysts believe that the method is flawed. They argue that because NAV models are based on the current market value of a REIT's assets, they are not forward looking and fail to take into account the value-creating power of good management. Proponents of DCF say REITs should be valued as operating companies that create value through buying, selling or renovating buildings and even developing, if they are allowed to do so by regulations.

It is common for analysts to come up with different computations of NAV because the capitalization rates they use differ, and it is particularly difficult to settle on a capitalization rate at the extremes of a property cycle, when rates in the market are either very high or very low.

But the argument in favor of NAV is that an investor should never lose sight of the fact that a REIT is fundamentally a collection of buildings that trade at real prices on a daily basis in the private market. And DCF calculations can also be widely off mark if discount rates are poorly estimated, with even the smallest variance in a REIT's risk profile wildly affecting valuations.

In essence, the argument between NAV and DCF boils down to whether a REIT is an investment in buildings, or an investment in the people who manage them. The answer is probably a bit of both.

Case study: REIT picking

This table of valuations for Singapore REITs, published on June 27, 2006, by Merrill Lynch, is a good example of how divergent DCF and NAV valuations can be. In this snapshot of the Singapore market in mid-2006, many of the REITs were trading somewhere between their DCF and the NAV valuations. CapitaMall Trust, for example, was trading at a 21.5% discount to its DCF valuation and a 25.6% premium to NAV. For most REITs, Merrill Lynch analyst Sean Monaghan set his share price targets close to the DCF valuation. Mapletree REIT was an exception because the trust expected to increase its asset size dramatically during the year in order to lift investor returns.

N.B. all data as on June 27, 2006	Unit price	DCF valuation	NAV valuation	Forecast 2006 distribution yield	Merrill Lynch target price
Ascendas REIT	S$1.90	S$2.70	S$1.34	6.1 %	S$2.50
CapitaCommercial Trust	S$1.61	S$2.08	S$1.64	4.5 %	$2.10
CapitaMall Trust	S$2.06	S$2.64	S$1.64	5.7 %	S$2.71
Fortune	HK$5.90	HK$7.52	HK$7.66	5.9 %	HK$6.85
Mapletree Logistics	S$0.93	S$0.72	S$0.70	5.5 %	S$1.20
Macquarie MEAG Prime	S$0.91	S$1.15	S$0.99	6.7 %	S$1.10
Suntec REIT	S$1.16	S$1.55	S$1.09	6.5 %	S$1.40

Macquarie Research analyst Tuck Yin Soong stuck rigidly to DCF valuations in his assessment of Singapore REITs. In research on three of the Singapore REITs under his coverage, published on December 1, 2006, he recommended "outperform" on Ascendas REIT and Macquarie MEAG Prime REIT, which were trading at discounts of 13.8 % and 27.2 % respectively to his DCF valuations for the trusts.

He believed K-REIT Asia's share price had climbed too far and too fast because of expectations of sharp office rent rises in Singapore, and rated the trust "neutral" because it was trading 6.4 % above its DCF valuation. It was also trading at 1.7 times its NAV.

"K-REIT is already trading at prospective a 2007 yield of 3.7 %, which is only about 60 basis points above the risk-free rate," Soong wrote. "We believe the strong DPU (distribution per unit) growth has already been factored into the share price."

N.B. all data as on November 28, 2006	Unit price	DCF valuation	Price/ book NAV	Forecast 2007 distribution yield	Macquarie target price (and recommendation)
Ascendas REIT	S$2.40	S$2.73	1.7	5.4	S$2.73 (outperform)
K-REIT Asia	S$2.35	S$2.20	1.3	3.7	S$2.20 (neutral)
Macquarie MEAG Prime	S$0.98	S$1.24	1.0	6.1	S$1.24 (outperform)

In contrast, Macquarie MEAG Prime had underperformed the REIT market for much of 2006 because investors were concerned about the two-year works closure of a link way from an underground train station to the basement of its shopping mall for. At the end of November, the trust was rare in that it was trading at its NAV, rather than above.

But the REIT had intensified a marketing and promotional campaign and was installing new escalators from street level to try to win customers. It was good value, but Soong described it as "one for the patient investor".

Although Soong was a proponent of DCF valuation over NAV, he kept a keen eye on how the wider market was valuing buildings.

"Macquarie MEAG Prime is currently trading at a 6.0 % yield (for 2006), much higher than recent Orchard Road transactions at 5.0 %," Soon said, referring to private market deals on Singapore's main shopping thoroughfare.

Soong was keen on Ascendas because the trust was poised to report a third year of double-digit DPU growth thanks to a spate of acquisitions. He also believed that a lack of supply in Singapore's office market would force some companies to consider moving into the kind of business park office premises that Ascendas dealt in.

"Given the strength in the office sector, Ascendas REIT could benefit from companies relocating to cheaper alternatives," he wrote. "We believe its industrial/office buildings could see stronger rent reversions at 4-5% per annum, rather than 2-3%."

(Note: These excerpts of research are meant as an illustration of analyst thinking on valuations and other issues related to REITs, and not as investment advice. The views were expressed on specific, time-sensitive circumstances, such as share prices, market sentiment and property portfolios, which are constantly changing).

Endnotes

1   "Hong Kong's Regal to launch REIT 'soon' to propel China drive," by Dominic Whiting, Reuters, October 25, 2006.
2   Credit Suisse research.
3   *Ibid.*
4   The capitalization rate is very similar to the net property yield but it is an appraiser's view of a building run during normal circumstances, whereas the net property yield reflects actual circumstances. For example, if a brand new building is being leased and is only 30% full in a district where occupancy rates are 96%, the net property yield will be much lower than the capitalization rate used by an appraiser, who will assume occupancy and rents will quickly adjust to market levels.

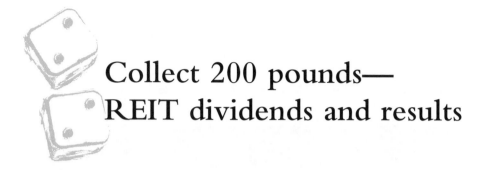

Collect 200 pounds—
REIT dividends and results

As REITs are designed to deliver steady income through their dividends, and are popular largely because of this stable and bond-like characteristic, small variances in a trust's earnings results can be more sensitive for investors than would be the case for other listed companies. A sharp increase in debt repayment costs or expenses for repairs at a building, for example, could take an unexpected bite out distributable income, and therefore dividends.

Because of this sensitivity, Asian REITs have tended to be cautious when forecasting their earnings and dividends, preferring to underplay the health of their businesses (see table on Early Growth of Dividends for selected REITs in Japan, and Company Projections). As a REIT's income is fairly predictable for those inside the business, the misforecasting could be seen as a little disingenuous, a tactic that tends to keep investors looking on the positive side.

Asian REITs have generally done a good job of increasing dividends for their investors, who have been particularly grateful because of the rock bottom interest rates prevalent in the early 2000s.

Much of the success was due to catching the property markets at the right time. In Japan and Singapore, REITs were encouraged at a time when property markets had slumped, in the hope that they would help stimulate interest and a price revival. That in fact did happen as acquisitions by the trusts started to fuel price rises, which then attracted other investors to property. Starting their lives at the bottom of property and general economic cycles, the REITs benefited from increasing rents that translated into dividend growth. While high-yield buildings were still available on the market, good acquisitions accelerated the trend.

In Singapore, average distribution per unit grew 4.2% in 2004 and 13.8% in 2005. Of the increase in 2005 from the previous year, only about four percentage points of growth was attributed to rent rises at buildings already owned by REITs, while nearly 10 percentage points of growth were due to the addition of higher yielding acquisitions.[1]

Early Growth of Dividends for Selected REITs in Japan, and Company Projections (in parentheses)

Accounting period	Nippon Building Fund	Japan Real Estate	Japan Retail Fund	Orix REIT	Japan Prime Realty
H2/2001	19,026 (16,200)	14,983 (14,900)	13,252 (12,881)	22,472 (21,957)	2,545 (2,140)
H1/2002	16,003 (15,660)	12,853 (12,400)	14,438 (14,134)	15,501 (14,024)	6,912 (6,500)
H2/2002	16,253 (15,220)	14,455 (14,300)	15,095 (14,504)	15,246 (14,262)	6,873 (6,300)
H1/2003	15,365 (14,301)	15,117 (15,000)	16,918 (15,724)	14,156 (13,064)	5,738 (5,600)
H2/2003	15,185 (14,300)	14,602 (14,200)	14,452 (14,008)	14,772 (13,821)	6,081 (5,600)
H1/2004	17,291 (13,600)	14,711 (14,600)	15,419 (14,920)	14,068 (13,012)	6,671 (6,400)

Source: Lehman Brothers Research

Any REIT investor should keep a close eye on financial results, to ensure that the trust is heading in the right direction and that managers are delivering on their promised dividend payouts. In line with the practices of their respective stock markets, REITs in Singapore and Japan report their results on a quarterly basis, while their Hong Kong counterparts report twice a year. Dividend payments are typically made twice a year.

Here are the main elements of a REIT's profit and loss (P&L), or income, statement:

Total revenue

This "top line" entry on the profit and loss statement adds together all the income flowing into the REIT, including rents, car park income, additional charges on tenants for items such as air conditioning, promotion and advertising, cleaning, rubbish collection, etc.. In some cases, total revenue could be boosted if a landlord selling a building to a REIT gives a rental guarantee, agreeing to a top-up charge if rent during a certain period does not reach a certain level.

Property operating expenses

As we work down the income statement, the property operating expenses are deducted from the total revenue. This item will include fees paid by the trust to property managers, the people who make sure a building is kept clean and secure and well maintained. Other operating expenses would include the actual costs of maintenance and the cost of providing utilities, such as electricity and water, for public areas of a building.

Manager's performance fees

Then the manager's performance fees are deducted. The fees, typically a percentage of acquisition values and revenue, are supposed to be incentives for carrying out a good growth strategy.

Net property income

Once property operating expenses and the manager's performance fees are deducted from total revenue, you are left with the net property income—a measure of how well the operational side of the business is doing (disregarding the purely financial aspects of a REIT's performance).

Borrowing costs

Borrowing costs are the payments made during the reporting period of interest and principle on a REIT's debt, which may be in the form of bank loans, a bond or commercial mortgage-backed securities.

Tax

In Hong Kong, REITs pay corporate tax. This is not the case in most countries, where "tax transparency" means that a REIT's income is taxed at the investor-level, and at the income tax rate of that investor.

Manager's base fee

The manager's base fee is typically a percentage of the REIT's asset size.

Income available for distribution

Once borrowing costs, any tax and the manager's base fee are subtracted from net property income, you are left with the income available for distribution. The amount actually distributed to investors by means of a dividend will depend on the REIT's dividend policy, but in most jurisdictions it must be over 90%. Some REITs will pay out 100% of their distributable income, while some will prefer to keep a "retained profit" for investment in the business or as cash in case of an emergency—for instance, a sharp rise in borrowing costs.

Distribution per unit

This is the amount a REIT intends to distribute to shareholders divided by the number of units in circulation.

Below is an example of profit and loss statements. It shows comparisons of the first quarter results in 2005 and 2006 of Fortune REIT, a trust listed in Singapore, which owns shopping malls in Hong Kong.

Item	Jan. 1, 2006–March 31, 2006 (thousands of Hong Kong dollars)	Jan. 1, 2005–March 31, 2005 (thousands of Hong Kong dollars)	% increase
Total revenue	154,129	75,336	104.6
Property operating expenses	36,897	17,551	110.2
Manager's performance fees	3,517	1,734	102.9
Net property income	113,715	56,051	102.9
Borrowing costs	25,457	5,560	357.9
Hong Kong taxation	15,383	8,789	75
Manager's base fee	6,356	3,095	105.4
Income available for distribution	72,474	41,499	74.6
Distribution per unit	0.090	0.087	3.3

Interpretation

The P&L statements from Fortune REIT reflect what happens to a REIT when it expands very quickly. In June 2005, Fortune REIT bought six suburban Hong Kong shopping centers, bringing the total number of assets in its portfolio to 11.

These acquisitions accounted for most of the 104.6% growth in total revenue notched up in the first quarter of 2006, in comparison with the same period a year earlier. But rents were also climbing. In the first three months of 2006, leases at Fortune REIT's shopping centers that were renewed were negotiated at an average 13% higher than previously. Its Ma On Shan Plaza shopping center was a particularly good performer, with net property income at the building growing 16.2% in the first quarter of 2006 from a year earlier.

But it is clear from the relatively high 110.2% increase in property operating expenses that Fortune REIT had not yet made savings from the greater economies of scale afforded by a bigger portfolio. In fact, property management fees, rather than falling on a comparative basis, actually jumped 131.9%— climbing further than total revenue. Fortune REIT was also spending money to revamp other shopping malls. At one, managers had negotiated to take back space from a supermarket so it could squeeze in smaller retailers at higher rents. At another shopping center, Fortune REIT was trying to promote a wedding theme, bringing in seven Taiwanese wedding operators.

Because of these high costs, the net property income in the first three months of 2006 was only 102.9% higher than a year earlier, also trailing the 104.6% rise in total revenue.

The higher borrowing cost incurred by Fortune REIT was a telling sign of the times. The REIT took on an additional HK$1.5 billion of loans to partly finance the purchase of the six shopping malls at a time when Hong Kong interest rates were rising dramatically. The three-month Hong Kong Interbank Offer Rate (HIBOR) rose to 4.4% in March 2006 from just 0.8% in January 2005. The REIT's weighted average borrowing cost for the first quarter of 2006 rose to 4.2% per annum, compared with 2.4% a year earlier.

Because Fortune REIT's properties were in Hong Kong, they paid Hong Kong taxes. And the manager's base fee doubled because of the addition of the six shopping malls.

The relatively high property operating costs and borrowing costs meant that distributable income grew only 74.6%, well short of the jump in total revenue. As well as borrowing to finance the shopping center acquisitions in June 2005, Fortune REIT sold new units in the trust. So the 74.6% rise in distributable income translated into a 3.3% rise in distribution per unit. At its share price on March 31, 2006, the distribution per unit translated into a yield of 5.9%.

The Balance Sheet

A balance sheet is a snapshot of the health of a company at any point in time, and REITs, just as any other listed firm, will publish their balance sheets together with their earnings results. By keeping an eye on changes in the balance sheet, an investor can track how a REIT manager's strategy is shaping the trust, and whether it is sustainable. For example, a balance sheet can show whether a REIT has more room to fund acquisitions using debt, or whether it will have to raise a bigger proportion of its funds on the equity market. That could have consequences for the additional income an investor will receive from the acquisitions, as "gearing" through the use of debt can help lift returns.

A company's balance sheet is comprised of assets, liabilities and equity. In a REIT's case, the main assets are obvious – its buildings. Liabilities are what the firm owes to others, such as creditors, suppliers and tax authorities. As essentially a REIT's assets, which are mostly buildings, are funded by total capital (debt plus equity), the central equation in a balance sheet is assets = liabilities + equity.

The main items to look out for in a REIT's balance sheet are:

Assets

1. *Receivables:* This is what is owed to the company by its customers. For REITs, this item is often irrelevant and does not appear on the balance sheet because they should be receiving rent from their tenants on time and regularly. If receivables are relatively high, in comparison to a REIT's assets, management may be having problems collecting rent.

2. *Cash or cash equivalents:* Because REITs are obliged to pay out a stipulated amount of their distributable income as a dividend, they hold a relatively small amount of cash compared with other companies. Whereas most firms would use cash to make acquisitions, REITs need to raise new equity or borrow funds. Because of this, investors have a high degree of certainty over the direction in which a REIT is heading. A cash equivalent is something that can be changed into cash very easily, such as a bond.

3. *Long-term investments:* Because of the way Asian REIT regulations have been drawn up, the main investment for a REIT will be in buildings, although in some jurisdictions they can have a certain amount of their assets in other property-related businesses, such as in a property fund management firm.

4. *Goodwill:* This is an intangible asset on the balance sheet because it is not a physical asset, such as buildings. Goodwill typically reflects the value of a strong brand name or good customer relations. Negative goodwill can also be

found on a REIT balance sheet—it is the difference if the transaction price for an acquisition is less than the fair value of its assets.

Liabilities

1. *Trade payables:* This current liability, or an item that has a timespan of one year or less, represents what the REIT owes to its suppliers. For example, it could include money yet to be paid for work done by building contractors.

2. *Short-term debt:* This is also a current liability, and represents any debt incurred by the REIT that is due within one year. The debt in this account is usually made up of short-term bank loans.

3. *Long-term debt:* This item brings together loans and financial obligations stretching over more than one year, including bonds, notes and bank loans.

Equity

1. *Shareholders' equity:* This is the initial amount of equity invested into a business. If, at the end of the fiscal year, a REIT decides to reinvest an amount of its net earnings into its business, these "retained earnings" will be transferred from the income statement onto the balance sheet in the shareholder's equity account. As REITs are governed by rules stipulating what percentage of their distributable income needs to be paid as dividends—generally 90%-95%— retained earnings for trusts are far smaller than would be the case for most listed companies.

The balance sheet at the end of 2005 clearly shows the impact of the acquisition of the six shopping malls in June of that year, which raised the trust's gross rentable area by 62% and accounted for the vast majority of the doubling in the value of fixed assets.

The purchases were funded by a mix of equity and debt, but with a greater emphasis on debt than the trust had previously maintained. As a result, the REIT's gearing (debt as a proportion of the value of its property) jumped to about 28% from 22%. Total shareholder's equity almost doubled, but long-term debt rose by 163%.

Although the gearing ratio rose, it was still well within Singapore's limit at the time of 35%, suggesting that Fortune could conceivably make another acquisition with a similar financial structure. In fact, in October 2005, after Fortune had bought the six shopping malls, Singapore raised its gearing limit to

60% on condition that a trust had an "A" rating from a major ratings agency.

Because the market value of Fortune's shopping centers was increasing, taking relatively more debt to equity had a softer impact on gearing than would have been the case had property prices in Hong Kong stayed stagnant over the period. On average, the asset value of Fortune's properties rose 10% in 2005.

While borrowing more, Fortune took steps to reduce its financial risk by cutting short-term debt that was most vulnerable to sharp interest rate rises. In 2005, the trust decreased one-month revolving debt to HK$12 million from HK$26 million.

As interest rates were rising, the trust also switched more into fixed interest rate borrowing, and by the end of 2005 about 75% of its debt, HK$1.8 billion ($230 million) worth, was maintained at fixed rates, against just 51% at the end of 2004.

Example of a Balance Sheet: Fortune REIT

(in millions of Hong Kong dollars)	end of 2005	end of 2004
Cash/short-term investments	213	104
Other current assets including receivables	136	34
Fixed assets	8,519.0	4,184.0
Other long term assets	0	(134)
Total assets	**8,868**	**4,188**
Short-term debt	12	26
Other short-term liabilities, including trade payables	195	72
Long-term debt	2,367	900
Other long-term liabilities	79	56
Total liabilities	**2,653**	**1,054**
Shareholders' capital	4,288	2,246
Retained earnings	1,927	888
Total shareholder's equity	**6,215**	**3,134**
Total capital (liabilities + equity)	**8868**	**4188**

Fortune REIT's share price

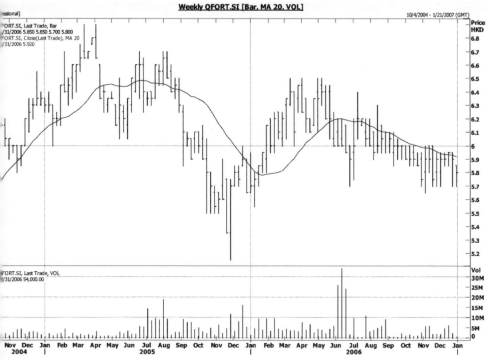

Source: Reuters

But by the end of 2005, about HK$541 million of debt was still subject to floating interest rates, and this item on the balance sheet was to have an impact on the trust's share price.

Fortune REIT's units were more volatile during 2005 than previously, in 2006, or in comparison with other Singapore-listed REITs. This was due to several factors, but especially the sharp rise in interest rates in Hong Kong— where the trust was borrowing—in a year when it took on much more debt.

The share price was fairly buoyant in the first half of the year, especially around the time the trust bought the six shopping malls in Hong Kong. It fell in line with other Singapore-listed REITs following critical comments by Temasek chief Ho Ching on financial engineering, although the market was probably also ready for a pause after a strong rally in 2004.

But when Singapore REIT share prices began to recover in October, Fortune REIT units continued to slide because of a sharp rise in Hong Kong interest rates.

The graph below shows that yields on three-month notes rose to about 3.6% at the end of 2005 from almost zero at the beginning of the year. Because of the

Hong Kong dollar peg to the US dollar, Hong Kong benchmark interest rates rose in tandem with US rates, but from a very low base because of an influx of cash into Hong Kong at the end of 2004. As a result, the average interest rate on Fortune REIT's debt climbed to 3.27% in 2005 from 2.02% in 2004.

Singapore interest rates also rose, but at a gentler incline, with three-month notes yielding 2.6% at the end of 2005, compared with 0.8% at the beginning of the year.

Interest rate on Hong Kong 3-month notes

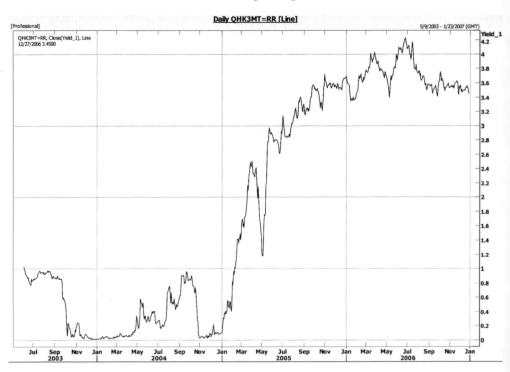

Source: Reuters

REIT players—The analyst

Soong Tuck Yin, head of research at Macquarie Securities in Singapore, explains what investors should look for from a REIT that is trying to increase its dividend payments through acquisitions.

When a new purchase is announced, investors should first look at the yield on the building's net property income, he said.

"That would definitely give you a first cut to whether the acquisition will be accretive to shareholders," Soong said. "Then you look at the detail of the property in terms of passing rent, and its valuation on a post-profit basis to see if it is in line with comparisons. You see if they've overpaid."

Soong said he usually then looks at the building's vacancy rate and whether there is room for occupancy to rise. A 10% vacancy rate means there is still some potential for rent to increase just by taking on more tenants. But a 5% vacancy rate is generally regarded in the industry as full occupancy.

Then come the details of the purchase contract. Soong examines who will pay outgoings such as maintenance of the buildings and security. In some cases the landlord will just sell a share of a building's income to a REIT, while maintaining control of the building and taking on the risk of possible utility charge rises. That landlord, for example, might decide to pay the outgoings to ensure the REIT manager keeps at arm's length from the day-to-day running of the building.

"The price will be higher if the REIT is not paying the outgoings," Soong said. "But sometimes it's better if the REIT pays. In a big portfolio it can spread insurance risk. The REIT can also buy electricity for several buildings in blocks, because of its better bargaining power. For larger REITs, operating expenses against revenue will fall slightly."

The acquisition should also fit into the strategy of the REIT. A specialist in warehouses would probably know little about managing a nursing home or a shopping center.

"It's a question of the REIT articulating a strategy and working it out, following a game plan. If you believe in the manager, you just follow what they're doing," Soong said.

"In the early stages of the REIT development of any country, the track record of a manager doesn't matter so much," he said. "It's really government policies and acquisitions that drive performance. But later you need to ask which REIT manager has the ability to drive growth organically through occupancy, asset enhancements and tenant mix."

Testing financial statements

The main measures used to value and compare REITs are discussed in the previous chapter: the yield, price to net asset value, and price to discounted cash flow valuation. But other tools commonly employed to evaluate listed companies can also be applied to REITs, such as ratios comparing information from the income statement and the balance sheet. Here are the major ratios, applied to the Fortune REIT financial statements shown above.

Interest cover: This income statement ratio shows how easily a company can pay interest on outstanding debt. It is calculated by dividing a trust's earnings before interest and taxes (EBIT) of one period by the company's interest expenses of the same period. The lower the ratio, the more the REIT is burdened by debt expenses. An interest coverage ratio of below 1 indicates a company is not generating sufficient revenues to satisfy interest expenses — such a situation is extremely unlikely for a REIT because regulatory limits on gearing or market-enforced discipline prevents heavy borrowing.

In the first quarter of the 2006 financial year, Fortune REIT's interest cover stood at 4.47 times (HK$113.7 million/HK$25.5 million), compared with 10.1 times in the first quarter of 2005, before the acquisition of the six shopping centers.

Debt/equity ratio: This balance sheet ratio can give another indication of whether a company is borrowing relatively more or less than its peers. It is calculated by dividing total borrowings minus cash by shareholders' equity and expressed as a percentage. For Fortune REIT, the debt/equity ratio stood at

A REIT also tends to perform better if it has a strong parent that can sell more buildings into the trust. Singapore's Ascendas REIT, for example, has bought many of its buildings from its parent Ascendas, a business park specialist whose forays into India will probably open up new REIT possibilities. Similarly, CapitaMall Trust and CapitaCommercial Trust could well benefit from CapitaLand's ventures across Asia, especially in China.

"A parent pipeline is very important," Soong said. "Why is CapitaMall Trust trading at a lower yield? It's because of its growth prospects."

38.2% (HK$2.379 billion/HK$6.22 billion x 100) at the end of 2005, reflecting the increase in borrowing for the acquisitions, compared with 29.5% a year earlier.

Gearing: This balance sheet ratio is another indicator of how heavily a REIT is borrowing. For REITs, market regulators define gearing as the proportion of total debt to either a trust's assets, or to the value of its property. In Singapore, the latter is applied, so Fortune REIT's gearing rose to 27.9% (HK$2.379 billion/HK$8.52 billion x 100) at the end of 2005 from 22.1% a year earlier.

Return on assets: Return on assets (ROA) is regarded as a profitability ratio, which shows how much a company is earning on its total assets. It is calculated as net income/total assets. ROA differs greatly across industries and for REITs the ratio is on the low end of the scale because being a landlord is a capital-intensive business dealing in expensive assets. On an annualised basis, return on assets in the first quarter of 2006 was 3.2% (HK$72.47 x 4/HK$8.87 billion x 100), against 3.9% a year earlier. This is a reflection of the higher operating expenses at the newly acquired shopping centers, as shown on the income statement.

Return on equity (2004: 5.5% 2005: 24.2%): Return on equity (ROE) reveals how much profit a company earned in a certain period (on the income statement) compared with the total amount of shareholder equity on the balance sheet. A business that has a higher return on equity is more likely to be one that is capable of generating cash internally.

On an annualized basis, return on equity in the first quarter of 2006 stood at 4.6 times (HK$72.47 × 4/HK$6.21 billion × 100) compared with 5.3 times in the first quarter of 2005.

Endnote

1   Merrill Lynch research, Singapore REITs, by Sean Monaghan, June 27, 2006.

Chance—Asian
REIT risk

Asia risk

Asia has had its ups, and its fairly dramatic downs.

For an idea of the volatility possible in Asia's property markets, look no further than land prices in central Tokyo since a property boom during the export-led "bubble" economy of the 1980s. By the early 1990s, a stretch of the Ginza district of the Japanese capital had become by far the most expensive plot of land in the world.

The Kyukyodo stationery store, which sells incense burners and calligraphy tools, stands on land that was worth more than $260,000 per square meter in 1992. But a subsequent property market crash during a decade of economic stagnation sent the price spinning down to less than $100,000 per square meter by 2004. Just two years later, a pick-up in the property market inflated the price to $130,000. To give an impression of how expensive that still was, a square meter of prime land would cost about $35,000 in London's Mayfair and $19,000 in Manhattan, New York.

A similar pattern of boom, bust and recovery has been spun out across much of the region, with the 1997-98 Asian economic crisis punctuating the recent history of property markets from Bangkok and Kuala Lumpur to Hong Kong and Seoul.

In general, investors see strong potential for quick capital appreciation in the world's fastest growing economies, but there is also a higher risk that property markets will slide further in Asia than in other regions if there is a turn for the worse.

For example, RREEF, the property asset management arm of Germany's Deutsche Bank AG, has a property investment risk model that gives Asia an average 3.75 point rating on a scale of ascending risk from zero to five. The global average for property market risk is 3.0 points on the scale.

The model takes into account the following assessments: the health of national economies, including gross domestic product (GDP) growth, investment and unemployment; political stability; country risk, including credit ratings and debt defaults and capital market access; tenancy risks related to lease lengths and rental guarantee periods; transparency, which takes into account information flows, regulations and corruption; and liquidity—how easy it is to buy and sell in property markets.

Application of the model in 2006 showed a great divergence within Asia. Hong Kong was ranked close to the global average for risk, while the Bangkok, New Delhi and Taipei markets were regarded as riskier than the Asian average. Tokyo and Singapore ranked in between.

Chart of RREEF risk model

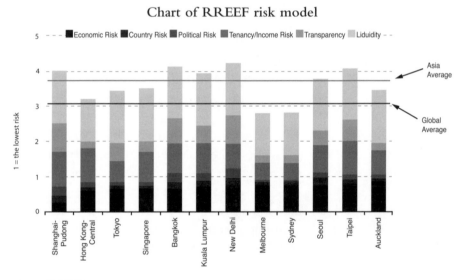

Source: RREEF

N.B. In the risk model, RREEF has applied different weightings to each risk category: a 30% weighting for liquidity risk, 20% each for transparency, economic and tenancy risk, and 5% each to political and country risk.

Although the model is useful for assessing property market risk across the region, it is important to remember that REITs will tend to stand in the low-risk zone within any particular property market. Because REITs are traded stocks, the property market "liquidity" risk is effectively eliminated by the fact stock markets are liquid. The financial reporting requirements for REITs mean that transparency risk is much lower than if an investor were to buy a building on the private property market. But a risk model for REITs would also have to take into account volatility of stock markets, which is much greater than for physical property markets.

However, elements of the RREEF risk profile, such as political and economic risk, will be just as relevant to a security listed on a stock market as they are to direct property investment. Developing country stock markets are also susceptible to fads and hot money flows. One year the Thai stock market might be in favor with international funds, and the next it will be Malaysia, even if the fundamental economies and corporate health within the two markets may not have changed a great deal.

Asia's property markets are, in fact, becoming less risky partly because of the advent of REITs, but also because of increased foreign investment, according to a global survey on property market transparency carried out by consultants Jones Lang LaSalle in 2006.

Describing a "virtuous cycle," Guy Hollis, director at Jones Lang LaSalle's international capital group, said increasing foreign investment across all of Asia was improving information flows, which would in turn give investors more confidence.

"Funds are much more aggressive and have certainly invested a lot of money, and in most places they haven't compromised on standards," Hollis said.[1]

International investors are getting more adventurous in Asia because the region's developing economies promise higher returns than developed markets in Europe and the United States. Cross-border investment in the Asia-Pacific region jumped 56% in 2005 to $20 billion, and Hollis said the growth was accelerating, pointing to about $9 billion pledged for China just in the first three months of 2006.

In the Jones Lang LaSalle global transparency index, China was classed as "low" but its score had improved to 3.50 points against 3.71 two years earlier. India was a notch above, in the "semi-transparent" third category of five, with its score moving to 3.46 from 3.90 in 2004, the previous time the index was published.

The top Asian scores were notched up by Hong Kong with 1.30 and Singapore with 1.44, while Australia and the United States occupied joint top place globally with a score of 1.15.

Japan had climbed three places in the index to rank 23 since 2004, with its score improving to a "high transparency" 2.40 from a "semi-transparent" 3.08.

The Jones Lang LaSalle index focused on availability of investment performance indices and market data, financial disclosure by listed companies, regulatory and legal factors and professional and ethical standards.

The report accompanying the survey said the development of REIT markets across Asia was already improving transparency, and could have a huge effect on market information and the way property investment was carried out:

> "A development which has the potential to have a very major impact on transparency levels in Asia is the emergence of the REIT sector... A major benefit of the introduction of REITs to markets such as Japan and South Korea is that the associated reporting requirements have seen significantly more information relating to real estate assets being released to the market. A related development which can assist in improvements in transparency levels is the establishment of professional bodies aimed at serving the needs of the sector. Such industry bodies provide a platform that facilitates the industry to lobby for greater transparency."[2]

The biggest gripes among foreign direct investors in Asia were over property titles, especially in China and India. India, which eased rules on foreign investment in construction in early 2005, lacks a centralized title registry. And with property prices soaring, land disputes are increasing. In China, land use rights cannot be directly traded, so investors must take the risk of acquiring the company that holds them. Relatively low accountancy standards hamper such deals.

But because REITs must deal with issues such as title before regulators allow them to list on stock markets, investors tend to mark down the risk premium on trusts. Hong Kong-listed GZI REIT, for example, managed to sell its IPO at a 6.5% yield, whereas a foreign investor would be unlikely to touch similar Chinese shopping centers on the private market unless they yielded at least 8% to compensate for possible regulatory and title risk.

But direct property market yields in many countries in Asia have begun to diverge from traditional assessments of investment risk.

That is partly because local investors in any given market will have a completely different perspective of the risks involved. While international investors can trawl property markets across the world for investments that will give a return commensurate with the risks they are taking, most investors in any given country will stay within their borders and will be used to practices that others may frown upon.

Hollis said the rush of foreign investors into some markets might also be pushing prices up too fast. Many investors were tired of low returns from developed European and North American markets.

"I'm not sure we're seeing the right risk and return equation in some of these developing markets," Hollis said, citing India, China, Russia and parts of South America.

"Yields aren't as low as London, Paris, or New York, but they aren't as high as they should be," he said.

Office buildings in Shanghai were changing hands at yields of around 8% in 2006, while yields of top-grade Tokyo offices had dropped to around 3.6% from 5-6% a couple of years before—lower than London's 4.6% yields. In Thailand, which ranked just above India on the transparency index in 2006 with 3.40 points, central Bangkok offices could yield just 6.5%.

Transparency rankings and office yields in mid-2006

Country	Transparency level	2006 transparency score	2004 transparency score	Prime office % yield in major city	World transparency ranking
Hong Kong	Highest	1.30	1.50	3.6	6
Singapore	Highest	1.44	1.55	5.1	10
Malaysia	High	2.21	2.30	–	22
Japan	High	2.40	3.08	Tokyo: 3.6	23
Taiwan	Semi	2.86	3.10	–	29
South Korea	Semi	2.88	3.36	Seoul: 7.8	31
Philippines	Semi	3.30	3.43	–	36
Thailand	Semi	3.40	3.44	–	39
India	Semi	3.46	3.90	New Delhi: 7.8 Mumbai: 12.0	41
China	Low	3.50	3.71	Shanghai: 8.6 Beijing: 9.5	42
Indonesia	Low	3.90	4.11	–	46
Vietnam	Opaque	4.69	4.60	–	56

Source: Jones Lang LaSalle

Note: *The Jones Lang LaSalle index tried to measure transparency, defined as: "any open and clearly organized real estate market operating in a legal and regulatory framework that is characterized by a consistent approach to enforcement of rules and regulations and that respects private property rights. It also includes the ethical and professional standards of private sector advisors, agents and brokers who are licensed to conduct business in each country."*

Property cycles

Better information flows and a more professional approach to investing, both by-products of THE development of REIT markets, should help to even out property cycles over time. In theory, there should be no more stratospheric peaks or plunges, although there is little chance of eliminating ups and downs altogether.

As is the case for many economic sectors, over periods of many years, the property industry experiences bouts of excess demand, when markets are characterized as "booming" or "hot," as well as periods of too much supply, when markets are "slow" or "cooling."

A property cycle occurs because markets tend to self-correct, but inefficiently.

When there is not enough space, developers will build more. When there is too much space, construction will stop until demand swells up again. If cities really could be built in a day, there would be no property cycle, because developers would supply exactly the right amount of space required at any point of time. But it takes time for market information to filter through to developers, and then even more time for them to arrange financing and construct a building. That time lag, often three to four years, can determine the length of an upswing or a downswing in a cycle.

The lag also gives time for economic fortunes to change, for inflation and interest rates to rise or fall. The best of plans can go awry, and what seemed like the perfect amount of space could be too much.

There is also a psychological element at work. Because developers usually achieve healthy returns in the early periods of an upward cycle, they tend to get carried away and build too much. If new supply continues to hit the market after demand begins to drop, the cycle might enter a recession phase, driving down prices, rents and occupancy rates. The cycle reaches bottom when construction slows to the point that demand can begin to absorb the excess space.

In an extreme case where market information is completely lacking, or developers and financiers lack the capability to properly judge risks and returns for projects, property markets can swing violently between boom and bust.

Thailand in the early to mid-1990s was a prime example. The economy was growing at more than 7% a year thanks to an export boom and a sharp rise in inward investment, some of it "hot money" looking to capitalize on the country's rapid economic growth. Japanese companies, especially vehicle and auto parts manufacturers, textile and semiconductor makers, set up production plants in Thailand to try to escape the steep production costs associated with a high yen currency.

The Japanese firms, and other companies from South Korea and Taiwan drawn by a booming Southeast Asia, brought wealthy executives who wanted plush housing. New wealth in the country meant a young Thai middle class was emerging that also liked the idea of moving away from traditional family compounds. Hundreds of thousands caught trains in from the countryside, leaving their rice farms to make their fortunes on construction sites, driving motorcycle taxis, or selling street food to the new army of city laborers.

Hundreds of developers sprang from nowhere, and banks seemed happy to take on as much new business as possible, believing demand for property in Bangkok would just keep rising. With no urban planning system to speak of, anyone with a plot of land in central Bangkok considered putting up an office or an apartment block. Land speculation went through the roof.

But a lack of good market information meant many projects were doomed. The expectations of the developers and banks completely outstripped immediate demand. One developer built a cluster of high rises on the outskirts of Bangkok that was intended to give tens of thousands of teachers affordable housing, but it became a ghost town.

Bank loans went sour. The property industry ground to a halt. So many developers went out of business that only a handful were left standing when the property market began to resuscitate in the early 2000s. Inward investment dried up, and sparkling new office developments were abandoned half-completed.

The property market crash was a precursor to an economic crisis, compounded by growing competition from cheaper manufacturers in China, which sparked a flight of capital from Thailand. The Thai experience was quickly played out to different degrees across the region, snowballing into the 1997–98 Asian crisis.

However, as Thailand began to recover, banks and property developers said they had learned a valuable lesson. Projects became much better thought out than they had been in the heady 1990s, and banks were more cautious in their lending, insisting on proper business plans backed up by market data and solid demand projections.

A Property Cycle Model

To give a clear idea of how property cycles work, here is a model used by Dr. Jack Harris, a research economist with the Real Estate Center at Texas A&M University, and his explanation of how physical and asset markets interact.[3]

Differences between the demand for space and the demand for properties are a source of confusion when analyzing real estate markets. This is because, in most cases, the user of the space is not the property owner.

One good way to sort this out is to use the four-quadrant model. This model recognizes there are actually two inter-related real estate markets: a space market and an asset market. The space market is where tenants contract for the use of developed space. The asset market is where investors purchase land, buildings and related interests.

Each market can be separated into a short- and long-run phase. Supply is constant in the short term, so decisions about construction are confined to the long-term side. Whenever something changes in one of the sectors (for example, when there is a rise in demand for space), the change must ripple through all the sectors before equilibrium can be re-established. Delays are introduced, inertia is reinforced and outside cyclical influences are introduced as the market responds.

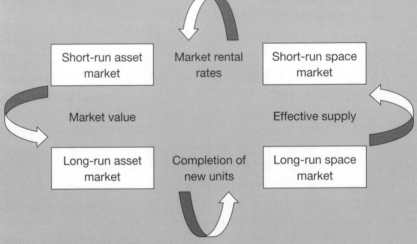

Consider how each part of the market operates.

1. Short-run space market

This is where supply, which is fixed in the short term, and demand for space interact. It is also where market rental rates are determined. Equilibrium is established when occupancy is at its "natural" rate, which can vary by how active and diverse the demand for space actually is. When the actual occupancy rate is lower, rents fall; higher occupancy rates prompt rent increases. The business cycle and how space is used affect demand.

2. *Short-run asset market*

Market rental rates support investors' expectations of future net operating income from real property assets. This expected income is capitalized into property values. Real estate capitalization rates are affected by a number of economic conditions, including inflation cycles, which affect the amount of appreciation real property investors can expect, and interest rate and stock market cycles, which has an impact on capitalization rates through changes in required investment yields.

3. *Long-run asset market*

In the long-run asset sector of the market, decisions are made that affect supply. Property values are translated into construction of new units. When existing property values rise to the point that new units can be produced profitably and when the value of existing buildings rises to more than the cost of replacement, construction begins to occur. Development costs determine this property value threshold. Changes in government regulations and construction costs, including interest rates, influence the point at which construction is triggered.

Both regulation and costs show some cyclical variation. Governments, for example, tend to apply stringent controls after market peaks while offering development incentives during recovery periods, reinforcing the real estate market cycle.

4. *Long-run space market*

In this quadrant of the market, decisions are made concerning maintenance, remodeling and demolition of existing buildings. While construction is adding new space to the supply, the forces of depreciation and attrition reduce the effective supply of space in the market. Long-range cycles of area prosperity or blight and the condition of the property influence decisions to invest money in maintenance or demolish the property.

Problems

Obtaining dependable and timely data on the market is often difficult. Detecting turning points in the cycle is not easy even with detailed, accurate data. Phases of a cycle are not consistent in length, making it difficult to predict when a new phase will begin. Overall market cycles may not influence the performance of individual properties.

Even so, there are distinct advantages to "thinking cyclically." Market participants who do not follow cycles tend to project current trends indefinitely into the future, leading to development and investment strategies that prove inappropriate when the trend inevitably turns. Those who understand cycles view market booms with caution and search for opportunities in down markets. They tend to resist excess optimism at the top of cycles and pessimism at the bottom of cycles.

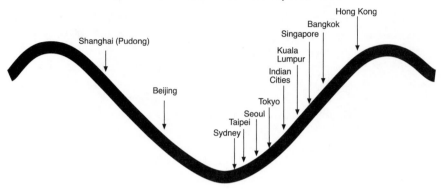

Asia Pacific Office Markets Cycle, 2006

Healthy recession?

Although rental income tends to deteriorate during downturns in the property market and in the economy, REITs have actually tended to be popular as "defensive" stocks during troubled times.

Like utilities, such as power firms or water companies, their income is relatively resilient to economic shocks, in comparison to say a technology company or a car manufacturer. For that reason, total returns from owning shares in REITs can still be healthy because of the capital gains from share price rises, even though income from properties owned by trusts might stagnate or fall.

In the US, most REIT stock prices gained between 40% and 50% in the three years after the onset of an economic recession in 2001, partly because investors sought a safe refuge from technology and other "growth" stocks following the bursting of the dot-com bubble.

In that period, property market fundamentals were extremely weak. As recession hit and began to empty office space, vacancy climbed to a crest of 17% in 2003 from 7.5% in 2000. Industrial property also suffered, with vacancies peaking at 12% at the end of 2003.

But the property market downturn in the early 2000s was nowhere near as severe as a crash in the late 1980s and early 1990s, when an explosion of construction gave way to high vacancy rates, pitifully low rents and poor demand for office and industrial space. Unlike a decade earlier, there were no mass bankruptcies and asset fire-sales.

REITs can take some of the credit. The US REIT market mushroomed as a result of the early 1990s crash as private landlords looked to offload their buildings. That ushered in a new era of professional management of real estate assets, and at the end of the 1990s, when an oversupply situation loomed, REITs began to pull back on their development activities, cushioning the blow of the property cycle downturn. In 2001, around 100 million square feet (920 million square meters) of new office space hit the US market, but in 2004 the figure had declined to about 40 million square feet. Industrial and warehouse construction also fell to about 90 million square feet in 2004 from 240 million square feet in 2001.

Low interest rates, at rock-bottom levels not seen for decades, also helped by allowing property prices to actually rise even at a time when rents were falling and vacancy rates were rising. Many investors were keen to take out cheap loans to acquire commercial buildings in the expectation of a market recovery, and the rush to buy worked as a self-fulfilling prophecy.

The fact property prices were rising made REITs attractive to investment from an asset valuation point of view, even if slipping rents were eating into dividend payments.

While most of Asia's REIT markets are too young to have tipped from a property cycle peak into a downturn, just as in the US, investors showed enthusiasm for REITs in Singapore and Japan at a time when property markets were just emerging from a sharp decline.

In Japan, for example, REITs experienced a three-year bull run to mid-2005, but then they went through a period of a few months when they underperformed shares in property developers as the economy ticked upwards. When investors began to believe a return to economic growth and an end to deflation was real, they preferred companies that could grow quickly, rather than the stable income of REITs. But when developer stocks began to be regarded as overvalued, REITs again became popular.

As discussed earlier, REITs can do quite a lot to soften the impact of a property market downturn, including making acquisitions, improving their buildings, streamlining operations and borrowing more at low interest rates to lift equity returns.

The opportunities for buying a building and improving it to add value can dramatically increase during the bottom of a property cycle as weaker market conditions adversely affect some assets more than others, creating the need for redevelopment or repositioning. In the most extreme cases, this could entail a complete overhaul of a building, for example, turning an office block into retail premises or even apartments, if office market vacancies are particularly high.

Redevelopment is often associated with higher risks resulting from matters such as planning approvals, cost overruns and production delays. But these risks can be mitigated by entering into forward contracts, whereby a REIT agrees to buy a building at a certain time and price, and possibly with a guaranteed number of tenants, from an intermediary who will take on the task of transforming on the building. Such arrangements are common in Japan.

Improving operations at existing buildings and newly acquired property should be a central part of any REIT management strategy. Leasing vacant or underused space is probably the most obvious way to add value, but the opportunity to do so is dependent on the property market cycle and the supply/demand balance. Office landlords can decide to lease space at very low rents, as they did in Hong Kong during the SARS outbreak in 2003, but that will drag down performance of a property when the property market stabilizes and begins to improve.

During the initial phases of a market recovery, new tenants may move in at the low rental rates over a period of several months, which means that effective rents will continue to fall even after the bottom of the property cycle is reached.

Good quality tenants and long-term leases are becoming highly valued in most developed property markets, with buildings often selling at a higher price if their tenancy profile is strong. And in a falling property market, when interest rates are likely to be low, a strong, durable property yield will be popular among investors.

For retail properties, getting the right tenant mix is crucial to bringing in the maximum number of shoppers, and sometimes a little shuffling of tenants can transform a shopping center. Other minor improvements might include, putting up better and more attractive signs to increase shopper traffic, and cutting costs—for example using energy-efficient light bulbs.

But investors can enjoy much bigger improvements on their returns if a REIT modifies its finances. If there is a wide spread between a REIT's property yield and interest rates, it would make sense to increase borrowing to boost return on equity. If a trust is making a lot of acquisitions, for which it needs to issue more shares, increasing borrowing will also soften the impact of share dilution.

Below is a model devised by Lehman Brothers analyst Yoshihito Oshima, based on the Japanese market, describing what could happen if a REIT increases its borrowing from 40% of assets to 50% during a 10-year period when it is also increasing its asset size by buying buildings.

The model assumes an interest rate of 1%, low by global standards but nothing new to Japan. The property yield (yield on net operating income) also remains steady, at 6%. But over the period, the acquisitions take the value of assets from 100 billion yen to 544.14 billion yen, while borrowing rises from 39.2 billion yen to 238.52 billion yen.

By gradually increasing borrowing, more of the REIT's increase in net operating income will filter down into dividends each year, producing annual growth of distribution per unit (DPU) of between 3.8% and 7.6%.

Distribution Per Unit Simulation as Leverage Increases for a REIT

	Year 0	Year 1	Year 2	Year 3	Year 4	Year 5	Year 6	Year 7	Year 8	Year 9	Year 10
Loan to value (LTV)	40%	41%	42%	43%	44%	45%	46%	47%	48%	49%	50%
Interest rate	1.0%	1.0%	1.0%	1.0%	1.0%	1.0%	1.0%	1.0%	1.0%	1.0%	1.0%
NOI yield	6.0%	6.0%	6.0%	6.0%	6.0%	6.0%	6.0%	6.0%	6.0%	6.0%	6.0%
Assets (billion yen)	100	125	156.25	195.31	244.14	294.14	344.14	394.14	444.14	494.14	544.14
Debt (billion yen)	39.20	49.41	62.42	79.03	100.20	122.33	144.88	167.83	191.13	214.77	238.52
NAV (billion yen)	58.8	71.10	86.20	104.76	127.53	149.51	170.08	189.25	207.06	223.54	238.72
NOI (billion yen)	6.00	7.50	9.38	11.72	14.65	17.65	20.65	23.65	26.65	29.65	32.65
Dividends (billion yen)	3.11	3.88	4.85	6.05	7.54	9.07	10.60	12.12	13.63	15.15	16.66
Distribution per unit (yen)	31,080	32,897	35,266	37,866	40,720	43,370	45,806	48,082	50,229	52,268	54,216
DPU growth (year on year)		5.9%	7.3%	7.4%	7.6%	6.6%	5.7%	5.0%	4.5%	4.1%	3.8%

Source: Lehman Brothers research (J-REITs: Yield Rush, by Joshihito Oshima, August 9, 2005)

REIT players—The manager

John Lim, chief executive officer of ARA Asset Management, the manager of Fortune REIT and Suntec REIT, talks about what a manager can do to boost investor returns when the property cycle peaks.

According to Lim, shopping malls have much more leeway for action than many types of property.

"You can improve the tenant mix and try to maximize efficiencies," Lim said in an interview in his office in the Suntec City complex in Singapore.

"Instead of leasing out to large tenants, you can cut down to smaller spaces and more tenants. Subdivide space and increase traffic flow. You can spend more on promotion."

Many in the REIT industry, impressed by CapitaMall Trust's success in turning offices into retail space, have suggested that other REITs carry out similar wholesale redevelopment to ratchet up revenues. But Lim said redeveloping sites was very complex, especially for Fortune REIT, because its shopping centers in crowded Hong Kong were attached to housing estates.

"You don't have to do sensational things like tear down an office block and build a shopping center. You can't do things like that in Hong Kong because suburban malls aren't standalone; they're part of integrated residential developments. It's technically difficult to tear something down and do something."

But entering lease agreements in which tenants shared a percentage of their revenues with the REIT was a viable option during times when a property cycle was peaking but the general economy was still healthy.

"Of course, rentals cannot grow forever," Lim said. "When you reach a peak there are ways of restructuring your leases. You can work with tenants, introduce base rent and turnover rent. If it's a restaurant with big volumes but smaller margins, it's a small percent. If it's a jewellery shop, the percentage would be higher. It varies from trade to trade. Then the tenants grow with the landlord and it can give shareholders a bigger return."

Lim said that investors often needed to be patient, because a property market upturn often took a couple of years to filter into rental streams.

"If there's a financial crisis, and the whole market is down 50%, REITs will come down like any other investment product," he said. "But in our experience, when interest rates rise, inflation rises and rentals also go up. Leases are of three years, so full rental growth is not immediate. It's in two- or three-year cycles."

Financial engineering

At the bottom of a property cycle and in the early stages of an upswing, REITs might also resort to financial engineering to try to lift yields for investors. There are various methods that can be employed where the aim is to do one thing: raise yield in the short term and pay for it later, when rents are higher. The desired effect is to even out the REIT's yields over a period of time, rather than have very low yields at the bottom of a property cycle that would dissuade people from investing and then very high yields when the property cycle is approaching its peak.

Financial engineering has often been frowned upon in Asia's REIT markets, with critics arguing that many of the tricks would backfire on investors if property markets fail to recover as predicted. In reply, bankers who structured REITs argued that financial engineering just needed to be properly understood.

One of the most popular strategies in Hong Kong's nascent REIT market was a "step-up" interest rate swap arrangement, employed by Prosperity REIT, Champion REIT and to a lesser extent Sunlight REIT as part of the structure of their IPOs.

Under a swap arrangement, a trust will pay a lump sum upfront and then fixed but gradually rising interest rates for a certain number of years to a counterparty. In return, that counterparty agrees to pay the trust's floating rate interest payments to its lenders. The effect is that a REIT can predict and manage its interest payments over the period of the swap arrangement, with those payments rising in tandem with forecast rent increases. This boosts the trust's yield at the beginning of the period, but limits dividend growth toward the end of the period. If rents do not rise as expected, there is a real danger that distributions can end up declining.

Furthermore, the upfront lump sum paid to the counterparty is regarded by some as a bit of a con. Because this sum is a prepayment it is amortized over the lifetime of the swap for accounting purposes. The charge is carried on the income statement of the REIT but then added back to the distributable income because the amortization doesn't involve any cash outlay. If the lump sum is funded by the money a REIT raises in its IPO, investors who subscribe for the issue are in effect funding a part of the distributions they will receive from the REIT. The headline distribution yield is actually not as attractive as it may seem, as part of the cash is coming from the investor's own pocket rather than operating income from the REIT's buildings.

Another popular method to shore up yield is for the seller of a property to the trust to accept payment in REIT units but with a "distribution entitlement waiver." The seller could be the sponsor, who retains a large share of the trust's units after its IPO, or the landlord of a single asset bought by the trust. If the seller agrees not to accept a dividend for a year or two, other shareholders will get a greater share of income, and therefore a bigger yield than usual. Obviously, when the seller takes up the right to a dividend, other investors will feel the pinch through dilution of income, but the idea is that by that time rents will rise sufficiently for no impact to be felt. However, question marks will be raised about the price the REIT is paying for a property if the former landlord is willing to accept a deal that involves missing out on dividends for a certain period.

Probably the riskiest deal a REIT can get into is a sale-leaseback agreement where the former landlord agrees to pay a high rent in return for a high purchase price for a building. The building may give a healthy original yield, but if for any reason the tenant has to vacate the premises, it will probably be impossible to find a new tenant willing to pay such an elevated rent. No REIT would subscribe to this as a tactic, but under investor pressure to grow the trust's portfolio, a manager might be persuaded to enter such a deal by a seller who is desperate for capital.

Among other structures used to lift yield, Hong Kong's Sunlight REIT gave investors a rental guarantee for almost three years to make up for leases that had not yet been negotiated to market rates. But obviously, there was a risk the yield would drop quickly after the guarantee expired.

Another, less dramatic, method to inflate yields in the short-term is for the REIT to pay its management firm in units rather than in cash. This can work as an incentive for the managers to perform well, but it gives the impression more cash is available for distribution than is really the case, while diluting the shareholding of investors.

The charts below show the extent to which financial engineering can be used to lift distributional yield.

The first shows a typical REIT with no financial engineering. Here the gross rental yield is 8.8%, before property operational expenses are deducted, to leave a net property yield of 7.8%. After trust expenses are deducted, the EBITDA/EV yield stands at 6.8%. The effect of debt leverage boosts the yield by 1.3 percentage points to 8.1%. Assuming a 100% payout, the investor will receive a 8.1% yield.

In the second scenario, a heavily financially engineered REIT starts out with a gross rental yield of only 2.6%, which falls to 2.2% once property expenses are paid. The upfront costs of the interest rate swaps bring the yield down to almost zero, before the difference between the cash and accounting interest costs on the interest rate arrangement adds 2.9 percentage points. The distributional yield rises to 3.2%, and then a distribution waiver by the sponsor, lifts the final distribution to other investors to 7.4%.

Champion was the first Hong Kong REIT of top-notch property, with developer Great Eagle Holdings Ltd. spinning off its Citibank Plaza office building, which housed several blue-chip companies, investment banks and law firms.

The trust sold its IPO at a yield of 5.45%, only a little over Hong Kong's 10-year bond yield of 4.9% at the time. But within two months its share price had fallen so much that it was trading at a 7.6% yield.

Conventional REIT

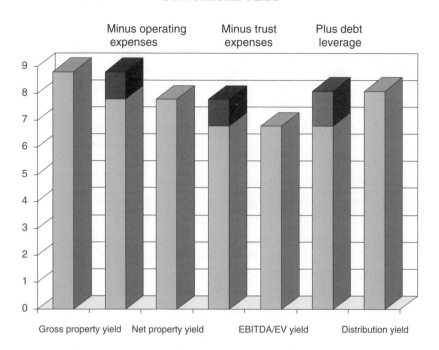

Financially Engineered REIT

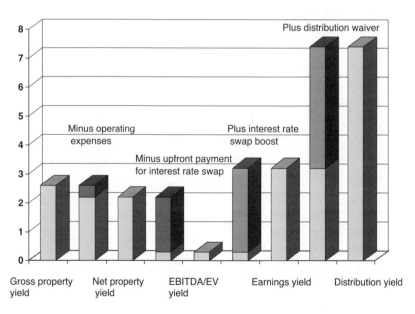

The deal faced several inconveniences, including a dip in stock markets across Asia and competition for investor attention from an $11 billion IPO by the Bank of China. But many investors were also deterred by Champion's financial engineering features, such as interest rate swaps and an initial waiver of rights to dividends by Great Eagle, which retained a 43.2% stake in the trust.

If Champion failed to grow by making good, yield-accretive acquisitions, its distributable income would start to slip within a couple of years, analysts predicted. And with its yield rising to 7.6%, finding an office block in Hong Kong with a higher yield than Champion would most probably be impossible.

Below is a table showing distribution projections for Champion REIT by Morgan Stanley analyst Kenny Tse *at the time of the IPOs*. The table shows fast-rising income for Champion in 2007 and 2008 because three-year leases signed during a property market slump around the time of the 2003 SARS outbreak would be renegotiated at prevailing market prices. But because Great Eagle would start to claim its dividend, and interest expenses through the swap arrangement started to rise, distribution per unit holds steady and then begins to drop off sharply in 2008.

Projections for Champion REIT

	2006	2007	2008	2009
Revenue (millions of HK$)	510.88	799.54	930.65	1,019.30
Expenses (millions of HK$)	−138.12	−159.13	−171.11	−178.31
Net property income (millions of HK$)	372.76	620.413	759.53	840.99
Distributable income (millions of HK$)	345.50	531.58	620.58	655.22
Units entitled to distributions	1,234,220	1,913,041	2,441,012	2,742,711
DPU (HK$)	0.2799	0.2779	0.2542	0.2389
Yield on IPO price of HK$5.10	5.5%	5.4%	5.0%	4.7%

Source: Morgan Stanley Research

REIT players—The investment banker

Investment bankers play a key role in structuring REITs and selling them to the public. They will arrange any financial engineering that the trust requires, and organize loans or bond issuance. They also arrange the initial public offering, possibly underwriting the deal as well—buying shares if they are not bought by investors. Of course, investment bankers receive fees for their work, and as such, they are some of the prime proponents of REITs, constantly marketing them as a good idea to landlords and investors alike. You will probably never hear a property investment banker talking down REITs.

Edmund Ho, head of property investment banking at Citigroup in Hong Kong, worked on the Champion REIT, which became associated with a downturn in Hong Kong's REIT market in May 2006. Many bankers and analysts said the Champion REIT overdosed on financial engineering, putting many investors off. But Ho was unrepentant.

"It's because the market valuation suggested 13,000 (Hong Kong dollars) per square foot, but the yield is low because they signed up all the leases during SARS or way back when the rental was still low," he said. "If they were to sell the property on the market they would achieve 13,000, so when we sell it to a REIT we have to sell at 13,000."

The financial engineering was needed because investors demanded a decent yield, and would not accept Champion's prevailing net property yield of just 2% before positive rental reversion started to kick in, Ho said.

"When you think of it from the investors' perspective, they want some yield, but the yield is low," he said. "So how do we do it? We ask the sponsor, if you want this you need to give the investors some benefit. So you do it using some structuring to provide some additional dividend to investors. And we sold it on that basis."

Ho blamed poor stock market conditions for the lackluster response to Champion's IPO and its subsequent share price fall.

"The market turned around quite quickly at that time and we were happy that it was kept on," Ho said. "It was fully booked, fully covered. Investors still bought into it at that time, despite the beginning of a correction. So we're not unhappy."

"Obviously the share price performance afterwards was not exciting and that I think was more for market reasons," he said. "It wasn't just Champion that fell, everything fell."

But would Hong Kong's REIT market now just become the domain of institutional investors who better understood financial engineering? Or would individual investors still be tempted?

"I think there are different reasons for each of them to invest into REITs," Ho said. "For institutional investors, they are more fundamental-driven. For retail, they are more followers. They look at the return compared to their investments now. It's a different angle."

Ho said investors should concentrate on the market value of Champion REIT's Citibank Plaza building.

"You look at valuation, 13,000 (Hong Kong dollars), is it cheap, is it fair, is it expensive? You make a judgment," he said. "You should always look at the underlying valuation at the end, because you're getting 100 percent of the cash flow."

Many analysts were also skeptical about Champion because it only had one building, and its lack of diversity would make it a risky prospect during an economic decline. But Ho rejected that argument, touting the high quality of Citibank Plaza.

"The single asset element…I wouldn't think it is riskier because it's a prime property and rises with the economy," Ho said. "Even if I have 10 properties in Central we're exposed to the same risk."

"I think what you need to look at is the tenant space, the spread of tenants. Do you have one single tenant, or 10 or 100? Citiplaza has many tenants, although Citigroup is one of the larger ones. Of course if one of them goes it is a risk, but you can easily replenish it, because it's a prime location."

Several people at rival banks had criticized the bankers working on Champion for overdoing the financial engineering and causing disruption in Hong Kong's REIT market.

"They always say that because they're not involved in the deal. So I normally don't worry about that. And frankly, if I can move the market like that, I'm really important. I'd love to be able to move the market," he said, tongue firmly lodged in cheek.

Risk in an upward cycle

Obviously, in the upward part of a property cycle, REITs should perform well, as property values and rents rise.

But for an investor in a trust, it is not all plain sailing. In an economic upturn, other, perhaps more exciting and riskier, investments will become flavor of the month, so REITs could end up underperforming the wider stock market. More fundamentally, when an economy is growing, interest rates are also likely to rise because the theory of supply and demand dictate that a higher need for money for investment pushes up the cost of borrowing and because central banks are likely to want to cut money supply to curb inflation.

The impact of rising interest rates is twofold: If bond yields and bank deposit interest rates climb, the attraction of REITs as a high-yielding investment can diminish in comparison; a trust can also suffer from higher costs, as interest repayments on its debt rise, and bite into the dividend it can pay to investors.

The model below, for a hypothetical Japanese REIT, shows what can happen to dividends if interest rates rise from 1% to 3% over a 10-year period. The level of borrowing remains steady at 40% of assets, but acquisitions lift the asset size fairly rapidly. However, the cost of paying interest on a growing value of debt rises, and by the fifth year of interest rate rises, distribution per unit begins to decline.

Simulation for Impact of Interest Rate Rise on DPU

	Year 0	Year 1	Year 2	Year 3	Year 4	Year 5	Year 6	Year 7	Year 8	Year 9	Year 10
Loan to value (LTV)	40%	40%	40%	40%	40%	40%	40%	40%	40%	40%	40%
Interest rate	1.0%	1.2%	1.4%	1.6%	1.8%	2.0%	2.2%	2.4%	2.6%	2.8%	3.0%
NOI yield	6.0%	6.0%	6.0%	6.0%	6.0%	6.0%	6.0%	6.0%	6.0%	6.0%	6.0%
Assets (billion yen)	100	125	156.25	195.31	244.14	294.14	344.14	394.14	444.14	494.14	544.14
Debt (billion yen)	39.20	48.20	59.45	73.51	91.09	108.74	125.98	142.83	159.28	175.33	190.97
NAV (billion yen)	58.8	72.30	89.18	110.27	136.64	163.11	188.98	214.25	238.92	262.99	286.46
NOI (billion yen)	6.00	7.50	9.38	11.72	14.65	17.65	20.65	23.65	26.65	29.65	32.65
Dividends (billion yen)	3.11	3.80	4.64	5.66	6.91	8.12	9.27	10.37	11.40	12.39	13.32
Distribution per unit (yen)	31,080	31,789	32,487	32,767	32,598	31,906	30,839	29,516	28,024	26,425	24,768
DPU growth (year on year)		3.2%	3.2%	1.8%	0.5%	−1.1%	−2.3%	−3.3%	−4.1%	−4.7%	−5.3%

Source: Lehman Brothers research

Simulation for Share Price Movements

	Year 0	Year 1	Year 2	Year 3	Year 4	Year 5	Year 6	Year 7	Year 8	Year 9	Year 10
Expected yield	3.5%	3.7%	3.9%	4.1%	4.3%	4.5%	4.7%	4.9%	5.1%	5.3%	5.5%
NOI (billion yen)	6.00	7.50	9.38	11.72	14.65	17.65	20.65	23.65	26.65	29.65	32.65
Share price (yen)	823,200	859,126	833,007	799,191	758,101	709,013	656,144	602,373	549,484	498,580	450,324
Share price growth (year on year)		4.4%	−3.0%	−4.1%	−5.1%	−6.5%	−7.5%	−8.2%	−8.8%	−9.3%	−9.7%

Source: Lehman Brothers research

At the same time, investors are likely to expect a much higher yield to compensate for the higher interest rates. If dividend growth is not sufficient, a REIT's share price must fall to achieve the higher expected yield. In the model, the share price falls to 450,324 yen from 823,200 yen, as investors demand a 5.5%

yield in year 10, when interest rates are 3%. A spread of 3.5 percentage points between interest rates and the REIT yield is assumed throughout the period.

Cutting interest rate risk

In real life, no trust would allow such a situation to develop. Managers will make sure a high proportion of borrowing is at fixed rates and therefore immune to sharp and unexpected rises in interest rates. Then, the main concern is whether trusts have staggered their debt maturities—the lifespan of a loan—so that all the borrowings do not need to be refinanced at once, which would increase the risk of suddenly being saddled with a much higher average interest cost.

Although REIT borrowing in Asia has been limited to a relatively low level by gearing restrictions imposed by regulators, trusts may be more prone than other types of businesses to cash crunches because they are obliged to pay out a high majority of their net income as dividends. As trusts are left little room to build up funds to deal with any emergencies related to debt repayment, analysts say looking at gearing levels alone is not enough to give a clear impression of the ability of a trust to pay their interest costs. Fitch Ratings, for example, urges investors to watch EBITDA (earnings before interest, tax, depreciation and amortization)/interest coverage, with a higher ratio indicating a greater ability to keep up debt payments in a higher interest rate environment. Other ratios to look out for include unencumbered assets/unsecured debt, and unencumbered net operating income/unsecured interest expenses.

The difference between secured and unsecured debt is important because of their different treatment of a REIT's assets. Secured debt, such as a bank loan and commercial mortgage-backed securities (CMBS), require a REIT's property as collateral. Bonds are unsecured, which means that assets remain "unencumbered"—a REIT is free to modify them without seeking permission from lenders, and more importantly can sell them if it wishes.

Asian REITs typically fund their initial creation through short-term bridging loans, repaid by the proceeds of IPO shares, plus term loans or CMBS. A similar process occurs when they want to buy buildings later. Hong Kong trusts have preferred bank loans, while Singapore trusts have opted for CMBS issuance, mostly denominated in euros.

But a popular $412 million bond issue by Hong Kong's Link REIT in mid-2006 was likely to encourage other Asian property trusts to issue more unsecured debt to help reduce risk.

Issuing unsecured bonds would free up bank credit lines for quick-fire acquisitions needed to lift returns for equity investors. It would also allow

REITs to widen their pool of lenders, providing financial flexibility, and give managers freedom to sell buildings if they needed to, maybe to raise funds to tackle an emergency or as part of a strategic move to reshuffle assets.

"As REITs evolve and want to redevelop or trade assets, they will find that the secured financing will be an impediment," said Craig Parker, Melbourne-based director at ratings agency Standard & Poor's.[4] "They'll move gradually to an unsecured platform."

But REITs, under pressure to pay high dividends, might still prefer traditional funding if interest costs are lower.

"At the end of the day, it depends on the all-in costs and plans of the REIT," said Richard Lai, chief financial officer of Singapore-based Mapletree Logistic Trust.[5] But Lai wanted freedom to borrow more, such as in the US and Australian markets where there were no limits on gearing. That would make it easier to drive through acquisitions without first going to the equity market to raise capital.

"Regulators should give more room to REIT managers to decide whether to take on more debt on their books," he said. "In jurisdictions where the time to market is longer, having more debt headroom is useful."

Below is a snapshot in early 2006 of the debt profiles of selected Singapore and Hong Kong REITs.

	Prosperity (HK)	GZI (HK)	CapitaMall Trust (Sg)	Suntec (Sg)	Ascendas (Sg)	CapitaCommercial Trust (Sg)
Secured financing (%)	100	100	100	100	77	88
Main source of financing	Bank loan	Bank loan	CMBS	CMBS	CMBS	CMBS
Leverage (%)	39.1	31.4	31.4	39.1	31.6	30.6
EBITDA/ interest coverage	4.4	6.1	4.3	3.7	5.6	4.6
% of debt at fixed rate	93.2	100	100	50	61.9	88

Source: Fitch Ratings

Inflation

Another worry for investors in times of economic growth is whether price inflation in the wider economy will make REITs unattractive relative to other investments, or might even outpace growth in rental income, thereby reducing how much dividends are worth in relative terms.

Much research has shown that inflation and stock prices have a negative relationship, with rising inflation hitting stock prices because investors are afraid of the impact of higher prices on the macro-economy: investment in the economy and trade tend to suffer because of the uncertainty. REITs, if treated as normal stocks, could decline in price.

But analysts point to evidence that in the established US market, REITs have diverged over time from average stock behavior, with investors increasingly viewing the securities as direct investment in property, which has inflation-hedging characteristics. Results from US REITs back this up, indicating that over an extended period dividend growth outstrips inflation rates, although in occasional years income from REITs has fallen behind.

As the chart below shows, in the decade to 2003, growth in dividends more than compensated for inflation as measured by the consumer price index (CPI) in every year but one. In 1998, at a peak in the property cycle, the difference was at its widest, with average REIT dividend growth touching 8% in a year when the CPI hovered around 1.5%. In 2002, when the property market was in a trough, dividends rose nearly 2% from the previous year, but consumer prices were up 2.75%.

Average Annual Dividend Growth Per Share and Consumer Price Index

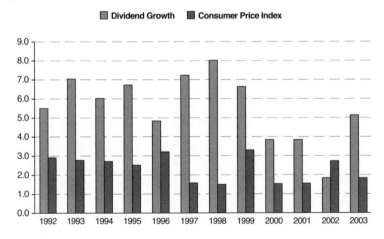

Source: NAREIT

Equity REIT Price Index Versus CPI, Monthly, 1985–2005

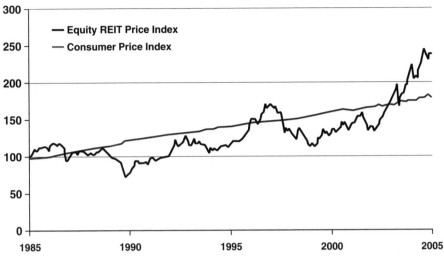

Indexed at December 1985 = 100.0

Source: NAREIT

During this period, inflation was primarily a reflection of the state of the economy, higher when the economy was healthy and REITs were prospering.

In times of growth, companies expand and hire more people, who fill up office space and produce more goods that need more warehouse space. Lower unemployment means more people could rent apartments and they could travel more, raising demand for hotel rooms. Higher prices, coupled with rising interest rates to curb inflation, also tend to put developers off starting new projects, which translates into rising occupancy at existing buildings and allows landlords to charge more.

Because the cost of construction rises, the property market marks up the price of existing buildings, so REIT valuations also rise, which can boost their share prices and therefore could help lift total returns for investors.

Because they are income paying investments, REITs are often compared with bonds, which will almost always suffer in times of rising inflation because the interest they pay to investors will be worth relatively less over time.

However, REITs are much more resilient. Unlike bonds, the payments property trusts make to investors are not fixed, but can, and usually will, rise sufficiently to compensate for higher inflation. While investors tend to mark down bond prices during inflationary and high-interest-rate periods because they demand a higher yield, there is often no need to downgrade the value of a REIT share. The chart above shows that this was certainly the case for the US

REIT market, with share prices keeping pace with the consumer price index between 1985 and 2005.

This trait was also appreciated by market players in Asia in the early 2000s, as the region emerged from post-economic crisis deflation into a period of inflation, fuelled partly by government spending on infrastructure.

"For reaching out for yield and a conservative inflation hedge, they're becoming quite popular," Desmond Soon, a bond fund manager at Pacific Asset Management in Singapore, said of the emerging REIT market.[6]

But Soon added that the Asian REIT market was not yet big enough for major investors to use as a proper inflation-hedging tactic, and warned traditional bond investors that investing in REITs was not straightforward.

"It's small steps at the moment. The market's a bit small for institutional demand," he said. "They (investors) have to understand that cashflows depend on location, the type of property, the state of the economy and the property market, and make sure the REITs are not overvalued."

However, the positive correlation between REIT dividends and inflation might break down if inflation is driven upward not by a healthy economy but by other factors, such as a spike in oil prices.

Researchers have created models that suggest that real returns from REITs could suffer during times of "unexpected" inflation because property managers cannot respond quickly enough.[7] Property trusts would be hamstrung by long-term lease and loan arrangements that they would find difficult to alter, and which were planned with only "expected" inflation in mind.

REIT players—The manager

Franklin Heng, a former investment banker, is chief executive officer at Pacific Star, which manages MEAG Prime REIT, a trust that listed on the Singapore stock market in late 2005. At its IPO, Prime REIT offered a share of two shopping malls in central Singapore, Ngee Ann City and Wisma Atria.

Heng explains how he expects to beat property cycles by expanding Prime REIT to include shopping malls and offices across Asia.

"We want to be in Singapore and outside, concentrating on prime retail and office," Heng said. "We want to be in different cities and different sectors on the property clock. We could buy offices in Japan and retail in Seoul, tapping into different markets and buying at the right point in the cycle. I hope that five or 10 years down the road, we can deliver prime regional commercial assets."

Investors would value Prime REIT's shares higher than other REITs if it could deliver a successful regional strategy, as they had done with Australian REIT Westfield, which expanded fast globally, he said.

"At our IPO we stated our strategy clearly; we want to be a regional player," Heng said. "We want to create a Westfield, and extrapolate our skill sets to many cities. That will command a premium over time, there's no such product on the market."

To soften the blow of any downturn in the property cycle, Prime REIT would consider extending leases past the typical three years, he said. "Some tenants are more comfortable if there is a longer tenancy and we will consider them. But we'll stay with the industry average unless there's a shortening in the property cycle or a lengthening. It depends on the outlook and our perspective."

But Heng said that top-notch buildings, such as Ngee Ann City and Wisma Atria, are fairly recession-proof compared with other types of assets.

"You have to look at risks very carefully," he said. "These two buildings have undergone multiple recessions: The 1986 crash, the Gulf war, the 1997 crisis, the dot-com crash, September 11, SARS in 2003. But occupancy has never dropped below 90%. They are well located with a direct link to one of the busiest MRT (underground railway) stations. We call this Prime REIT because we're focusing on prime locations, prime buildings and prime partners."

In an economic downturn, industrial and logistics REITs such as Ascendas and Mapletree would suffer more, Heng said.

"People say you don't have a lot of growth because the properties are already well managed," he said. "But I say that with these properties you can sleep well at night. If there's another Asian crisis I don't know if Ascendas or Mapletree can survive, because that'll be the first sector to hollow out. There's a focus on the growth of their asset base, but industrial and logistics properties have a high yield because they're more risky. The tenants are more risky. Investors are looking at growth more than the underlying quality of the assets."

Endnotes

1 "Asia property gets less risky but expensive," by Dominic Whiting, Reuters, July 13, 2006.
2 Jones Lang LaSalle Real Estate Transparency report 2006.
3 "Real Estate Cycles: Riding the ups and downs," by Jack Harris, Tierra Grande, July 2000, reprinted with permission from Texas A&M University.
4 "Asian REITs seen looking more to unsecured debt," by Umesh Desai, Reuters, July 21, 2006.

5   *Ibid.*
6   "Asian property trusts a growing inflation hedge," by Dominic Whiting, Reuters, March 17, 2005.
7   "REIT Investments and Hedging Against Inflation," by Bahram Adrangi and Arjun Chatrath, *Journal Real Estate Portfolio Management*, May–August 2004.

Houses and hotels—
Assembling a portfolio

Just as holding a REIT is a very good proxy for directly owning property, it can also be a comfortable fit for long-term investment purposes, such as for a personal pension plan. Just as a house or apartment, rented out, can provide enough for a retirement income, or at least a decent supplementary income, the same can be true for investing in a REIT.

Take a hypothetical example of a 30-year old woman who invested $10,000 in Australia's first listed property trust, General Property Trust, in 1971. If she ploughed back all her dividends into buying more shares, she could have retired at the age of 65, in 2006, with an accumulated $1,174,390 worth of shares over 35 years. That represents a compound annual return of 14.7%.

In 2006, General Property Trust was yielding about 6%. So the woman would receive a dividend yield of $70,463—enough for a comfortable lifestyle, while still holding more than a million dollars worth of property. Alternatively, she could sell the shares and live off the proceeds.

Many Asian REITs have surpassed those levels of returns in their early, high-growth, years. For example, Singapore REITs gave on average an annual return of 29.45% between mid-2002 and November 2005. But as a better indicator of their long-term potential, US REITs have offered similar returns to General Property Trust, with a compound annual return of nearly 13% between 1971 and 2003.

But REITs are not just useful as very long-term investments. By including them in a multi-asset portfolio, an investor can take advantage of their relatively low volatility and low correlation to other assets in order to reduce risk.

Volatility, which is measured by standard deviation—the dispersion of a set of data from its mean, is usually regarded as something to avoid as it represents the potential for an investment to miss its expected returns. The more spread apart the data is (a higher standard deviation), the higher the uncertainty in the amount of returns and therefore the greater the risk.

A study by JPMorgan Private Bank illustrates this.[1] Take two $10 million portfolios that are originally expected to give a return of 8%, but one travels a more erratic path than the other. The lower volatility portfolio, which has potential to swing up to 8% in either direction, has a higher median compound return than the other portfolio, which has the potential to move 12% in either direction.

In fact, the less volatile portfolio would be worth $200,000 more, on average, after five years, $700,000 more after 10 years and $1.6 million more after 15 years, according to the bank.

As already discussed, REITs tend to be less volatile than other stocks because of their element of steady income and valuation. Property markets are fairly predictable because supply can be foreseen far in advance and demand shifts slower than for most other products, so barring a dramatic change in economic circumstances, rents and the value of buildings should be stable.

And Asian REITs have already shown that they are less volatile than comparable investments as measured by standard deviation.

In its first three years, Singapore's REIT market displayed a standard deviation of 12.7%, compared with a 21% standard deviation for Singapore property company stocks, according to Henderson Global Investors. The Japanese REIT market's standard deviation was 12.9% in its first two years, compared with 26.2% for Japanese property stocks in the period. For Korean REITs the figure was just 4.5%, but mostly because of the relatively illiquid nature of the investments, compared with 32.8% for Korean construction stocks in roughly four years from early 2002.

Not only is this inherent low volatility helpful for creating the right blend in a portfolio of investments, the fact that REITs are not often correlated with other investments will also decrease the overall volatility of a mixed portfolio.

Put simply, it is best not to put all your eggs in one basket, and REITs offer an extra component to the usual mix of stocks, bonds and cash.

If an investor put all her money in the stock of one company, which was expected to give 8% over a certain period, she would be exposing herself to full risk. If something happened to damage that investment, (for example an economic downturn, a natural disaster or bad company management) the investor would suffer the whole impact. But if it were possible to split the investments between two assets, both of which gave 8% returns over a certain period but which always moved in opposite directions to each other, she would be exposed to zero risk. When one investment did badly, the other would compensate.

The following table shows how global REIT returns, as represented by the EPRA/NAREIT index, correlate with returns on global stocks (MSCI World index), global bonds (Citigroup World Global Bond index) and US stocks (S&P/TSX composite index) over a 15-year period to the end of 2005. REITs are positively, but lowly, correlated with the other assets classes.

Table 1: **Correlations of Global Asset Classes 1990–2005**

	15-year average annualized total return (%)	Correlation to EPRA/NAREIT index
EPRA/NAREIT index	11.5	1.0
MSCI World index	8.6	0.6
Citigroup World Global Bond index	7.0	0.2
S&P/TSX composite index	10.9	0.5

Source: NAREIT

In the case of US assets, the correlation between REITs, stocks and bonds is even lower. And as the next two tables illustrate, the correlation has decreased over time as investors gradually treated REITs differently as they realized the securities had their own, separate, characteristics. Over 20 years, the correlation between REITs, as measured by the NAREIT equity index, and stocks in the S&P 500 index, stood at 0.50, but in the last decade of that period, the correlation was only 0.29. REITs and bond returns were hardly related at all in the 10 years from 1995.

But Table 4 suggests that an investor can also reduce volatility of a portfolio through geographical diversification within the allocation given to REITs. Correlations between property shares in different regions are low mostly because of differences in property market cycles.

An "asset allocation tool" created by US property-focused fund management firm Cohen & Steers Capital Management, Inc., demonstrates clearly that the inclusion of US REITs in a mixed portfolio of stocks and bonds has helped to reduce volatility and also boost returns.

Table 2: Correlation of US Assets March 1975–March 2005

	NAREIT	S&P 500	Merrill Lynch Government/Corporate bonds
NAREIT equity index	1.0	0.50	0.20
S&P 500		1.0	0.23
Merrill Lynch Government/Corporate bond index			1.0

Source: NAREIT

Table 3: Correlation of US Assets March 1995–March 2005

	NAREIT	S&P 500	Merrill Lynch Government/Corporate bonds
NAREIT equity index	1.0	0.29	0.07
S&P 500		1.0	−0.06
Merrill Lynch Government/Corporate bond index			1.0

Source: NAREIT

Table 4: Correlation of Global Listed Property Markets 1993–2005

	North America	Europe	Asia	Australia
North America	1.0	0.49	0.33	0.40
Europe		1.0	0.34	0.51
Asia			1.0	0.43
Australia				1.0

Source: NAREIT

The models used market data over a five-year period from 2001 to 2006, and over a 10-year period from 1996-2006, and compared returns and risk for the following indices:

S&P 500

An unmanaged index of 500 large capitalization companies listed in the US representing a variety of industries.

MSCI EAFE

The Morgan Stanley Capital International EAFE Index represents the performance of 900 companies whose stock is listed on stock exchanges located in Europe, Australia and Asia.

Russell 2000 Index

An index of the 2,000 smallest companies in the Russell 3000 Index, a commonly used measure of US small stock performance.

Citigroup Broad Investment Grade Index

An index designed to reflect the performance of investment-grade, US government and domestic corporate bonds.

The NAREIT Equity Index

An unmanaged, market capitalization weighted index of all US publicly traded equity REITs that have 75% or more of their gross invested book assets invested directly or indirectly in the equity ownership of real estate.

In the following model portfolios, which compare different allocations to the five types of investments including REITS, volatility is represented by standard deviation.

Because US REITs outperformed other investments over the period examined, the model portfolios show that the higher the allocation to REITs, the higher the returns. Adding REITs will also reduce risk, as measured by volatility, but this impact starts to wear thin when the allocation reaches 20% or 30%. The 10-year data show that a portfolio starts getting more risky again between a 30% and 50% weighting for REITs, whereas the five-year data show that the inflection point lies around the 20% mark.

In general, US fund managers and analysts have tended to say a 15-20% allocation to REITs is wise in a mixed portfolio. This level of exposure to physical property is slowly being adopted by long-term institutional investors such as pension funds, with Dutch and German funds in particular leading the way.

In Asia, REIT markets are growing quickly but are still much smaller than that of the United States, so some investment advisors are suggesting lower allocations to REITs.

Portfolio	Case A	Case B	Case C	Case D	Case E	Case F
S&P 500 large cap	50	50	46	43	31	28
Russell small cap	10	10	8	7	5	3
Citigroup bonds	30	25	22	19	13	9
MSCI EAFE	10	5	4	3	1	0
NAREIT equity	0	10	20	30	50	60
1996–2006						
Volatility	10.63	10.56	10.43	10.16	10.51	10.99
Annual return	8.05	8.92	9.82	10.49	11.98	12.68
2001–2006						
Volatility	9.42	7.6	7.6	9.79	10.65	11.28
Annual return	5.0	9.75	9.75	8.97	11.88	13.33

Source: Cohen and Steers

REIT players—The investment advisor

Sanjay Lodha is a senior investment advisor at one of Switzerland's largest private banks, 200-year-old Pictet & Cie, which manages investments for wealthy individuals as well as institutions.

Lodha, who moved to Pictet's Hong Kong office in January 2005 after a stint as a portfolio manager in Montreal, Canada, believes that Asian REITs will become increasingly popular among investors. But allocations will vary according to familiarity with the region's property markets.

"Overall exposure to Asian financial markets is low, but for Asians this is home," Lodha said. "A European investor will maybe have a 10 to 12% exposure to Asia and maybe just two percent in Asian REITs. But if you're Asian, you might have six, seven, or eight percent in REITs," he said.

"I believe the REIT market will take time," he said. "A trend that will pan out over five or 10 years is that there will be an increased level of interest in financial securities that provide exposure to real estate in Asia."

Lodha recommends that investors with a low-risk agenda, especially those who would normally like bonds, take a close look at Asian REITs.

"Usually I wouldn't recommend too high an exposure because you do have asset classes with higher return-risk profiles," he said. "But for a fixed-income type of investor, REITs would be an asset class of choice. It provides diversification, and increases stability of returns. Why would you invest in fixed income? With bonds you always have the risk that interest rates will go against you. There's some amount of stability and capital protection. But given that REITs have the ability to rise in valuation, they provide the best of both worlds."

Lodha particularly likes the Singapore REIT market, but believes that property trusts would gain ground across the region and make good investments because the fundamentals of the property markets were so positive.

"As people get an easier way to gain exposure to real estate, you'll find a lot of money chasing this and it will improve valuations of REITs," Lodha said.

Giving an example of trends in his native India, Lodha said Asia's property markets often had more to offer than markets in developed countries.

"In Asia, overall demand for real estate is only going to improve," Lodha said. "There's a density of population that is very high compared to the rest of the world.

"In India, five years back you couldn't take a loan to buy property," he said. "My father couldn't buy a property unless he had cash. But now you can get credit and as more people can afford to buy property, demand will go up.

"My father was one of seven sons living together, but now in India the family is going nuclear," he said. "Then there's migration from rural areas to urban areas. There's very little downside in property in India compared to the US."

Asia's *nouveau riche*—Future buyers of REITs

Real estate remains the leading alternative investment (to stocks and bonds) for the world's wealthy, despite all the talk about private equity, hedge funds and commodities, private bankers say. For example, Credit Suisse's clients have on average 15% to 20% of their assets in real estate, which compares with 5% to 7% in private equity, hedge funds and structured products.

And REITs are becoming the investment product of choice.

"The mass affluent—those with up to $30 million in investible assets—tend to use REITs or funds of real estate funds, while the even wealthier will be more inclined toward direct investments," said Christopher Meares, chief executive of HSBC Private Bank UK, Channel Islands & Luxembourg.[2]

Asia is also minting millionaires at a faster pace than any other region in the world, a trend that will boost demand for REITs in the region. Here are some figures about Asia's wealthy:

- In 2005, the Asia-Pacific region had 2.4 million high-net-worth individuals—people with more than $1 million in financial assets excluding their homes—with total financial wealth of $7.6 trillion, according to a survey by Merrill Lynch and consultants Capgemini.

- Globally, there were 8.7 million millionaires, worth $33.3 trillion.
- China had 320,000 wealthy individuals in 2005, compared with India's 83,000. In 2005, the number of wealthy grew fastest in South Korea (21.3%) and India (19.3%).
- In Asia, 16,800 people are included in the ranks of ultra-rich, those with more than $30 million in financial assets. That made up about one-fifth of the world's ultra-rich.
- Asia's 115 billionaires are worth a collective $364 billion, according to *Forbes* magazine. India's 23 billionaires are worth nearly $100 billion, and China's 10 billionaires are worth $12 billion.
- British bank Barclays plc forecast in March 2006 that within three years, high-net-worth clients in India would have assets of $256 billion, while in China the figure would be $150 billion.
- While North America is the most popular region for investment, millionaires are increasing their exposure to Asia at North America's expense. In 2005, North America attracted 44% of investments by high-net-worth individuals, compared with 46% in 2004, while the share of Asia rose from 21% to 23%.

The REIT selection process

When selecting investments, professional fund managers will often talk about taking either a "top-down" or a "bottom-up" approach, and these methods should also be considered by individual investors.

In a top-down strategy, investors will firstly try to narrow down their "investible universe"—assets they would consider investing in—before making their choices. This could entail discounting certain regions or countries that are deemed too risky or avoiding certain economic sectors because their outlook is poor. This approach is often used as there are simply too many individual investment options to look at in depth, and because macro-issues, such as political and economic instability, can affect whole markets, however good a particular investment looks.

With a bottom-up strategy, investors will trawl through all the different investment options, looking for factors they like. That could be good management, a company with a new innovation, or a stock with a particularly low valuation. The main argument for this method is that investors often miss out on real gems if they tar whole countries or economic sectors with the same broad brush. While Asia's REIT markets are in their nascent phase, with quite a small number of trusts, this approach is viable.

A top-down bias to investing in Asian property securities has been adopted by fund management firm Henderson Global Investors, which uses economic outlooks, views on currencies, property cycle projections and stock valuations to narrow the investment choices down to 75 stocks (including REITs) from 150.

Henderson's fund managers will then use these opinions to establish different allocations, or "weightings" for particular countries and property sectors that will divide the 75 stocks, before putting together a portfolio of 30 to 40 stocks based on which meet the fund's risk and return objectives.

Henderson Global Investors Investment Process

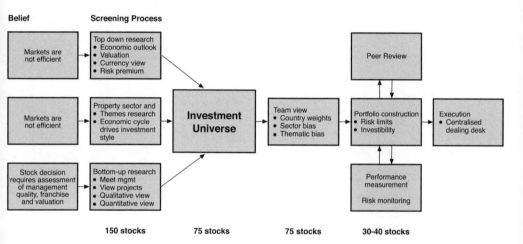

Source: Henderson Global Investors

In contrast, Australian fund management firm MacarthurCook, which is also working to set up and manage REITs in Asia, follows a bottom-up approach for a fund listed in the United States which invests in Asian property, including REITs.

In its approach, the MacarthurCook fund firstly gathers all the investment options, including unlisted property funds, listed property companies and REITs, and assesses "micro" factors such as the skills of the manager, the quality of properties, financial strength and the business model. Analysts then move to comparative valuations, before drawing up a list of recommended investments. Only then are "macro" elements brought in, with sector and geographical risks and allocations discussed.

1. Investment ideas	2. Analyst review			3. Portfolio construction	
REITs	*Quality tests*	*valuation*	*investment recommendation report and peer discussion*	*Weighting in portfolio*	*Ongoing review*
listed property-related companies	skills of manager			risk control parameters	still meeting income and capital growth expectations?
	quality of fund			sector allocation	
wholesale property fund	quality of properties			geographic diversification	relative attractiveness to alternative
unlisted property trusts/ syndicatess	debt management skills			target income yield	investment ideas
	commitment to income growth			target tax advantage component	
	financial strength				
	proven management				
	business model strength				

As of June 30, 2006, the fund was split along sector and geographical lines as follows:

Sector	
Diversified	52%
Retail	17%
Office	13%
Other	9%
Short-term investments	9%

Country/territory	
Japan	39%
Hong Kong	27%
Australia	17%
Other	8%
Short-term investments	9%

In mid-2006, at a time when the Japanese economy was showing signs of a sustained rebound after a decade of stagnation, property developers were generally in favor because they were seen as a more aggressive play on the country's economic upturn than REITs. Not only did major property developers own big portfolios of buildings, which were raising their rents steeply, they could also build the offices and apartments that were in demand. REITs were also seen as fairly fully valued after a good four-year run, although they were still very popular because of the rising rents.

The MacarthurCook fund's portfolio reflected these ideas, with sizeable holdings in Japan's major property firms, Mitsubishi Estate Co., Ltd., Mitsui Fudosan Co., Ltd. and Sumitomo Realty & Development Co., Ltd., as well as a much smaller investment in the Tokyu REIT, a property trust which owned offices in the Japanese capital.

The fund's exposures to Singapore and Hong Kong were more weighted towards REITs. In Singapore, it held developer CapitaLand Ltd., a major sponsor of REITs, as well as the Mapletree Logistics Trust, a REIT specializing in warehouses across Asia, and the retail-focused Frasers Centrepoint Trust.

In Hong Kong, the fund favored Champion REIT, which owned the Citibank Plaza building in the Central district, as well as the trust's sponsor and major shareholder, Great Eagle Holdings Ltd.. It also owned a stake in GZI REIT, of Chinese shopping malls, as well as stakes in Hong Kong's big two developers, Cheung Kong (Holdings) and Sun Hung Kai Properties.

Interestingly, the fund's Australian allocation included a stake in the Babcock and Brown Japan Property Trust of Tokyo assets, as well as General Property Trust among other Australian REITs. In Thailand, it took a stake in retailer Central Pattana PCL, which had launched a REIT and was interested in spinning off more of its shopping malls and office buildings into the trust.

Fund managers have also tried various ways to fuse the top-down and bottom-up approaches to try to glean the best of both methods, and Invesco, a US-based fund management firm whose global real estate securities funds invest in Asian REITs, is one such example.

The firm starts with a "fundamentals analysis," feeding its views on about 400 property securities from around the world, including REITs, to come up with a points system, which ranks each security from zero to 10. Only a ranking of five or over will qualify a security for consideration, and around one-third of the 400 choices are usually eliminated at this stage.

The fundamentals analysis has three components:

A top-down market cycle analysis, taking into account the economic and demographic factors affecting metropolitan and regional property markets, commands a 40% weighting in the score. Management and corporate structure also accounts for a weighting of 40%, with Invesco analysts rating each REIT or property company on factors such as the quality of its management, the capital structure and expansion opportunities. Finally, a bottom–up assessment of property fundamentals of the REIT or property company accounts for a 20% weighting, with the quality of the assets and tenancies taken into account.

In the next step, a "securities analysis," looking at earnings data and valuations, will narrow the field of securities for investment down to a portfolio of 60–80 securities.

A REIT picking checklist

The following is a checklist of issues to consider when looking at putting money into a REIT, divided into three different levels: a "macro view" on the general investment environment, a "sector view" of the property market and property types in that market, and a "REIT view" of the prospects of individual trusts.

Macro
Regional economic outlook
Regional political risk
Country economic outlook
Country political risk
Expected currency movements
REIT market regulations
Tax regime for REITs

Sector
Stage of country in property cycle
Popularity of REIT market
Liquidity of REIT market
Sub-sector (e.g. retail, office, etc.) stage in property cycle, including supply and demand projections

REIT
Management quality
Growth strategy
Valuation of REIT
Asset quality and position in market
Occupancy
Tenancy concentration

REIT players—The fund manager

Joe Rodriguez, director of real estate securities management at Invesco, discusses the merits of Invesco's investment process and gives tips for individual investors who are interested in REITs.

Rodriguez, who is based in Dallas but travels to Asia frequently, said employing a pure top-down approach often allows good companies with strong prospects to slip through the net.

"We would discount a company because of balance sheet quality, management quality, and if the property type in that country was not very strong, but not because it was located in a certain geographic area," Rodriguez said. "You can find opportunities in a particular country which is experiencing negative sentiment. It might have good property types even though the general state is negative."

The investment process used by Invesco involves intense research of REITs and other property companies. It also requires the formation of a view of the property sectors, for example retail or industrial, in any given country.

"Once we pick a property type we like, we have a good idea which companies are located in favorable markets," he said. "The process lets the cream rise to the top. A top-down manager would say he likes Japan, and then fill it. We look at the relative value of each security across each country and property type to build a portfolio."

Rodriguez said he not only looks at measures of stock valuation, such as discounts to net asset value, but also takes into account what is happening in the wider world of stock research. If many analysts are saying the same thing, the investment story might well be drawing to a close.

"The biggest opportunities are when you uncover big anomalies between your view and the views of sell-side analysts," he said. "We would hope to be able to identify market fundamentals before published reports that sell-side analysts use."

Once a REIT is chosen for potential investment, because of the fundamentals of the trust's business and the market in which it is operating, Invesco analysts will examine if it will enhance the overall portfolio.

"We use statistical tools to test every stock in terms of volatility and covariance," Rodriguez said. "It's a very sophisticated approach to managing risk. We're not of the mentality of picking a few good stocks and concentrating the portfolio and hoping they win out over the near term. That approach has a lot of volatility built into it, so we tend to hold a lot more stocks than our competitors. It's more about process, the team and research input, not one or two people making big bets. We look at every stock individually, not only for relative value, but the risk or risk mitigation it adds to the portfolio."

Rodriguez said he looks for REITs that expanded because of a strong competitive advantage, rather than just for the sake of it.

"Our overall philosophy when we buy is that a real estate company is more than just a collection of assets," he said. "What we're looking for is franchise value and competitive advantage. If a company is expanding internationally, to add an office or two in a market where it doesn't have a competitive advantage is not an optimum use of capital."

But, for example, Singapore REITs, partly spurred by ventures by the parent property developing firms, are expanding into China in the right way, Rodriguez said.

"Singapore developers have brought expertise in development capabilities, technology and capital access to create a competitive advantage vis-à-vis Chinese developers," he said.

"International retailers also get a higher level of comfort with Singapore developers because of a relationship that is pre-established," he said. "China's growing, so there are a lot of development opportunities. It dilutes the pure play on Singapore, but a pure play on Singapore might be just 1.5% of a portfolio. In time, China will be a bigger part of everyone's portfolios."

Large-scale US investors are tending to devote as much as 15% of their portfolios to property, Rodriguez said, and many are starting to introduce an international element to those investments—a sign that heavier investment will flow into Asian REITs in the future.

"When we're talking to most institutional investors, what we're hearing is that most investors are comfortable with 5% to 15% allocations to the asset class within an overall portfolio," he said.

"What we've been seeing for the last couple of years is an increasing number of investors, individuals or institutions are looking abroad. The US REIT market outperformed for six years and they are saying, 'We want property, but we think there's potentially better valuation outside the US.'"

"We share our thoughts on the growth prospects in Asia and it makes a lot of sense for many investors, especially if there are concerns about currency, the US dollar weakening," Rodriguez said.

Individual investors interested in REITs should learn as much as possible about the asset class and put their money into funds, he said.

"I would suggest that an individual would have to make the decision about how much time to devote to finding out about the underlying assets," he said.

"If you're not comfortable getting to know them, why not let a professional manager do it? All they do, all day long, is follow a sector. The chances are very good that active management would lead to performance higher than the specified benchmark."

But he also offered a tip to individual investors who want to assemble their own REIT investments: think long-term.

"One thing we tend to notice is that some investors are very trading-oriented. If investors are to do it themselves, I would encourage people to look longer term. Property at its core is a stable asset class," Rodriguez said.

"You know what the rents are; buildings aren't put up over night. You can have an understanding of fundamentals over the next few years. Base your investments on solid research. Be more patient. A short-term trading mentality can lead to inferior results versus buying over the long term," he advised.

The fund management industry has so far offered little in the way of exposure to Asian REITs, mainly in the form of mutual funds specializing in Asian property securities, with REITs as one of the investment options.

But as Asian REITs proliferate, more professionally managed investment options will become available, as they have over the years in the US and Australia. These will probably include:

- Actively managed funds focusing entirely on Asian REITs, which could, for example, be sector-focused and pan-Asia, country-focused or completely diversified;
- Index funds, which would mimic the performance of REIT market indices in Asia;
- Exchange-traded funds (ETFs), most likely listed in Singapore, Hong Kong or Tokyo, which would allow investors to buy tradable securities that track either an index or a basket of REITs,
- Funds of funds, which give investors exposure to a portfolio of funds, which would be focusing on REITs.

But in the meantime, for pure exposure to listed investment property in Asia, investors will need to make their own (hopefully well-informed) choices as they play the REIT game.

Endnotes

1 "Options abound for stable portfolios," *Financial Advisor Magazine*, April 6, 2006.
2 "Property seen top alternative for rich investor," by Martin de Sa'Pinto, Reuters, October 4, 2006.

APPENDIX:

The options— Some of Asia's main REITs

HONG KONG

Champion REIT
Stock code: 2778
Originator: Great Eagle Holdings
Stock market listing date: May 24, 2006
Website: www.championreit.com

Champion REIT started out life as a single-asset REIT, owning a 91.5% stake in the rentable space in Citibank Plaza building in Hong Kong's Central district. The REIT's financial engineering, as well as a stock market dip just before the REIT's market debut, put many investors off Champion. The trust's share price fell on its debut, sending the yield up to over 7%—a high yield for prime Hong Kong property but one which made it practically impossible for the REIT to find yield-accretive acquisitions in the city.

GZI REIT
Stock code: 0405
Originator: Guangzhou Investment
Stock market listing date: December 21, 2005
Website: www.gzireit.com.hk

A spin-off by the investment arm of the Guangzhou city government, GZI was the first REIT formed entirely of buildings in mainland China. The $230 million IPO was popular with investors thirsty for rare exposure to Chinese property. GZI owned units in three fairly modern commercial buildings in the southern city of Guangzhou—Victory Plaza, Fortune Plaza and City Development Plaza. But its main source of income was the White Horse building, a bustling warren of textile and clothing wholesalers located near the city's main railway station.

Link REIT

Stock code: 0823
Originator: Hong Kong Housing Authority
Stock market listing date: November 25, 2005
Website: www.thelinkreit.com

The Link was formed by the privatization of 151 government-owned retail facilities and 79,000 car park spaces, which serve tenants on some of Hong Kong's biggest public housing estates. The trust had a troubled beginning when a court case brought by a 67-year-old pensioner delayed its IPO for nearly a year, but saw its share price soar on its market debut, as investors bought into promises that the management would overhaul its shabby shopping centers. The Link has first option on shopping centers owned by the Hong Kong Housing Authority that were not put into the original package, and is also considering expanding to nearby Shenzhen and Macau.

Prosperity REIT

Stock code: 0808
Originator: Cheung Kong (Holdings)
Stock market listing date: December 16, 2005
Website: www.prosperityreit.com

Prosperity REIT was launched on the coattails of the Link, when REIT fever was at a peak in Hong Kong. By late 2006, Prosperity owned seven commercial properties in Hong Kong with a total of 1,200,633 square feet. The trust's flagship property at the time was The Metropolis Tower, a 15-story office block, which is part of The Metropolis shopping, office and hotel complex in the Hung Hom district of Kowloon.

Sunlight REIT

Stock code: 0435
Originator: Henderson Land Development, Shau Kee Financial Enterprises
Stock market listing date: December 21, 2006
Website: www.sunlightreit.com

Sunlight REIT began as a spin-off of 20 office and retail properties in Hong Kong. The most prominent building in its portfolio is 248 Queen's Road East, a 40-story, gleaming office block in the city's Wanchai district completed in

1998. The trust employed several measures to boost its yield at IPO, including a rental guarantee for a couple of years, interest rate swaps and a temporary dividend waiver by sponsors Henderson Land Development and sister firm Shau Kee Financial Enterprises.

JAPAN

Fukuoka REIT
Stock code: 8968
Originator: Fukuoka Estate
Stock market listing date: June 21, 2005
Website: www.fukuoka-reit.jp

Fukuoka REIT Corporation promoted itself as the first "regional J-REIT"—the first not to focus on Tokyo. It aimed to put together a portfolio of blue-chip retail and office properties in the city of Fukuoka and the rest of Kyushu Island, in the western-most part of Japan, which has an economy of comparable size to the Netherlands and Australia. The trust's flagship property is the Canal City Hakata shopping complex, where a walkway passes along a canal through fountains, trees and, of course, shops.

Japan Logistics
Stock code: 8967
Originator: Mitsui Corp, Kennedix, Mitsui TB
Stock market listing date: May 9, 2005
Website: www.jlf.co.jp

The strategy of Japan Logistics REIT is to take advantage of sale-leaseback deals sealed with companies that would like to cash in on their warehouses and distribution centers. By late 2006, the trust had put together a portfolio of 15 buildings, mostly in the greater Tokyo area but also in Osaka and Saitama. Its newest building was the Funabashi-Nishiura Logistics Center in Chiba on the outskirts of Tokyo, with a total rental area of 35,322.18 square meters, which was completed in January 2006 and purchased by the trust a month later.

Japan Prime Realty

Stock code: 8955
Originator: Tokyo Tatemono, Meiji Yasuda Life
Stock market listing date: June 14, 2002
Website: www.jpr-reit.co.jp

Japan Prime Realty focuses on office and retail properties in Tokyo but also wants to diversify geographically into other major cities. The REIT began life in November 2001 with 13 buildings, but owned 45 worth 215 billion yen just five years later. Office space accounted for about 60% of leased area, with retail space accounting for the rest. About 26.2% of its portfolio was in central Tokyo, but this was worth 45.1% of the REIT's total assets—an indication of the disparity in property values between the capital city and the provinces.

Japan Real Estate

Stock code: 8952
Originator: Mitsubushi Estate, Dai-ichi Life
Stock market listing date: September 10, 2001
Website: www.j-re.co.jp

Japan Real Estate expanded its portfolio rapidly in its early years, more than doubling the number of its buildings to 52 by the beginning of 2006 from 20 when it listed in September 2001, with about 80% of its space in Tokyo. Most of its buildings are office blocks, but some are mixed-use. For example, in early 2006 the trust paid $694 million for the Kitanomaru Square building near the Imperial Palace in Tokyo, which contained office space, retail stores and apartments.

Japan Retail Fund

Stock code: 8953
Originator: Mitsubushi Corp, UBS
Stock market listing date: March 12, 2002
Website: www.jrf-reit.com

Japan Retail Fund owns urban and suburban shopping centers, many of which are occupied by retailer AEON. Of the 37 properties owned by the REIT in mid-2006, just over half were in greater Tokyo, and nine were in the Osaka-Nagoya area. The firm hopes to expand by taking advantage of major corporate restructuring by Japan's major retailers, which will probably involve sale-lease back agreements on shopping centers.

Mori Trust Sogo REIT
Stock code: 8961
Originator: Mori Trust
Stock market listing date: February 13, 2004
Website: www.mt-reit.jp

The 17-story, modernistic Nissan Motors New Headquarters in the Ginza district of Tokyo is the flagship building of the Mori Trust Sogo REIT, which specializes in offices in the center of the Japanese capital, but also owns some retail property. As part of a diversification policy, the REIT also bought a residential building, the Park Lane Plaza in Shibuya district, in 2004 and bought the Hotel Okura in Kobe in 2006.

Nippon Building Fund
Stock code: 8951
Originator: Mitsui Fudosan
Stock market listing date: September 10, 2001
Website: www.nbf-m.com/nbf

Japan's first REIT, Nippon Building Fund specializes in office buildings, and had built up a portfolio of 55 buildings within five years of its listing in 2001, mostly in central Tokyo. One of its major tenants is Mitsui Fudosan, the company that set up the trust, but the properties also house blue-chip firms such as IBM, GlaxoSmithKline and Fuji Xerox. The trust was keen to expand its portfolio outside of the Japanese capital, and bought buildings in Osaka, Nagoya, Hiroshima and Sapporo.

Nippon Residential
Stock code: 8962
Originator: Pacific Management
Stock market listing date: March 2, 2004
Website: www.nric.co.jp

The property portfolio of Nippon Residential is a study in the cramped living conditions for the majority of Japanese living in Tokyo, which has some of the highest land prices in the world. By late 2006, the REIT had accumulated 56 apartment blocks of single rooms, or "live-alones" designed to give office workers affordable access to central Tokyo. It also had 34 one-bedroom "compact-type" apartments for working couples without children, and 17 slightly bigger "family-type" buildings. The trust operated 14 "large-type" apartment blocks, but said these were aimed at "the upper income group and foreign nationals employed by foreign-backed companies."

Nomura Office Building Fund

Stock code: 8959
Originator: Nomura Real Estate
Stock market listing date: December 4, 2003
Website: www.nre-of.co.jp

Nomura Office specializes in central Tokyo offices and owns a share of the giant headquarters of Japan Airlines, which in 2006 accounted for 15% of the floor space of a 30-building portfolio. However around a third of the REITs buildings at the time were located in provincial cities, including Nagoya, Sapporo and Kobe. The REIT more than doubled its asset size to 268 billion yen from 120 billion yen in a little over two years after listing in December 2003.

Orix JREIT

Stock code: 8954
Originator: Orix
Stock market listing date: June 12, 2002
Website: www.orixjreit.com

Orix JREIT concentrates on office property, which in 2006 accounted for 87% of its portfolio, but the trust also dabbles in residential, retail and hotels. Almost all of its buildings are in Tokyo, with a third located in the central three wards of the city. The REIT said it will always focus on offices because of the large size and liquidity of the office market, but was also planning to diversify into the Osaka-Nagoya area. In early June 2006, Japanese regulators called for disciplinary action against the managers of Orix J-REIT, saying the trust had not conducted proper due diligence before acquiring properties from its parent, and had not held as many board meetings as it said it had.

Tokyu REIT

Stock code: 8957
Originator: Tokyu Corp, Tokyu Land
Stock market listing date: September 10, 2003
Website: www.tokyu-reit.co.jp

The assets of Tokyu REIT are split almost evenly between the office and retail sectors, with most of its properties in the Tokyo area, in particular the Kanagawa, Saitama and Chiba prefectures, where its parent, Tokyu Corp., is active. As of late 2006, the REIT owned 17 buildings, bought for a total of 160 billion yen. The REIT's newest shopping center is the Cocoti, approximately a three-minute walk from Shibuya Station in Tokyo, an area popular with young Japanese. This building, which opened for business in 2004, houses brand-name clothing shops, cafes and sports gyms.

United Urban

Stock code: 8960
Originator: Marubeni, CSFB, Trinity Fund (US)
Stock market listing date: December 22, 2003
Website: www.united-reit.co.jp

United Urban is a truly mixed-asset REIT, with shopping centers, offices, hotels and residential buildings in Japan's major cities. One of the distinguishing characteristics of the REIT is its varied residential portfolio, including company dormitories catering for single workers, and other single-room apartments close to major railway stations. The trust also owns the 1,296-room Shinjuku Washington Hotel, close to Shinjuku Station in Tokyo.

MALAYSIA

Axis REIT

Stock code: AXSR
Originator: Private investors
Stock market listing date: August 3, 2005
Website: www.axis-reit.com.my

Axis was the first of a new wave of property trusts to be launched after Malaysia revamped its REIT code in 2005. The trust began with a portfolio of five office/industrial properties located in Petaling Jaya and Shah Alam, but quickly began to accumulate buildings, including industrial premises in North Port, Port Klang, in December 2005.

Starhill REIT

Stock code: SRHL
Originator: YTL Corp. Bhd
Stock market listing date: December 16, 2005

The retail-focused Starhill was worth RM1 billion when it listed, the most valuable Malaysian property trust to date. Its original portfolio included the JW Marriott Hotel in Kuala Lumpur and two shopping complexes, the Starhill and Lot 10. The trust's originator, property group YTL Corp Bhd., said Starhill would be looking abroad for acquisitions, even to Europe and the US.

Tower REIT
Stock code: 5111
Originator: GuocoLand (Malaysia) Bhd
Stock market listing date: April 12, 2006
Website: www.guocoland.com

Tower REIT was created with two office buildings in Kuala Lumpur, the 32-story Menara HLA in central Kuala Lumpur and HP Towers in the commercial area of Damansara Heights. The trust planned to double its asset portfolio within two years of listing, with GuocoLand expected to sell more property to the trust it created.

UOA REIT
Stock code: UOAR
Originator: UOA Holdings Sdn Bhd
Stock market listing date: December 30, 2005

The UOA REIT was created with parcels of space amounting to 770,000 square feet and 1,207 car park spaces in three properties built by its originator company, UOA Holdings Sdn Bhd. The three buildings are the Wisma UOA Centre and Wisma UOA II in Kuala Lumpur, and Wisma UOA Damansara in the Damansara Heights neighborhood of the Malaysian capital.

SINGAPORE

Allco REIT
Stock code: ALCR
Originator: Allco Finance Group
Stock market listing date: March 30, 2006
Website: www.allco.com.au

Allco REIT promotes itself as a pan-Asian REIT, and plans to carry out a region-wide acquisition strategy. But when the trust listed, it had exposure to the office market in Perth, Australia, through a 50% interest in the Central Park office tower, as well as owning two properties in Singapore: the China Square Central office tower and retail complex and the 55 Market Street office block.

Ascendas REIT

Stock code: AEMN
Originator: Ascendas
Stock market listing date: November 19, 2002
Website: www.ascendasreit.com

Ascendas REIT was Singapore's first business space and industrial REIT when it listed in November 2002, with a portfolio of eight properties worth S$545 million. Within four years, the trust had increased its properties to 66 with a book value of S$2.9 billion.

It owns a diversified property portfolio in Singapore comprising business and science parks, high-tech industrial properties, light industrial properties, and logistics and distribution centers. In 2006, the properties housed a tenant base of more than 700 international and local companies. The tenants were typically involved in research and development, life sciences, information technology, electronics, engineering and light manufacturing. Ascendas REIT was tipped to add overseas properties to its portfolio, especially Indian assets built by the trust's parent firm.

Ascott Residential Trust

Stock code: ASRT
Originator: The Ascott Group
Stock market listing date: March 31, 2006
Website: www.ascottreit.com

Ascott Residential was established as a pan-Asian REIT specializing in serviced apartments, with its original portfolio scattered over Singapore, China, Vietnam, the Philippines and Indonesia. A typical asset in the portfolio was the 21-story Ascott Beijing, which had 272 units located in the prime Chaoyang district of Beijing, with easy access to the Forbidden City and Tiananmen Square. The building, with an appraised value of S$217.7 million, contained apartments ranging from one-bedroom units to penthouses.

CapitaCommercial Trust

Stock code: CACT
Originator: CapitaLand Ltd.
Stock market listing date: May 11, 2004
Website: www.capitacommercial.com

CapitaCommercial was Singapore's first REIT focused on office property. As of March 31, 2006, the trust's portfolio was valued at about S$2.1 billion. In the central business district of Singapore, CapitaCommercial owned Capital Tower, the HSBC Building, Starhub Center, Robinson Point and Bugis Village. At the time, the trust also owned the Wisma Technip, in Kuala Lumpur, Malaysia. CapitaCommercial said it would expand its holdings abroad, and would branch out into mixed developments and high-tech industrial buildings.

CapitaMall Trust
Stock code: CMLT
Originator: CapitaLand Ltd.
Stock market listing date: July 2002
Website: www.capitamall.com

Singapore's first property trust, CapitaMall invests primarily in retail properties in Singapore. By 2006, the trust had built up a portfolio worth S$3.4 billion of nine shopping malls in Singapore, with rental payments received from a diverse list of more than 1,200 leases with local and international retailers. CapitaMall carried out much renovation work on its first buildings, such as the Bugis Junction shopping mall, which helped to lift rental income. Some analysts believed that Chinese shopping malls bought by CapitaLand would be sold to CapitaMall at some point.

CapitaRetail China Trust
Stock code: CRCT
Originator: CapitaLand Ltd.
Stock market listing date: December 8, 2006
Website: www.capitaretailchina.com

CapitaRetail China Trust was the first REIT solely comprising Chinese property to list on the Singapore stock exchange. At its IPO, the REIT packaged together seven retail malls with a total of 453,000 square meters, in five cities. Three malls were located in Beijing, while the others were in Huhehaote, northwest of the capital, Zhengzhou in central China, Shanghai and Wuhu. Anchor tenants included US retailer Wal-Mart Stores Inc., and France's Carrefour.

Fortune REIT

Stock code: FORT
Originator: Cheung Kong (Holdings)
Stock market listing date: August 12, 2003
Website: www.fortunereit.com

Fortune was the first REIT of Hong Kong properties, but it preferred to list on the Singapore stock market in mid-2003 because REIT regulations in Hong Kong were still being finalized at the time. However, the trust said on various occasions later that it would seek a dual listing in Hong Kong at some point. By 2006, Fortune REIT held a portfolio of 11 retail malls and properties spread across Kowloon and the New Territories. A typical property in the portfolio is the City One Shatin, a retail center that serves a residential development of 10,642 apartments. The premises include two free-standing podiums, a fresh market, various single shops and 986 car parking spaces.

K-REIT Asia

Stock code: KASA
Originator: Keppel Land
Stock market listing date: April 28, 2006
Website: www.kreitasia.com

K-REIT Asia started life owning four buildings on three properties in Singapore's central business district, namely Prudential Tower Property (approximately 44% of the strata area of the building), Keppel Towers, GE Tower and Bugis Junction Towers. The prime office blocks were almost completely full when the trust listed, a reflection of the very low supply of prime office buildings in Singapore at a time when businesses were expanding. The trust's buildings represented about 1% of Singapore's grade A office stock, so its managers were following an acquisition strategy based on the city, rather than overseas.

Mapletree Logistics Trust

Stock code: MAPL
Originator: Temasek
Stock market listing date: July 28, 2005
Website: www.mapletreelogisticstrust.com

Singapore government-backed Mapletree Logistics listed with 15 assets in Singapore worth S$422 million, but within a year the portfolio had more than doubled to S$1 billion, with additions of properties in Hong Kong, China and Malaysia. The trust specialized in logistics buildings such as distribution centers, warehouses, food and cold storage properties, and oil and chemical storage properties. The trust said it was interested in building up a large portfolio across Asia, and would also look at acquisitions in Thailand, Vietnam, India, Indonesia, the Philippines, South Korea and Japan.

MEAG Prime REIT
Stock code: MMPR
Originator: Ergo Tru, Macquarie Bank
Stock market listing date: September 20, 2005
Website: www.macquariepacificstar.com

MEAG Prime REIT was originally created by Germany's Ergo Trust with two prime retail properties, Wisma Atria and Ngee Ann City, both on Singapore's main shopping thoroughfare, Orchard Road.

Suntec REIT
Stock code: SUNT
Originator: Cheung Kong (Holdings)
Stock market listing date: December 9, 2004
Website: www.suntecreit.com

Suntec REIT is focused on office and retail property, and it was initially created with ownership of the Suntec City Mall and the majority of the Suntec City Office—parts of Singapore's largest integrated commercial development known as "Suntec City."

SOUTH KOREA

KOCREF CR-REIT 7
Stock code: 086720
Originator: Koramco
Stock market listing date: November 11, 2005
Website: www.koramco.co.kr

KOCREF CR-REIT 7 is focused on office buildings, but it was the first Korean trust to be allowed to invest in a mix of property sectors and still qualify for tax privileges. Its portfolio includes the LG Insurance Dadong Building and the Gwacheon Kalon Building, bought for 85 billion Korean won and 60 billion Korean won, respectively.

Macquarie Central Office
Stock code: 076850
Originator: Macquarie Bank
Stock market listing date: January 8, 2004

The Macquarie Central Office CR-REIT was Korea's first property trust by a wholly owned foreign manager, Australia's Macquarie Bank. It acquired the 23-story Kukdong Building in the Seoul Central Business District as its initial asset for about A$180 million in 2003, in what was the largest commercial property transaction in Korea that year. The IPO raised A$95 million, including A$18.5 million bankrolled by Macquarie Bank itself.

Realty Korea CR-REIT
Stock code: 072450
Originator: Realty Advisors Korea Ltd.
Stock market listing date: May 13, 2003
Website: www.realtyadvisors.co.kr

Realty Korea owns fairly new buildings, including the 20-story Rosedale office block in Seoul, which was completed in 2000 and houses Samsung Securities. The firm also owns the Say Department Store in Daejon City, and the 10-story Turbotek Building in Seongnam City.

TAIWAN

Cathay No.1 REIT
Stock code: 01002T
Originator: Cathay Financial Holdings Corp.
Stock market listing date: October 7, 2005

The Cathay No. 1 REIT's main property is the Sheraton Taipei Hotel, worth about 75% of its total assets when the trust was launched. The trust, worth NT$13.93 billion when it was listed, also owned two office buildings: the Taipei Ximen Building and the Taipei Chunghwa Building.

Fubon No.1
Stock code: 01001T
Originator: Fubon Financial Holding Co.
Stock market listing date: March 10, 2005

Taiwan's first REIT, Fubon No. 1, raised NT$5.83 billion in its IPO with two office buildings and a serviced apartment block in Taipei. But soon after its listing, the trust raised its borrowing so that it could add a retail property, the Ruentex City Link.

Fubon No.2
Stock code: 01004T
Originator: Fubon Financial Holding Co.
Stock market listing date: April 13, 2006

When it listed, Fubon No. 2 was solely comprised of office facilities. Its three properties were fully leased at the time but the portfolio displayed a relatively high tenant concentration, with member companies of the Fubon FHC and Ruentex groups collectively accounting for 62% of the rental revenue.

Shin Kong No.1 REIT
Stock code: 01003T
Originator: Shin Kong Financial Holding Co. Ltd.
Stock market listing date: December 26, 2005

Shin Kong No. 1 REIT is dominated by office buildings, including the Shinkong Jasper Tienmu Building, which in 2006 made up 52% of the total portfolio, as well as the Tainan Shinkong Mitsukoshi Building, the Shinkong International Building and the Taiwan Securities Building. It also owned a very popular serviced apartment called the Shinkong Jasper Tienmu Building, which between 2000 and 2006 was almost always completely full, with an average vacancy rate of only 5% because of its handy location.

THAILAND

CPN Retail Growth
Stock code: CPNRu
Originator: Central Pattana PCL.
Stock market listing date: August 23, 2005
Website: www.centralpattana.co.th

The CPN Retail Growth property fund was created when its originator, shopping mall developer Central Pattana, sold it the leasehold rights for 20–30 years to two shopping centers for 10.915 billion baht. The centers, Central Plaza Rama II and Central Plaza Rama III, are both located in Bangkok, with the Central Department store as the anchor tenant.

Ticon Property Fund
Stock code: TFUNu
Originator: TICON Industrial Connection PCL.
Stock market listing date: May 12, 2005
Website: www.rent-a-factory.com

The TICON Property Fund owns tens of factories in Thailand's major industrial estates, including the Bangpa-In Industrial Estate in Ayudhaya, the Amata Nakorn Industrial Estate in Chonburi and the Bangpoo Industrial Estate in Samut Prakarn.

Glossary of REIT terms

amortization – the liquidation of financial debt using periodic payments of principle.

anchor tenant – the major tenant in a building.

beta – a measure of volatility of a public stock relative to an index or a composite of all stocks in a market or geographical region. A beta of more than one indicates the stock has higher volatility than the index (or composite) and a beta of one indicates volatility equivalent to the index (or composite). For example, the price of a stock with a beta of 1.5 will change by 1.5% if the index value changes by 1%.

board of directors – a group of individuals, typically composed of managers, investors, and experts, which have a fiduciary responsibility for the well-being and proper guidance of a corporation. The board is elected by the shareholders.

capital gain – investment earnings resulting from the purchase and sale of assets.

capital markets – public and/or private markets where businesses or individuals attempt to obtain debt or equity capital.

capital market yield – a REIT's dividend payments as a percentage of its current unit price.

capitalization rate (cap rate) – for a property asset, the capitalization rate is the net operating income of the property expressed as a percentage of its value. The capitalization rate for a REIT can be derived by dividing its market capitalization by its net operating income. Comparing a REIT's capitalization rate and the capitalization rate for its properties can be a useful measure of how appropriate the REIT's unit price is.

cash flow – with reference to a property, the owner's rental revenues from the property less all property-related operating expenses. The term ignores depreciation and amortization expenses, as well as interest on loans incurred to finance the property.

central business district (CBD) – the area of a city where major private sector office premises are clustered.

commercial mortgage-backed securities – securities collateralized by mortgage loans on commercial real estate.

commercial property – land and buildings which are either zoned, designed or intended for use by businesses such as retailers and office workers. Property other than that used for residential purposes.

cost of capital – the cost to a company, such as a REIT, of raising capital in the form of equity (common or preferred stock) or debt. The cost of equity capital generally is considered to include both the dividend rate as well as the expected equity growth either by higher dividends or growth in stock prices. The cost of debt capital is merely the interest expense on the debt incurred.

decanting – moving tenants, usually in order to increase rental income from the property.

depreciation – the decrease or loss in property value due to wear, age or other factors. In accounting, depreciation is a periodic allowance made for this real or implied loss.

development – property development refers to either the construction of new buildings or refurbishment of existing buildings in the pursuit of gains.

direct property – direct ownership or control of physical property.

discount rate – the interest rate used to determine the present value of a series of future cash flows.

discounted cash flow (DCF) – a model of valuing a REIT by calculating the present value of distributable income in the future. By expressing the net present value per share, investors can measure whether the current share price is undervaluing or overvaluing a REIT.

dividends – dividends are distributions made out of a company's profits to its shareholders in proportion to the number of shares they hold.

dividend yield – the annual current dividend rate for a security expressed as a percentage of its market price.

EBITDA – earnings before interest, taxes, depreciation and amortization.

exit strategy – a term often used by private equity investors for a plan for generating profits for owners and investors of a company. Typically, the options are to merge, be acquired or make an initial public offering (IPO). An alternative is to recapitalize (releverage the company and then pay dividends to shareholders).

flipping – the act of selling shares immediately after an initial public offering. Investment banks that underwrite new stock issues attempt to allocate shares to new investors that indicate they will retain the shares for several months. Often management and venture investors are prohibited from selling IPO shares until a "lock-up period" (usually six to 12 months) has expired.

freehold – an owner's interest in land where both the property and the land on which it stands belong to their owner indefinitely, i.e. the outright ownership of a property.

gearing – for REITs, this term is used to describe the ratio of debt to the value of property assets. Gearing is sometimes also referred to as "leverage." A highly geared or leveraged REIT is one that carries a lot of debt in relation to the value of its property. However, for other types of listed company, the term is used to describe the relationship between debt and equity.

gross property yield – a building's gross rent as a percentage of its capital value.

income property – property owned or operated to produce revenue.

indirect property – indirect ownership of property, the most common form of which is through a REIT.

initial public offering (IPO) – a company's first share sale to the public when it lists on a stock market.

institutional investor – professional entities that invest capital on behalf of companies or individuals. Examples are: pension plans, insurance companies and university endowments.

interest coverage ratio – a measure to gauge a company's ability to meet its debt interest obligations. Usually computed as the ratio of EBITDA to interest expense.

leasehold – the right to occupy a portion of a building for a given length of time. Leaseholds generally occur in buildings that comprise more than one unit.

leases – leases can appropriately be classified into finance leases and operating leases. The distinction between a finance lease and an operating lease will usually be evident from the terms of the contract between the lessor and the lessee. An operating lease involves the lessee paying a rental for the hire of an asset for a period of time which is normally substantially less than its useful economic life. The lessor retains most of the risks and rewards of ownership of an asset in the case of an operating lease and this category would apply to most property rental situations (see "rent"). A finance lease usually involves payment by a lessee to a lessor of the full cost of the asset together with a return on the finance provided by the lessor. The lessee has substantially all the risks and rewards associated with the ownership of the asset, other than the legal title.

leverage – the practice of using borrowed funds or debt capital to increase the book value of assets above the book value of equity and to boost the rate of return on the amount of invested equity capital.

liquidity – the ability to convert assets into cash without appreciable loss in value. Higher liquidity implies greater ease of transferability, whereas lower liquidity indicates greater difficulty.

loan to value (LTV) – generally refers to the proportion of borrowings to real estate or total assets. A lower value indicates lower risk.

net asset value (NAV) – for REITs, net asset value is defined as the value of the real estate in the portfolio minus borrowings and other debt. By expressing NAV in terms of NAV per share, investors can measure the degree of premium or discount to NAV at which the share prices is currently being traded.

net operating income (NOI) – net operating income is calculated by subtracting property taxes, maintenance fees and other operating expenses associated with the management of a REIT's buildings from gross rental income for the year. These expenses do not include depreciation or interest expenses.

probable maximum loss (PML) – PML is an indicator which measures how much loss is possible from an earthquake, and was originally developed as an indicator for the property and casualty insurance industry. It is also used for REITs using disclosed information on property holdings. In Japan, PML assumes that there is a 10% chance of a major earthquake occurring every 50 years, and is a measure of the project expense of restoring buildings damaged by this assumed earthquake divided by the current cost of rebuilding the property. The smaller the number, the more earthquake-resistant the building.

private equity – equity investments in nonpublic companies.

rating agencies – independent firms which rate the financial creditworthiness of securities for the benefit of investors. The major rating agencies are Fitch Ratings, Moody's Investor Services and Standard & Poor's.

real estate investment trust (REIT) – a REIT is a corporation or business trust that combines the capital of many investors to acquire or provide financing for all forms of income-producing property. In most countries, a REIT generally is not required to pay corporate income tax if it distributes the vast majority of its taxable income to shareholders each year.

rent – an agreed charge for the use of a capital asset, typically property. (See "lease.")

rental reversion – the net relationship between the rental rate of a group of lease contracts with the rate of previous lease contracts. Rental reversion is positive if new rental rates are on average higher for a portfolio of property, and it is negative if they are lower.

return on equity (ROE) – the proceeds from an investment, during a specific time period, calculated as a percentage of the original equity investment.

residential property – property usually occupied for private or domestic purposes. Yields and returns often vary from other types of property investments, and often a different type of investor or financier is involved.

sale-leaseback – when a seller deeds property to a buyer for a consideration, and the buyer simultaneously leases the property back to the seller.

securitization – the process of financing a pool of similar but unrelated financial assets by issuing to investors security interests representing claims against the cash flow and other economic benefits generated by the pool of assets.

share dilution – the reduction in the ownership percentage of current investors, founders and employees caused by the issuance of new shares to new investors.

spin-off – when a company sells a portion or all of a division to the public in the form of an IPO. The parent company would do a spin-off for several reasons: to raise capital, to rationalize its operations by selling off a non-core business, or to draw attention to the newly independent entity and perhaps to raise the stock price of the parent.

special purpose vehicle (SPV) – an SPV is any entity established for the purpose of undertaking a single property transaction. There are many types of SPVs and each has its own tax status.

sponsor – the company that puts together a REIT, often by selling buildings to the trust, also known as an originator of a REIT.

total return – in reference to investment performance, a stock's dividend income plus capital appreciation over a specified period as a percent of the stock price at the beginning of the period, before taxes and commissions.

title – a legal document evidencing a person's right to or ownership of a property.

trustee – a fiduciary whose role is to ensure a REIT complies with regulations.

underwriter – a brokerage firm that raises money for companies using public equity and debt markets.

weighted average cost of capital (WACC) – the average of the cost of equity and the after-tax cost of debt. This average is determined using weight factors based on the ratio of equity to debt plus equity and the ratio of debt to debt plus equity.

yield-accretive acquisition – the purchase of property that will increase the dividend yield for investors.

yield spread – the difference between a REIT's dividend yield and a benchmark, usually a local 10-year government bond yield.

Index